The Tune That

Ronald Bassett

Copyright © Ronald Bassett 2015

The right of Ronald Bassett to be identified as the author of this work has been asserted by his in accordance with the Copyright, Designs and Patents Act, 1988.

First published in the United Kingdom in 1973 by Macmillan London Ltd under the name 'William Clive'.

This edition published in 2015 by Endeavour Press Ltd.

The quotation on page one from 'The Widow at Windsor' in Barrack-Room Ballads by Rudyard Kipling is by kind permission of Mrs. George Bambridge and Methuen & Co Ltd.

Table of Contents

CHAPTER ONE	7
CHAPTER TWO	14
CHAPTER THREE	27
CHAPTER FOUR	40
CHAPTER FIVE	58
CHAPTER SIX	79
CHAPTER SEVEN	83
CHAPTER EIGHT	90
CHAPTER NINE	95
CHAPTER TEN	105
CHAPTER ELEVEN	109
CHAPTER TWELVE	117
CHAPTER THIRTEEN	129
CHAPTER FOURTEEN	139
CHAPTER FIFTEEN	148
CHAPTER SIXTEEN	162
CHAPTER SEVENTEEN	175
CHAPTER EIGHTEEN	179

POSTSCRIPT	182
AUTHOR'S NOTE	183
BIBLIOGRAPHY	185
ACKNOWLEDGEMENTS	186

CHAPTER ONE

It was a fair and fruitful land, and wanting for nothing. To the eastward the long, white-capped rollers of the Indian Ocean clawed and creamed along two hundred miles of empty coastline, and drank from the great rivers — Pongola, Umkusi, Umfolozi and Tugela. Inland there was thick timber and undulating veldt, rock-strewn mountains wreathed in mists that fled with the sunlight, streams and cataracts, shaded, moss-carpeted ravines untrodden by man. Beneath the rich earth lay gold, silver and copper, while above it, among the trees, those colours flashed in the plumage of countless wild birds, and the plains teemed with eland, springbok, kudu and hartebeest, zebra and wildebeest, who multiplied, their numbers scarcely diminished by the demands of leopard and hyena. In the dry season the streams might narrow to struggling trickles, the coarse buffalo grass shrivel and the trees droop with tiredness — and, it was said, there would be a truce among the beasts at the shrinking waterholes, when none would kill another whilst he drank. None, that is, save man. But the rains always came, and the thirsty earth was quenched, steaming in the sun, the grass flourished and the trees greened — mimosa, acacia, euphorbia and baobab. The streams would swell, rushing and swirling, mud-coloured, between their banks, cascading from the mountain tops to the veldt beneath, to the rivers and the sand-ridge of the shore, to the devouring sea.

Sometimes, when the sun was high and hot, the land would shimmer before the eyes and the trees would dance. This was the hour when animals sought the shade, no birds flew, and only lizards basked, motionless, and only ants continued their endless counter-marching among the oven-dry rocks. The lions slept and the monkeys ceased their bicker, the vultures floated earthward and buffalo sank to their bellies in the river mud. All waited for the sun to sink, for dusk, the time for drinking, for hunting, and for running swiftly for life.

With darkness came the moonlight, silvering the veldt, and the hunters slept, sated — except die striped hyena, who was never sated — and the scattered, nervous herds of deer and zebra could doze in reasonable safety until the yellow-smeared eastern sky told of another day of claw and fang, of fleeing hooves amid the dust as leopard or cheetah charged. And with the dawn the carrion birds lifted their soulless eyes and the hunters yawned and stretched. The calf nuzzled for its dam's teats, unaware of the death that stalked in the sunshine.

There were men in the land — black-skinned, vigorous men — who lived in settlements of thatched huts on the hillsides close to the water, groups varying in size from a half-dozen people to townships of several thousand. They lived by the results of simple agriculture, by hunting the plentiful game of the veldt, and they kept cattle mainly for a supply of milk that was highly valued. Iron weapons and tools were crudely forged from surface-gathered ore, and there was an abundance of hard woods, horn, ox-hide and animal skins. They were a people of complex superstitions, and every kraal was part of a vast feudal network, subject to laws and disciplines the flouting of which could mean vicious reprisal. They called themselves amaZulu — the People of the Heavens — after an obscure and long-dead chieftain named Zulu since whom the tribe had greatly multiplied and additionally absorbed the people of many other clans. Their history had been handed down from mouth to mouth, distorted, embellished, and often hopelessly tangled with mythology and make-believe, but it told a story of restless movement, of continual struggle against the elements, against wild beasts and fellow man, of wars, of famine and times of plenty, of births, blood, and death. And it told of the coming of the White Men.

The white men, most of them, were to the westward and southward, beyond the Buffalo and Tugela rivers. They were a strange, humourless, unmannerly breed, bearded and unclean, riding small, wiry horses, herding cattle and raising crops — fruit trees, corn, tobacco — with a stubborn determination that overcame all obstacles. Some it seemed, were content to settle in farmsteads and great, dirty kraals, but others probed incessantly, trekking northward and eastward with their shapeless women and their lumbering lines of big, tented wagons drawn by oxen. To them, all natives were, contemptuously, *Kaffirs*, inferior people, ignorant, pagan, who had no right to occupy the green and fertile lands that the white men coveted.

They were comparatively few, as yet, these white men; they were not numerous enough to constitute a threat to the security of the Great King,

Cetshwayo, who could put fifty thousand warriors into the field. And why should the white men threaten the Great King? Had he not been crowned ruler of the amaZulu lands at Mahlabatini by the *induna* of the white men's Queen? True, all the white men had guns — including big brass ones on wheels — but these also were few, and they moved slowly and clumsily, perhaps ten miles in a day, when a Zulu impi could trot fifty. All the same the white men would have to be carefully watched.

Some had trickled into Zululand, tolerated. There were the traders, with calicos and beads, steel knives and axes, and smooth-bore trade guns manufactured specially for the market in Birmingham and Liège. And there were missionaries, who had a god named Ofartawtchartee-neven, and complained continuously and absurdly that a man should not have more than one wife, that women should cover their nakedness, that stealing cattle was a sin, and killing was a sin, and adultery and sodomy were sins. Almost anything worth doing it seemed was a sin.

The white men were greedy — for gold and ivory, silver and copper — but most of all they were greedy for land. And not just enough land to accommodate a house and a cattle pen, and to grow a few mealies and melons. Each wanted thousands of acres so that none might see the smoke of another, be nearer than a half day's ride from a neighbour, and they wanted only the best land, the rich pastures with ample water, where cattle grew sleek and fat, and the plough furrows ran black like sable-skin. The Kaffirs could have what remained — the dust-plains, or the icy high veldt, or the sea marshes, it was all that Kaffirs were fit for. Well, the trickle of white men across the Buffalo and Tugela was small, as yet, but it would have to be watched. Africa was vast, and could absorb many — but not so vast —

There was one of the whining missionaries at kwa-Jimu, the crossing of the Buffalo River into the white men's territory, southward — Otto Witt — although the station still retained the name of the original owner, James Rorke, and the white men referred to the crossing as Rorke's Drift. They were stupid names, unpronounceable. To the north-east of die river were the Nqutu Mountains, the threshold of Zululand, with an outflung spur, grassed, scrub-scattered, and oddly shaped. The white men had not yet awarded it a name but the Zulus had. It was Isandhlwana.

* * *

Most of the white men to the south and westward were originally of Dutch stock, but their links with Holland had been severed generations before, their language bastardised, and their communities infiltrated by immigrant British, Swedes, Portuguese, Germans and Frenchmen, until they had become a hybrid, unaffiliated breed known simply as Boers — farmers. They had in common a dislike of governmental authority, an inherent conviction that they alone were the title-holders of southern Africa, and a bitter resentment towards the natives who still occupied much of it. It was preposterous that thousands of square miles of land should be retained by ignorant, pagan Kaffirs who had neither the means nor the desire — nor the right — to exploit them. They were being wasted, these lands, when they might be producing com and cotton, fruit, tobacco, tea, coffee and flax. Under Boer ownership, of course.

They had clashed with the Kaffirs on numerous occasions. Boer homesteads and wagon-trains had been attacked, white people massacred, and there had been vicious reprisals, but the Boers had not yet collided with the full weight of the Zulu nation. It must happen soon. As the lands in die proximity of the Cape became settled, and Authority became increasingly demanding, the Boers pushed steadily inland, northward, across the Vaal river, into Natal, and beyond the Drakensberg Range. There were carelessly-worded treaties with the natives and there was always the gun.

They were the chosen race, their laws those of the Old Testament, and they admitted allegiance to none other. The lines of their great, clumsy wagons, their dusty cattle, inched their way across unmarked maps, over veldt and mountain, river and desert, always probing, seeking. As communities halted and settled succeeding families would push still further, then further still — until, incredible to believe, there was no more land. No land, that is, fit to farm and where the local Kaffirs retreated before them or relinquished their rights for a few worthless trade goods. It was incredible, but it was true.

Mind, there *was* land — thousands of square miles of the richest land in Africa — beyond the Buffalo and Tugela rivers. It was the kingdom of the Zulu. There lay the rub. The disciplined impis of Cetsthwayo were a far cry from the cowed Kaffirs of the Cape and Natal, many of whom had become the menial running-dogs of white man, deprived of their birth right, demoralized by gin and the new order. The Zulus were a coordinated, proud and powerful people, quick to anger and crushing vengeance, as they had shown in their treatment of insubordinate clans and their resistance to punitive Boer commandos in the past. Indeed, the boot was on the other foot. There was little to stand in the way of the Zulu hordes if they decided to invade the white man's lands. No, only a professional army could deal with the Zulus, and an army meant government and taxes, and laws —

Still, there was the prize, dangling tantalisingly across the Buffalo, where the Nqutu Mountains began with the oddly-shaped mound that the Kaffirs called Isandhlwana.

* * *

The British wanted law and order, markets and profits, with the Union Jack flying over provinces neatly parcelled and indexed, magistrates and the Queen's justice, rather on the pattern of India. Under British administration, native populations were ruled on the principle of benevolent neglect, neither ill-treated nor their problems particularly considered, less subjugated than by other colonising powers and invariably more secure than they might have been under their own native kings. It was a system which, with brief lapses, worked very well in India — but the Indian yardstick somehow refused to be applied to southern Africa. To begin with the British arrival had found a small European population, of a kind, already in residence — some members of which still nursed a vague affiliation to another European country of which they knew nothing, but strongly resented the intrusion of a second. They did not hide their resentment, and they did not care for the British brand of law and order. The Boers, in fact, were an embarrassment, and the British could have done without them.

Whilst some Boers remained, resigned, others did not. They trekked inland, sometimes with dreams of establishing their own republics, always with a determination to escape British jurisdiction, taxation, and the threat to their independence that the rules of civilisation implied. They cared nothing for any plans the British had for the interior. It was none of their business — and who were the British, anyway? Annoyed, the British had to follow. There could be no unpredictable, ragbag republics in a British sphere of influence, no broils with native rulers who held scraps of paper promising the Queen's friendship — and who complained bitterly about the Boer land-stealers. The impoverished republic of the Transvaal was scooped into the British net, to the indignant protests of the resident Boers who, although they had earlier poured scorn on their own ineffectual administration, had no desire to see it replaced by a British one. Tribal wars flared on the northern perimeter of Natal, threatening to overspill into the European settlements. Land-hungry, resentful Boers, harassed British, and the jealous native tribes — some independent, some nominally under Crown rule — snarled and spat at each other. There was friction between London-appointed officials and locally-elected ones. British regular troops disliked and distrusted the colonial militia, most of whom were recruited from the unemployed and dissolute of the European population, badly paid, and likely to run like rabbits at the first gunshot, while the Kaffir irregulars were utterly unreliable. In return, the colonial forces were irritated by the Britishers' arrogance, claiming that the redcoats were unsuitable for campaigns against will-o'-the-wisp natives in the wild bush of the interior, and the task should be left to experienced colonials. Both, to a degree, were right.

The British position was an uncomfortable one. The scattered African territories were vast, in varying stages of development, teeming with political and social problems, and almost ungovernable. There was only one solution, decreed London. It was federation, with a central government, common policies and a coordinate existence. The piece-meal, go-as-you-please doctrine *must* be abandoned. Everything must be neat and tidy, as in India. Why couldn't southern Africa be like India?

London was losing patience with its bickering offspring; but London was far away. The annexed Transvaal was a powder-keg, with the frustrated Boers now claiming ownership of a huge slice of Zululand which, they said, had been legally ceded to them by the Zulus. True, territorial maps differed as much as seventy miles in their location of the border, but the Boer's demands were preposterous. Cetshwayo, who had kept the peace despite the progressive gnawing at his borderlands, possessed a curious faith in British integrity. He had asked for arbitration eighteen times in fifteen years, to no avail, largely because the Boers did not wish to submit their evidence of ownership to close examination. Now, however, Cetshwayo was becoming alarmed. His young men were asking that their spears be washed in blood.

The clouds were gathering, but the storm was not quite yet. The Boers' territorial claims, considered the British in Capetown, might be a blessing in disguise. If federation was to be achieved, then clearly an independent and unpredictable Zulu state in its midst could not be tolerated. Furthermore, if the Transvaal Boers achieved the disputed territory they, at least, would be placated. And if Cetshwayo denied the territory by force, then he would be providing the perfect excuse for an invasion and annexation of Zululand. It was all very simple.

It was also unfortunate that the investigating Boundary Commission was led by an attorney who was astute, honest, and impervious to influence. He declared that the Boers' claim was not only spurious, but that they already occupied lands that were rightfully Zulu, and which should be evacuated forthwith. Cetshwayo, his faith in British justice confirmed, returned to his kraal. Both British and Boers were incensed.

Faced now with a choice of insurrection in the Transvaal with Zululand remaining an obstacle to colonial planning, and an invasion of Zululand, Capetown determined on the second. The forces in Africa, however were far from adequate. Military reinforcements would have to be asked of London — and London did not want a war with Cetshwayo or anyone else. Wars were expensive. The African colonists wanted more land, and they wanted British troops to fight for it, but they were incapable of paying for a military campaign even if the thought of doing so had ever entered their heads. No, said London firmly. Further troops would not be supplied. The colonists should adopt a course of forbearance and reasonable compromise, and thus avoid the very serious evil of a war with Cetshwayo.

But London was far away, and there were ways of forcing an issue. One was called *fait accompli*.

CHAPTER TWO

He was Sibindi — the Brave One — but how could a man be brave when his spear had not yet drunk blood? Sibindi was tall, Sibindi was strong — but what matter, when the men of the inDlu-yengwe regiment were forbidden to take wives, or even occasional women without the King's express approval? He was Sibindi, in the prime of thirty-three years, and he was not yet *iKhehla* — the coveted reward of proven warriors, when they were granted the head-ring, *isiCoco*, and could live in their own kraals as men. The uThulwana regiment — they of the white shields and ostrich plumes — had their head-rings, as did the uDloko. They walked haughtily, saying that all that were not *iKhehla* were no better than herd-boys, knowing nothing of killings such as there had been against the iziGqoza warriors, whom they, the chosen *iKhehla*, had massacred at the place now named Mathambo — the Place of Bones.

'It is not just,' Sibindi complained, but not too loudly. 'To be *iKhehla* a man must kill — and there have been no killings for many years. Must a man grow old and toothless before he can take a woman, or live in his own hut, just because there are no killings? And must a man be forty, or forty-five, and still be named a herdboy by others who have bled a few cowardly aba-Qulusi?'

Nzobo, his companion since boyhood, took a pinch of snuff from the small bag that hung by a string from an ear-lobe. 'Men who kill are also killed,' he said. 'Where is the *isiCoco* of them who made meat for hyenas? Where are their women?' He thrust finger and thumb into each nostril and sniffed violently. 'But if you want a woman' — he waved a hand airily — 'here there are hundreds of women.'

Sibindi put his tongue between his lips and ejaculated a contemptuous noise. The penalty for even attempting to appropriate a woman was to have genitals sawn off by the iron knife of Nyoka the witch-doctor, while that for accomplished rape was worse — like having a sharpened stake hammered up the rectum. Sibindi was not that foolish. Women there might be, and he had often thought about them — but not in Ulundi, at the time of *uMkhosi*, the festival of the First Fruits, and under the eyes of the Great King.

It was not good to speak of death. A slain warrior must be disembowelled by his slayer so that his spirit was released, and the victor then return to his kraal for the rituals of cleansing. The first of all men, Unkulunkulu — the Very Old — had sent death. He had said to the chameleon, 'Go, and tell men that they shall not die!' The chameleon had started on his journey, but had halted to eat the fruit of a mulberry. Meanwhile, Unkulunkulu had changed his mind, and ordered the lizard to take a different message to man. Because of the chameleon's laziness, the lizard reached men first and gave them the God's message — 'Men *shall* die!' — and departed. When the chameleon arrived with his own belated message of immortality, men did not believe him. 'The lizard has told us already,' they cried, 'that men will die!' And it had always been so thereafter. No man had ever avoided death.

'Perhaps,' he mused, 'there will be white men to kill.' He knew how to kill. He had practised thousands of times the upward slash — the *iKlwa* — of his stabbing spear, the blow that the Zulus had perfected in the time of Shaka, but there were very few white men, not nearly enough for the many warriors who fretted for *iKhehla*. He had practised with a stick when he was a small boy with no other covering than the tiny box of banana leaves that contained a diminutive penis. With others of his age he had herded the kraal's cattle, wrestled and chased and, when he had experienced the perplexity of his first nocturnal emission, his father gave him a loin kirtle and he had submitted to the puberty rites that had qualified him to carry a spear in battle.

'But there have been no battles,' Sibindi repeated. Few tribal chieftains on the borders of Zululand dared to provoke the wrath of Cetshwayo; a handful of stolen cattle was not worth the risk of annihilation. Nor had the Great King sought quarrels with his neighbours. The *indunas* of the white men's Queen had forbidden all military conflicts and, although Sibindi did not understand why the white men should be allowed such impertinence, why they had not been stamped out like ants, Cetshwayo had kept his warriors in idleness.

And so Sibindi and his fellows had herded cattle, grown crops — maize, com, pumpkins and paw-paws — brewed sorghum beer, and hunted. It was the hunt that he enjoyed most. The other things were rightly for boys and women. Sometimes as many as a thousand men, in a vast, shouting and stamping circle, would drive the stampeding game before them, across the hot veldt, and there would be a great slaughter, with feasting afterwards, beer-drinking and dancing. The men would boast of their exploits, occasionally real, more usually aspiring. Drunken jeers might lead to fighting, and the *indunas* would report to the King that his warriors were weary of the years of peace, that it was time to wash the spears, to unleash the dangerous frustrations of fifty thousand men. Cetshwayo would scowl but, aware that the rumblings of discontent could not be ignored indefinitely, would order the impis to enjoy a day of *ukHlobonga*, of masturbation by the unmarried women. It was not enough. The warriors wanted *iKhehla*, to wear the head-ring, to buy the wives of their choice, to father sons, as men should.

Now it was December, with the moon full, and the warriors had gathered at Ulundi, the King's kraal, for the ceremony of the First fruits — *uMkhosi*. In four or five weeks the crops would be fully ripened, and throughout Zululand both men and women would be bringing in the harvest for the year to follow. Now, however, was the time for communicating with ancestral spirits, for eating flesh and fruits taboo at other times, for the witch-doctors' ritual of smelling out evil-doers, for cleansing celebration, and to hear the Great King speak.

There were jealousies between the regiments from widely separated kraals and varying in man-strength from the thousand inDlu-yengwe to the 3,500 of the uVe, and their *indunas* had good reason to camp them apart. The inGobamakhosi threatened to settle old scores with the uThulwana, and when the cooking fires vomited sparks into the night sky, and the beer was flowing, they shouted their war chants, taunting. In the daytime they strode in belligerent groups, eyeing each other sullenly, and it would need little to have them at each other throats with a thousand corpses at the end of it.

The King's kraal covered ninety acres of the plain of Mahlabatini, the scattered buffalo-grass trampled into the sandy soil by countless stamping feet. A dense thornbush hedge surrounded hundreds of thatched huts, interrupted by a single gate and embracing cattle and sheep pens, and the *kgotla*, die men's meeting place. Here idlers gossiped or, at more critical times, the *indunas* — the regimental commanders — held conference, or Cetshwayo emerged from isolation to punish, to reward, to issue his commands, and all who approached lowered their faces to the dust, save the witch-doctors.

And the smelling-out ceremony was the occasion most feared by all, for none were immune from the witch-doctors' accusing fingers, and all must attend. Evil was caused by spirits who inhabited trees, rocks and rivers, animals, birds and — unfortunately — human beings who were ignorant of the evil's presence in their bodies. The witch-doctor crouched and prowled before the assembled, cowering tribes-people, sniffing, screeching, pausing to speculate and then, with a spiteful howl, flicking at a victim with the tail of a wildebeest. The terrified accused would be dragged away to an agonising death, his family massacred, his hut and crops burned. Only the Great King's person was safe on the day of smelling-out.

But this year the *indunas* and counsellors of the Great King had more to occupy their thoughts than vagaries of the smelling-out. The white men were threatening war, and the impatient impis might well be given an opportunity to wash their spears, all too soon.

A month earlier the British had issued a report on the findings of their Border Commission. The Zulus' ownership of the disputed territory was not denied, but the Boers had residential rights and the British would protect them. If any of the Boers chose to leave the Zulu lands they must be compensated — by the Zulus.

And this was not all. There was far worse to follow. Several minor border incidents, which earlier might have passed almost unnoticed, had been seized upon by the British as examples of Zulu criminality. Cetshwayo was mildly surprised. A renegade clan on the Zulu border had been accused by the Boers of cattle-raiding. Cetshwayo had sent the Boers a hundred cattle and permission to destroy the thieves' kraal. Two women had deserted their Zulu husband and, with their lovers, fled across the border into Natal. The deprived husband had followed, dragged back his wives and, in accordance with Zulu law, killed them — although leaving the lovers unharmed in Natal. Finally, two Englishmen, surveying in debatable border territory, had been detained for an hour by Zulus and searched before being released. They were trivial incidents, but they were enough.

The *indunas* were fearful of telling the King the remainder lest he ordered them to be speared. Now, the British had continued, there must be justice done. The vengeful husband and his followers must be surrendered for trial under British law. Heavy fines were imposed for the behaviour of the cattle-stealers and for the insult offered to the white surveyors. And there were to be many changes in Zululand — implemented within thirty days — including the disbanding of the Zulu army and the substitution of another defence system approved by the British, a resident British officer in Zululand, the fullest freedom given to missionaries, and no expulsion from Zulu territory without British agreement. There were other demands, impossible demands which, if ignored, would mean an invasion by a white army. The British would march in twenty days' time, and would enter Zululand after thirty.

On the great plain of Mahlabatini the massed regiments of Cetshwayo stood in their drilled ranks — inGobamakhios, umCijo, uDloko, umHlanga — their black skins shining with sweat, each carrying the coloured oxhide shield of his regiment, white, white and red, black, black mottled white, and wearing its distinguishing headdress, ostrich plumes, otter-skins, monkey-fur. They carried the short-hafted stabbing assegai, honed to razor sharpness, and the skull-crushing knobkerrie — twenty thousand lean, muscular men who had been trained since early boyhood to charge, stab and kill, to move swiftly across sun drenched veldt, forty, fifty miles between dawn and dusk, to live and fight on a handful of mealies. They stood now in silence, motionless as stone, their shields raised. They were proud and confident of their unmatched fighting ability, contemptuous of all lesser men. Every Zulu male was a warrior and he desired to die like a warrior. When an honour-jealous impi avalanched towards an enemy, nothing could halt it save complete destruction. The impis waited now, a weapon forged only for war, for killing. They waited for the Great King to tell them.

'Who are these white men,' growled Sibindi, the Brave One, 'that they think they can insult the amaZulu?' He had seen a few white men, and he had not been impressed, but he had never seen a battalion of redcoat soldiers armed with breech-loading Martini-Henrys, nor a ten-barrelled Gatling gun that fired a thousand rounds per minute. He knew that there were considerable numbers of white men in large kraals to the far southward, but they could not be more numerous than the amaZulu, nor could their kraals be larger than Ulundi. 'If the Great King will say so, we will choke diem in their own blood and scatter the land with their bones.' What if the white men did have guns? There were Zulus with guns also — although Sibindi could not know that there was a wide difference between the natives' cranky trade weapons, made from lengths of gas-piping, and the British infantry rifle. He only knew that guns were unreliable, inaccurate, dangerous to use, and that an assegai in the hands of a trained warrior was far more effective.

From the front rank of the leading regiment a single *induna* paced forward, halted, then raised his spear to the sky. '*Bayete!*' It was the signal for twenty thousand assegais to flash silver in the hot sunshine and a mighty roar of cheering that rolled like summer thunder across the veldt. '*Bayete! Nkosi enkulu! Bayete!*'

At another time Cetshwayo might have viewed the spectacle of his saluting legions with proud pleasure, but today he was perturbed and angry. The British were issuing orders to him as if he were no more than one of their Natal Kaffirs. His *indunas* knew it, and probably many of the warriors on the Mahlabatini plain knew it. Now they waited for his word. He did not unduly object to the fine imposed, but three weeks had been insufficient to muster six hundred head of cattle and drive them to the border — and, in any case, two weeks had already elapsed before news of the ultimatum had reached him. It seemed almost as if the British had no intention of allowing him to pay the fine. Nor did he object to delivering up Zulu miscreants to British justice, although this was nothing short of impertinence — but why should he have to surrender the offenders *and* pay a fine? Even in Zululand nobody was punished twice for the same crime. And had not the British officials declared that the amaZulu yearned for release from the oppression and tyranny of their King? He, Cetshwayo, had heard no complaints from his people — only blood-chilling threats against the white men if they dared to venture across the Buffalo or Tugela rivers.

In his fifty-second year, Cetshwayo was a tall man, muscular, with an impressive dignity despite a tendency towards the stoutness that had always marked his family. Like his predecessors, his rule was harsh; no weakling could bridle fifty thousand of the most savage fighting men in Africa. Death was the commonest of punishments, and only the method of execution varied with the degree of the offence committed. A man could be simply speared or clubbed, or he could be thrown to crocodiles. He could have wooden pegs hammered up his nostrils into his brain, or he could be castrated, flayed, and buried in an ant-hill. It was not apparent to Cetshwayo or his subjects that the age-old penalties were inhuman. They had always been thus, and only academically different from the white men's practice of choking to death with a rope. Nobody, certainly, was complaining. Indeed, there were some who whispered that Cetshwayo did not possess the stoic qualities of his illustrious uncle, Shaka, who would kill three hundred at a single smelling-out or, at a whim, slash open the bellies of a hundred pregnant women to ascertain the development of an embryo. Those were the days when no white man insulted the amaZulu.

The Great King had given little thought to the British demands for disbanding the Zulu army or the accompanying threat of invasion. The demands had clearly been made in complete ignorance of the Zulu social structure in which every healthy male was automatically a warrior, and disbanding the army — whatever that meant — could not make the men any less warriors and would only serve to release them from the rigid, restraining discipline of their regiments, with possibly frightening consequences. No, the threat could hardly be more than a bluff. He, too, had met with white men. He had seen contingents of the Victoria Mounted Rifles, the Richmond Mounted Rifles, and watched the ox-drawn Durban Volunteer Artillery fire a seventeen-gun salute. He had not been awed by the performance, and although he was aware that the British had red-coat soldiers of better quality than the clumsy Volunteers, it was unlikely that they seriously considered them a match for the Zulu impis.

Before him, as far as his eyes could see, a vast curtain of dust was rising from the dun-coloured plain. The massed ranks of warriors, perfectly co-ordinated, shuffled forward, chanting. Thousands of feet stamped rhythmically, spears stabbed at pretended enemies, and occasionally a man would jump high in the air, with a screech, to avoid an imaginary blow. A brilliant sea of ostrich plumes and crane feathers tossed in the sunshine, black bodies twisted and whirled, and anklets rattled like hailstones. Then, suddenly, there was utter silence. The ranks froze into deathlike immobility, and every eye turned towards Cetshwayo.

He lifted his hand. 'Turn loose the bull.'

It was a black bull with massive, scimitar-curved horns — not from the cattle-pens or the grazing herds below the river, but a half wild animal that had spent a year on the open veldt, unafraid of cheetah or hyena and unfamiliar with man. Its heaving flanks were scored by thorns, the heavy head lowered and eyes red with spite. It snorted, pawed, and drooled saliva. No bull, this, to be driven by a child with a stick. It had trodden the slopes of the Inhlazatye and mingled with the great eland on the banks of the White Umfolozi river, heard the coughing roar of hunting lion and the trumpet of the dust-rolling elephants. It had driven the fanged baboons from the birth-slimed foals of the zebra, and regained a measure of the cunning of its ancestors who had roamed the hill-slopes a thousand years before men came. Now these puny men had dragged it with ropes from the wild veldt to the smoke of their fires and their noisy yapping. For an hour the boys had tormented it until, now maddened with rage, it wanted nothing but to hurtle its twelve hundredweight of bone and muscle at the first humans within its limited vision. A handful of warriors, one chosen from each regiment, were to fight it with nothing but their bare hands.

Sibindi stalked forward, imperiously, from the ranks of the inDlu-yengwe, dropped his shield and weapons to the ground and shrugged free of the broad cow skin collar that covered chest and shoulders. Behind him the warriors sank to their haunches, humming like a horde of bees. Sibindi's mouth had dried. In previous years men had died in the ritual of the bull, and the black monster that now tore at the earth with enraged feet had the appearance of a killer; but Sibindi and his fellows must show no fear, no hesitation. They were the chosen of their regiments, and the Great King watched.

With a spear, or even a knife, it would be easier. He had sometimes crouched for hours in the veldt-scrub, downwind of a herd of wildebeest, until an animal had strayed sufficiently near for him to spring, run like the wind to close with his prey before it could bunch its muscles into acceleration, and slash, swiftly, at the jugulars below the head. He did not always succeed, and it was more certain to drive game towards prepared pits floored with sharpened stakes, but that involved labour unbecoming a Zulu warrior. He had never killed kraal cattle and only rarely tasted beef, a forbidden meat unless an animal died or, like this bull today, had been killed in ritual.

And the black bull, suddenly released, bellowed at the sun-glare that dazzled its eyes. Behind it there was the torture of rope and whip, ahead the open veldt denied to him only by an approaching group of men, and his hatred of men was matched solely by a desperate anxiety to regain his freedom. His nostrils flared, vehemently, as he lowered the sword-points of his horns, and then he charged.

The uDududu man was in the bull's path, and in those brief seconds he might have flung himself aside, but he dared not. He was a warrior of the uDududu, the chosen one, and he must die before he shamed his brothers. He halted, rose to his toes, and opened his mouth as if to shout, but no sound had reached his throat when the bull's horns smashed him headlong and sprawling, like a tangled rag doll, to lie in the dust from where he never rose. The humming of the men of the uDududu changed to a melancholy wail.

Momentarily uncertain, the bull slewed in its tracks with horns scything wildly and the sand scudding from churning feet. The warriors sprang, grappling, and the King laughed as the chaos of animal and men writhed and boiled in the dust. A slashing hoof sent a man reeling with face crimsoned and, as the bull rolled, frantically, another screamed with a crushed pelvis, but in the next moment the bull was blinded, its eyes clawed from their sockets. Crazed with pain and frustration, it flung off its attackers, plunging, kicking, spattering blood. Its horns were lethal still, but the warriors' fists were flailing, hammering blows at head and flanks, with the beast helpless. Fist after fist, reddened, smashed at jowls and muzzle, and the bull lifted its face to bellow for the last time at an unseen sky. With its senses dazed, its forelegs trembled and then buckled. The watching thousands hummed more loudly, and a final crescendo of blows sank the animal to its belly, defeated and gasping. The King nodded, satisfied, and an *induna* motioned the victorious warriors aside as he lifted his assegai.

'It was quickly done,' Cetshwayo said. 'Let the blood be drained and given to them.' He wore ibis feathers and a kirtle of lion-skin. Soon he would retire to isolation again, to drink the black medicines that would cleanse him, and the woman would perform their shuffling dance-first the married women, perhaps some of the forty-nine wives of the Great King himself, considered Sibindi. He was bruised and sweating, with the skin torn from both knees and a gashed scalp. The isaNgqu man had a broken wrist, but gave no sign of it as the King eyed them. After the wives would come the virgins, in a long, snaking file, stamping, singing, their breasts tossing and beaded kilts swaying. Then the medicine men would consult their magical objects to predict the future. They had already warned of a late harvest but, since the rains had been late, delaying the crops, the prediction might have been made by any child.

The dying, feebly-kicking bull defecated noisily in the dust. Yards away the broken unCijo man lay, grey-faced, knowing that there was only one fate for him. The *induna* stood astride him, lifted his assegai and thrust downwards.

* * *

He was drunk, boasting, 'Am I not Sibindi, the Brave One?' The inDlu-yengwe howled and cat-called good-humouredly, and plied him with still more beer until it trickled over his chin and chest as he staggered wildly in his dancing, hammering his spear against his shield. 'Am I not Sibindi, of the inDlu-yengwe?' Who were the others — the unHlanga, the uVe, and the uThulwana — but old men or herd-boys? He, Sibindi, would fight any of them. He stabbed ferociously at the air in the vague direction of the distant, rival cooking-fires, where other beer-fundled warriors would be shouting similar claims.

Dusk was falling, and the smell of tallow-soaked torches was added to the fire-smoke that whirled sparks into the sky. The men who had fought the bull, the King had ordered, should have a cow from the royal herd, except those with no head-rings, who would enjoy *ukHlobonga* instead. What good was a cow to a warrior who lived in a military kraal, with the King's herds of thousands to tend? Sibindi spat disgustedly. He had seen the women for only a few seconds before they turned, giggling, and vanished into their huts — but long enough to observe, with a pang of disappointment, that they were not fat. There were some women — like some cattle — who persisted in a failure to be fat. But then, fine women with big legs and bellies, and breasts like pumpkins, would not be long unmarried. They would command a high *lobola*, cattle-price, and be beyond the reach of men like Sibindi, who owned not so much as a goat. Fat women were bought by the old men, the wealthy ones, who already had many wives and many cattle. It was not just.

'Let the white men come, and they shall be swallowed up!' He stabbed again. 'Then, see, will this spear drink deep, and the hyena and the vulture be gorged!' Rumours were circulating that messengers had already reached the Great King with news of red soldiers, with guns on wheels, hundreds of wagons, carts, mules and oxen, congregating on the borders of Zululand — at the kwaJimu crossing of the Buffalo beyond the Blood River in the north-west and, to the far southward, deliberately crossing the Tugela River by repeated journeys of a great, flat boat. That the white men were seriously contemplating an invasion was inconceivable. Their numbers were doubtless exaggerated, and probably amounted to the usual escort of soldiers for road-building parties, or perhaps a swift raid into Zulu territory, a burned kraal, cattle stolen, and an equally swift withdrawal before vengeful warriors appeared. It was a pity.

'The white men are fools!' Nzobo shouted. 'They want to know what the moon is!' The Bambala people claimed that mankind once wanted to determine the character of the moon. They stuck a pole in the ground, and a man climbed it, carrying a second pole that he tied to die first. Another man climbed with a third pole, then another, and yet another until, at a considerable height, the whole structure collapsed and mankind perished. 'They will be swallowed up!' Sibindi bellowed, reeling. 'Their blood will wash our spears, and their bones will whiten the plains to the edge of the sea!' It was customary for a warrior to boast and threaten, to bolster his own determination and hopefully undermine an enemy's.

It was good beer, made from boiled maize and yeast, and the King had provided great quantities for the ceremony of the First Fruits. For weeks the pots had been steaming, fermenting, then strained off and stored in pits to cool, closely guarded. If there could be no killing, the warriors' frustrations could be vented in drunken carousing and empty bluster. There might be brawls, perhaps a few stabbings, but most of the men would be too fuddled to initiate any concerted violation of discipline. Sibindi danced, stumbling and shouting nonsensical defiance and slaying numerous illusory foes, until his legs buckled and he collapsed. He was hardly aware of the dozen pairs of hands that hauled him gleefully towards the gate, dropping him several times during the erratic journey, to the huts where the *ukHlobonga* women waited.

It was dark in the hut, choked with smoke from the fire-pit that had not filtered through the grass-thatch of the roof. Sibindi, thrust unceremoniously through the small door-opening, lay on the floor, bemused, until the noisy banter of his comrades faded and disappeared. He was not sure where he was, and he had forgotten *ukHlobonga*. Even if he had remembered, he would have been indifferent. Prior to pubescence, as a small boy, his elders had permitted, and even encouraged, the fullest association with females of his own age, laughing condescendingly at his infant efforts to emulate the mating exertions of the adults, but they had rigidly enforced celibacy at the first signs of maturity. If, after the rigours of the veldt, cattle-herding and constant drilling, a warrior still had sexual energies to expend, he could do so with a male comrade. Women were for child-bearing, for hewing wood, cooking, crop-gathering, and only incidentally for sexual enjoyment. Many of them had been circumcised during early maidenhood and derived no pleasure from intercourse, their qualities measured by their fatness, which meant strength, work stamina, and child-bearing potential. Cattle were similarly assessed.

He could still hear the distant noises of festivities beyond the flimsy, wattle walls, of drums and rattling gourds, a tangle of voices incessant and incomprehensible. Nearby, cattle were lowing. Through the billowing smoke of the fires the sky was black, scattered with stars, with the moon in its last quarter. Had not the medicine-men predicted that the moon was dying; but in seven days it would steal feathers of fire from the sun, and shine full again? Then would the night veldt be silver again, almost as day — but, unlike the day, silent and motionless, except for the prowling, sniffing hyena that men detested but did not kill.

Sibindi's addled head floated with half-visions of a bull with red-gouged eyes, an assegai against a hot sky, dripping crimson, and the unCijo warrior with his crane feathers torn in the dust and his face expressionless as the *induna* struck. There was a vast sea of plumes and ox-hide shields, and the inDlu-yengwe hummed. He had been drunk before, and he recognised that he was drunk now. He wanted to vomit. Bull's blood and beer, churned by his hours of wild dancing, threatened to explode into his throat, but if he could achieve the oblivion of sleep quickly it might not happen. He did not want *ukHlobonga*.

Tomorrow, like his fellows, he would awaken with an aching head. The great kraal of Ulundi would be littered with broken beer-pots, the ashes of cold fires, sleeping-mats and food-bowls. All the belligerence and boasting of the previous night would have disappeared, and the regiments would be preparing to depart for their own kraals, where the harvests were waiting. Another year would pass before they mustered again, another year of fretting for the head-ring, *iKhehla*. The Great King had promised nothing, and the spears would not be washed in blood.

Sibindi slept, snoring gently, and the woman who had waited in the darkness, resigned, turned into her sleeping-mat and closed her eyes.

* * *

But as Sibindi slept, an exhausted runner had thrown himself at the feet of the Great King, Cetshwayo. He had come from the kraal of Sihayo, to the southward, and he begged that the King should spare his life, for the news he brought was bad. An army of red soldiers had crossed the Buffalo river at kwaJimu, with big guns, wagons, and dogs of Kaffirs under white officers. They had attacked and burned the kraal, killed twenty of the village men — including one of the chiefs sons — and driven off the cattle. Now the white men were ten miles inside Zululand and, while the red soldiers waited for their hundreds of wagons to struggle from the crossing, they camped on the open slopes of Isandhlwana. The white men had come, O King, and they march for Ulundi.

* * *

Cetshwayo sat with his chin in his hands, deep into the night, meditating. The Ma-Buru — the Boers — had come with their masters, die Ma-Nyisimane — the English, and the red soldiers of the Big Woman of the Waters, the dreaded Kwini Vittori. The English had made one mistake already. They had anticipated that the King's warriors would be dispersed throughout Zululand for the harvesting, not knowing that the season was late, and the finest of the regiments were still gathered, fully armed, at Ulundi for the ceremony of the First Fruits. It might have been better if they had been dispersed. Cetshwayo could then, with reasonable excuse, have met the English with gifts of cattle and fair words. Now he had no choice. His regiments were ready, fortuitously, and his angry young men would demand that their spears be washed.

Tomorrow — no, today; Ikwezi the Day Star was already showing in a greying sky — he would move his regiments towards Isandhlwana. There could be no fighting on this day, for the moon was dead, and the day before a new moon was bad for any activity. It must be the next day, in the morning.

CHAPTER THREE

The most annoying thing about a period of boredom, Noggs had decided, was that its duration was unpredictable. It might drag on for weeks, even years, or it could end suddenly at any unsuspecting moment. He had known those moments before, when stultifying monotony had exploded in his face — in the Meerut cantonments, for instance, when a dishevelled, exhausted man had run into the drill-ground, shouting that the sepoys had mutinied and were butchering every European within sight. He had known such a moment when, crouched on weary legs by the side of an Australian creek, he had seen the gleam of yellow in his swirling pan, and known that his weeks of sweat and frustration were to be at last justified — and in the China Sea, when a drug-crazed lascar had scythed down the ship's captain with a meat axe, and even, briefly, when the platform had collapsed under Lady Camden at a meeting of the Social Purity Alliance.

And *Lohengrin* was just another boredom. Unimpressed by an ageing Elsa and her portly knight, he had abandoned the opera house after twenty minutes and strolled into the Strand. It had earlier been raining, and the softly hissing gas-lamps were smearing the wet pavements with sickly yellow. It was too late for a Turkish bath or the London Fencing Club, too early for White's or the Travellers' and anyway, he was in no mood for whist at a pound a point. His lodgings would be cold and empty now that his man had gone. It would be Ireland tomorrow, then Donegal. He pulled his collar around his ears and eased on his white gloves. Donegal promised only further boredom, and mud.

Not that London in late September 1877 suggested that his feelings of depression might be relieved if he remained. Summer had faded early, with the Aldwych beeches already turning to burnished copper, and winter blacks had replaced the tweeds and cottons of a few weeks ago. There were already throngs gathering at the soup-houses, where a basin of prime soup, potatoes and a slice of bread could be had for twopence, and the old reek of coal smoke was in the air. The Queen, a recluse for many years, was at Balmoral — although it was more than likely that her middle-aged son was, at this moment, somewhere in the Mayfair mile, in the Café Royal, the Bristol, or his private room at Romano's. In Hyde Park, anti-Russian orators were baying, 'We don't want to fight, but by Jingo if we do, we've got the ships, we've got the men, we've got the money too!' It had all happened before, and would doubtless happen again. But tomorrow he, Noggs, would be on the boat-train to Holyhead.

His real name wasn't Noggs. It was Charles Leonard Norris-Newman, but if anyone had shouted Charles, or Norris-Newman, he would not have turned his head.

He had been Noggs since his teenage subaltern days, and Noggs in India, Shanghai, Sydney, and Richmond, Virginia. There had once been a time when he'd resented it. Nicknames, pimples, giggling girls, and the communal shower-bath are only a few of the many embarrassments of sensitive youth, but he'd outgrown them all; and now, in London, he was still Noggs, forty-three years old, lonely, and bored.

He groped for his watch. It was nine pm, and the beer-houses in the Strand and its side-streets were closing. A handful of tipsy citizens gathered about the flare lit entrance of a theatre to which, at this hour, they could achieve admission for half price. Noggs paused to light a cheroot and to eye the playbill. 'The Oriental Military Spectacle,' he read, 'of the Tiger of the East, or the Wolf of Hindostan, promising scenes depicting Jungle Ambushes, a Horrific Explosion, and a Terrible Broadsword Combat of Three — during which an Engine and Carriage will cross the stage at FULL SPEED!' It would be, Noggs mused, the same mixture as in a score of similar theatres: a titled aristocratic villain, a naive, handsome hero and an unbelievably helpless heroine, blood-stained knives and a missing will, an absurd plot with a final curtain descending upon tearful bliss and the preservation of true justice. It was what the common people wanted; anything more subtle would be incomprehensible to the half-drunken audience who stamped and booed, cheered and hissed, and spat eel-bones onto their neighbours' feet. Still, Noggs shrugged, perhaps *Lohengrin* was no more realistic.

He puffed thoughtfully on his cheroot, then turned away to signal a hansom with a wave of his cane. It would have to be the Club, a brandy and seltzer, and the usual satirical discussions of current affairs — the six million pounds voted for increased armaments, the admission of women to the University of London, the crank American named Edison who claimed to have invented a talking machine — followed by the tired, predictable jokes about ail married men already possessing talking machines anyway. They were not subjects to hold his attention for very long; he didn't care a damn about the follies of Parliament, blue-stocking women or cranky Americans. Noggs had brightened briefly when he had read of 'Chinese' Gordon going to the Sudan and the possibility of a campaign against Arabi Pasha; but only briefly. His soldiering days were over, and his old Adams' pistol would still be gathering dust if Britain went to war with half the world, blast it.

The hansom ground into the kerb and above him the driver leaned forward but, before Noggs could order him to Pall Mall, a voice shrilled from only yards away. 'Captin! Captin Noggs!'

He turned his head with a quick smile, his hand rising to the brim of his hat. 'Ah,' he nodded. 'Rosie, my little demimonde. The coryphée of Charing Cross — a last breath of summer in this cold, tenebrous gloom.' She'd be a Rosie, a Clara or an Emily, he decided. In Leicester Square she'd be a Natalie or a Celina, in Piccadilly a Calliope. The Director of Criminal Investigations had reported, 'From three o'clock in the afternoon, Villiers Street, Charing Cross and the Strand are crowded with prostitutes, who are openly soliciting in broad daylight. At half-past twelve at night, a calculation was made that there were five hundred prostitutes between Piccadilly Circus and the bottom of Waterloo Place.' No unescorted woman, in the Strand after dark, could be anything else.

She pouted — a waifish slip of a girl in a shabby bonnet of yellow straw and a skimpy feather boa swathed tightly around her neck. She exuded a pungent aroma of attar of roses and gin. 'Don't yer know me,' Rosie enquired, 'when yer' wearin's yer swell duds?' She examined him. 'Christ. A silk 'at and cloak. Where yer goin'? Buckin'am Paliss?'

'That was yesterday, my dear,' he jested. 'No. I've just abandoned the Opera — thus the "swell duds". They're customary, dammit.'

'Bleedin' opera?' she sniffed. 'Can't say I've ever been partial ter bleedin' opera,'

Noggs removed a polished foot from the step of the hansom. 'An indifference with which I sympathise.' He sighed. 'And I was about to terminate a drab evening at an equally drab club for pompous gentlemen — but if you're not otherwise engaged, my little libertine, and have no objection to my company, then I'll buy you a drink.'

She straightened her bonnet. 'Gin? And yer payin'?'

'Gin, if you must,' he nodded. 'And I'm paying.'

'And yer don't want nothin'?' He was a queer sod this Captin Noggs. Any man who never asked for nothin', except talk, must be a queer sod. Still, the Captin was gentry, that was certain. During earlier encounters he'd never wanted a quick 'arf hour, and he kept his hands to himself. Rosie was suspicious of such eccentricities in the opposite sex, but nor had the Captin shown any tendency towards abnormalities in other directions — and a girl like Rosie could tell a few stories about the twisted ones. There were the loose-mouths who claimed acquaintance with Paris *grandes horizontales*, hinting at unequalled experience but failing in tears of frustration when faced with a little London gutter-slut. Alternatively, there were the sadistic ones who left her bruised and clawed, and those who winked and offered a guinea, not for her but for a ten-year-old and an undisturbed hour. Noggs was none of these. 'There's a little place in Maiden Lane,' she suggested, then hesitated. 'Will I meet yer on the comer?' Shabby little women on the game didn't walk in company with gentlemen in silk hats.

Noggs laughed, and his opera cloak whirled as he threw an arm towards die waiting hansom. The driver hawked and spat. Maiden Lane. Not more than two 'undred bleedin' yards, and no more than a tanner's worth in it. Still, a tanner was better than a kick in the arse. He flicked his whip at his horse. He'd keep the roof-trap open, sod it. No bleedin' toff was going to indulge in a bit o' stink-finger in exchange fer two 'undred yards.

In the small Private of 'The Feathers', Noggs wrinkled his nose at the quality of the brandy while Rosie, warming her hands at the fire, examined him surreptitiously. He weren't young, but he weren't really old. Anything, in fact, between thirty-five and fifty — it was difficult to say. The same applied to his appearance. It was *ordinary* — height, build, features.

There was nothing that made him *stand out*. She saw dozens like him, stage-door Johnnies and fancy men, who frequented the Carlton and the Savage, seldom rose before ten in the morning and drank champagne at eleven, played baccarat at White's and occasionally strolled the seedy backstreets of Covent Garden in search of 'a lark'. But Captain Noggs was a little different. He had a tan that was no product of a few weeks in

Deauville or Cannes — likely he was an 'ol' yaller' from the India service. He'd sometimes let slip less fashionable names, like Ghazi-uddin Nagar, and Foochow, and the Parramatta. Most different of all, he didn't seem interested in women. Not in the usual way, that was. He only talked.

She'd seen him a dozen times or more, but knew nothing about him. 'Captin,' she ventured, 'was you a Navy or an Army gent?'

Noggs raised his eyes from a thoughtful contemplation of his glass. 'I've been a lot of things, Rosie — some of them not fit for ladies' ears, even —' He stopped himself, and she grinned. 'Even Covent Garden whores?' She snorted. 'Christ, there's not much I ain't 'eard about, or seen, Captin, And yer can't tell me it's any soddin' different in Turkey or Africa, or anywhere else.' She grinned. 'I know Chinese wimmin are shaped different, an' the Hindoos 'ave twenty-five ways. Gawd, I weren't born yesterday.' It was getting late, and she still had her lodging-money to earn. It was all very well sitting here, drinking the bleedin' Captain's gin, but if he didn't want a bit o' the usual —

He might, of course, be one of the difficult ones, who didn't know how to *start* Some of 'em bleedin' near wanted their breeks pulled off, and yer'd think they kept the perishin' Crown Jewels in their crotch —

'If yer' bashful,' she winked, 'I know 'xactly what yer've got under yer trousers, Captin. I've seen it orl before —'

The stem of Noggs' glass snapped in his fingers, and cheap brandy spattered the floor. He stared at the broken glass, then choked. 'Goddam — !' There was a white ring around his mouth, and Rosie stifled the giggle that had followed her last words. She'd drawn her skirt as high as her stockinged knees to afford him a tantalising glimpse of the pleasures that could be his, and another inch would betray that, for the patron who wanted only an impatient few minutes in some dark alley, she wore nothing under her crumpled petticoat.

The Captain, however, seemed far from intrigued. Noggs drew a deep breath, coughed, then reached for his cane. 'I've just remembered,' he muttered, scarcely audible. 'If you'll forgive me —' He turned, and was gone.

Rosie stared at the door of the Private. 'Christ,' she breathed, 'that didn't larst bleedin' long — !'

* * *

When Noggs entered the Travellers', only a few members still lingered in the Lounge, wreathed with stale cigar smoke. Three stood in a group, and he recognised two of them — Francis Frances of *The Times* and Drew Gay of the *Telegraph*, recently returned, he knew, from the Balkans, The third was a stranger. The thick, turkey-red carpet deadened Noggs' approaching footsteps, but Gay, red-haired and freckled, threw up a hand in greeting.

'Ah — enter our special correspondent for the *Standard*, disguised as a native! Noggs, old fellow — have you been briefed?'

'Briefed?' Noggs nodded at the wine steward already reaching for a decanter. 'Briefed for what?'

'Constantinople, o' course, then Plevna. The Russians under Gourko have crossed the Danube.' He chuckled. 'But India's more your meat, ain't it? Jezzails and talwars and hawk-eyed Pathans, eh? Frances and I have managed to get berths on the *Spain* — slipping Portsmouth on Monday.'

India. The name was like a knife-thrust. Delhi, Lahore, and the Grand Trunk Road to Peshawur, the punkahs creaking, deft brown fingers serving whisky-sodas, stifling heat and lips cracking, malaria, and the prak-prak of rifles among dun rocks, the reeking smell of the bazaars, tinkling bells and nautch-girls swaying —

'No,' Noggs said. They'd be surprised, then sympathetic, and finally condescending. In Cairo and Constantinople and Bombay they'd say, T)o you remember old Noggs? The damn' fool's gone rustic — farming, in Ireland of all God-forsaken places. Donegal — a land agent, or something —' And then they'd forget him, permanently. He was no longer one of Them. He was just one of the faceless millions who read penny newspapers over their bacon and eggs, yawning, with never a thought to the labour and sweat that had brought the ink-smudged copy to their daily breakfast-tables. But *he'd* remember, Goddammit!

Drew Gay was suddenly apologetic. 'I'm damn sorry, Noggs — I'm forgetting.' He waved his hand again. 'May I present Mr George Dyson? He's been hoping for an opportunity of meeting you this evening.' He turned. 'Mr Dyson, this is Noggs' — he laughed — 'or, rather, Captain Charles Norris-Newman —'

Mildly surprised, Noggs bowed slightly. 'I am at your service, sir.' He eyed the elderly, portly stranger, florid-faced and generously side-whiskered. The man's tailor, he decided, should be hanged with his own tape-measure and buried with a pair of rusty scissors through his heart.

'Dyson,' the other confirmed, chuckling, 'of Dyson & Bradley. I'll wager there's not a single soul in Birmingham, above three years old, who hasn't heard of "D & B".'

Noggs bowed again. He wanted to be left alone. 'It's a little late, sir, and I have a tiring day ahead of me tomorrow.' He was being churlish, and knew it, but why should a paunchy little man like Dyson, who looked like a prosperous wholesale grocer, want to meet him?

Dyson drew a handsome watch from a waistcoat pocket, glanced at it, then returned it with a nod. 'I'll be as brief as I can, Captain. I'd like to consult you, if I may, on a matter of some importance —'

'Consult *me*?' Noggs shrugged, and Gay threw back his head and laughed. 'Who else, Noggs?' His expression was impish. 'What's more, old son, Mr Dyson comes to you with the compliments of Fred Burnaby.'

It was stranger still. Dyson's smile was replaced by a frown of annoyance. 'Colonel Frederick Burnaby, of the Royal Horse Guards,' he affirmed. 'I made the mistake of consulting him first. As you may know, he has recently been adopted by the Tories as a candidate for Birmingham, and I feel that my modest request deserved rather more civility than he showed.' He paused weightily. 'Unfortunately, Burnaby is an eighteen-stone simpleton with no more intelligence than is necessary to ride behind a gingerbread coach or sit in Whitehall in a tin belly whilst a London mob gawks at him. That he could advise anyone on anything other than the winners at Sandown or the price of claret I now realise is impossible.'

Francis, who had remained silent, spluttered, then pushed his nose into his whisky. Noggs, not quite sure whether or not the two newspapermen were hoaxing him, ventured a diffident protest. 'Fred Burnaby's a determined devil, Mr Dyson, and occasionally short-tempered, but I'd hardly call him a simpleton. It takes more than that to ride to Khiva, follow the Car-lists in Spain and the Turks in Bulgaria — and reach Gordon in Khartoum. It also takes more than a simpleton to be an accredited correspondent to *The Times 9* Dyson snorted. 'Penny-dreadful stuff. Any schoolboy could do the same. If he's contemplating being a Member of Parliament, then he'd better learn that the name "Dyson & Bradley" means something.' He glanced up at Noggs. 'Incidentally, there's no Bradley, but in business two names always sound better than one, Captain — more solid, y'know.' Noggs raised his eyebrows in the direction of Gay, but that gentleman was showing an unusual interest in the ceiling. Dyson went on. 'It was a perfectly simple request, and I told him that money was no object. Damme, I've never been afraid to put my hand in my pocket, Captain. And I mentioned that, in return for the commission, I'd see the Regiment had something — a new flag, say, or a few trumpets — and likely twenty dozen of port for the Officers' Mess. That's the way we do things in Birmingham —'

'Commission?' Noggs enquired. 'Do you mean the *Queen's* commission?'

'That's right, Captain — for my son. He's eighteen, and determined on the Army, more's the pity. I've argued, threatened, and pleaded. There's no damn brass in the Army, I've told him, except the kind that's polished every day. Commerce is the thing for a young man today, Captain. It's commerce that makes money, not stamping up and down in a red coat. I might have saved my breath. Then, I decided, if it *had* to be the Army, it might as well be the best —'

Noggs was hardly listening. He shook his head. 'You mean that you actually asked Colonel Burnaby for a commission in the Royal Horse Guards?' And this was the man who had named Burnaby a simpleton?

'At Regent's Park Barracks, yesterday —'

Gay, having difficulty in maintaining his gravity, interrupted. 'The Colonel was annoyed, and rather lacking in courtesy. He called Mr Dyson a greasy little gun-pedlar, a profiteering vampire, and then threatened to assist the poor gentleman's departure with a size eleven jack-boot. Not unnaturally, Mr Dyson feels somewhat aggrieved.'

'I am considering a complaint to the Duke of Cambridge,5 Dyson added, but the vision of a massive, fire-eating Burnaby confronted by a Birmingham grocer demanding a commission for a spotty-faced son, and even promising to renew the Blues' revered regimental colours, was too much for even Noggs' pessimistic mood. He laughed.

Still, when all was said, Burnaby needn't have been so blasted irritable. Why call Dyson a greasy little gun-pedlar — ?

'Why,' he asked, 'did he call you a gun-pedlar?' He felt his mouth begin to dry and, a yard away, Francis was humming softly.

Dyson lit a cigar very carefully, watching the smoke curl upwards towards the existing haze above their heads. 'The Colonel seemed to resent,' he said, 'that I am an arms broker.' He halted, meeting Noggs' narrowed eyes, then went on defiantly. 'It's the old law of supply and demand, Captain. All kinds of people want guns, and I have guns — any number that you care to mention. Not always Martini-Henrys or Sniders, of course.' He paused again. 'I've sold Bess muskets to the government of Mexico, Brunswicks to Garibaldi, flintlocks to the Canadian and African trade, to revolutionaries in Argentina and Serbia, tribesmen in Turkestan. Whenever anybody wants guns, Dyson & Bradley can supply them.'

Noggs was beginning to understand. Gay and Francis had led him into this, not spitefully — they weren't spiteful men — but mischievously, and perhaps from curiosity towards his reactions. The story would be worth a few brandies in Sofia. 'You should have seen old Noggs' face,' they could chuckle, 'when we faced him with a real, live gun-merchant —' Did they suspect? Possibly. It hadn't been easy to conceal in the gregarious conditions of bivouacs, camps and shared billets.

Men like Dyson he could have killed without hesitation when, in the scorched scrub-hills of the Punjab, he had been pinned down by Pathan sniper-fire — not of native jezzails made by some Afghan gunsmith, but of modem, European breech-loaders as accurate as those of his own men. And who had supplied the Waziri hostiles with the exploding bullets that tore a man's guts to crimson slubber? Or the Belgian fifteen-barrelled volley-guns that might have scythed down his entire company if they'd been better handled?

Dyson was reading his thoughts. He plucked at the lobe of a fleshy ear. 'Ah — no. I never sell guns to anyone who is likely to be in conflict with our own military, that's bad business, Captain. Mind you, it's sometimes difficult to predict. I can sell guns to an Algerian, who'll resell them to a Greek, and they'll end up in Kabul —'

'And be responsible for murdering British troops on the frontier?'

'I confess it's possible, Captain, but the same can be said for selling frigates to China or, for that matter, of training Indian sepoys to butcher women and children.' He pulled out his watch again. 'Another thing,' he added. 'I can be strictly impartial. I sold Enfields to both sides in the American Civil War. That evens things out, doesn't it?'

Noggs drew a deep breath. Blast it, he'd not be provoked. That's just what Gay and Francis were waiting for. It was exactly as he'd told himself earlier. A period of boredom could end at any unsuspecting moment, and this, for certain, was one of those moments. It had been a long time since the filth-reeking *Lord Clive* had docked with her cargo of wounded and disease-wracked men from India. He had been carried aboard in Bombay, not wanting to live, and lay sweating in his cot as the ship wallowed southward to the Cape, then northward to cross the sweltering Equator again. Men moaned and vomited, cursing a commissariat that could transport maimed humans under conditions unfit for cattle, feed them on maggot-riddled beef and rancid potatoes, and deduct 5s 4d from a weekly pay of 7s 6d for food, maintenance and necessaries. It had been bitterly cold on their arrival in the Solent, and the disembarked sick had been laid on an open jetty to await transport that nobody seemed to know, or care about. Noggs had given a cabman a guinea to carry him to Netley, and probably saved his own life. He had simply not wanted to die in the cold.

He hadn't been so fortunate as some of his brother officers after the capture of Delhi, but he'd brought some useful pieces of jewellery and a few uncut stones, and converted them into cash in London. It was as well that he had, b'God. The Army had abandoned him like a worn-out boot, and had not even paid the prize money for the Indian campaign. But he'd lived well enough during the monotonous years that followed, until his resources had dwindled. Then there'd been the *Standard*, and finally the offer of the place in Ireland.

But Dyson was still talking. 'There's nothing illegal about it, and if I didn't sell guns, there's plenty of others willing to — Swedes, Germans, French, Austrians —'

There were things a man could hide, the surgeon-major had said, like poor eyesight, or recurring malaria, but not this. Nobody could hide this. He was sorry — damn sorry. Noggs could, of course, write to the Military Secretary, but it would be a waste of time. He had emerged into Victoria Street stunned and ashamed, and for hours had tramped the pavements without knowing where he was, or why.

'You mentioned that you wished to consult me?' Noggs was relieved to find that his own voice was measured and sober, at a moment when he wanted to smash a fist into the bland, puffed face of Dyson — but that would be an unforgivable sin in a gentlemen's club, and the news of it would reach every corner of Mayfair within hours. 'It is with regard to your son's commission?'

'That's right. I'll be damned if he'll take the Royal Horse Guards now, even if Burnaby went on his knees — and, mark my words, Mr Burnaby might be whistling a different jig when it's nearer election time. That's when he'll discover that "D & B" means something in Birmingham. Burnaby might make a loud noise in Whitehall, but he'll not be so damn arrogant in Aston Park —'

Christ, didn't this flabby bastard ever stop? Noggs drew another breath. 'There are some regiments that are difficult, Mr Dyson — difficult, that is because there's usually a long waiting list. The Household Cavalry, for instance, the Guards, the Greys and Hussars, the 60th Rifles, the Royal Scots —' He shrugged. 'There are others. Fathers sometimes submit a son's name at birth, and preference is often given if there's family connections with the regiment. Also, with the Household Cavalry and the Guards, the names of potential officers usually have to be approved by the Commander-in-Chief —'

'And what, may I ask, is wrong with the name Dyson? I've had dealings with important people, Captain — titled people — and I could tell stories that would start a few embassy gentry sweating.' He snapped his fingers. 'Goddammit, I could equip the entire British Army with Gatling guns tomorrow — *and* throw in free ammunition. I doubt whether that pompous imbecile, Burnaby, could afford a double-barrelled duck-gun!'

'You're possibly right, sir,' Noggs said drily. 'Your son is fortunate in his parentage. Many young officers have nothing but their army pay, and have a thin time of it.' He hoped that, if the younger Dyson ever achieved his commission, he never revealed to his brother officers the source of his father's income; if he did so the boy might bitterly regret the day he received that treasured parchment signed by Her Majesty, who addressed him as Trusty and well-beloved, and reposed especial Trust and Confidence in his Loyalty, Courage and Good Conduct. 'But there are a number of fine line regiments, with splendid records, in which your son might find service more satisfying than "riding behind a gingerbread coach in a tin belly", as you put it.'

'Line regiments?' Dyson sniffed disdainfully, but his eyes rose to Noggs' again. 'Such as which?'

'Well —' Noggs considered. 'With your high regard for Birmingham, why not the 24th Regiment — the Warwickshires? The Second Battalion is at Chatham —'

'Second? I'll not have any damn seconds, Isn't there a First?'

Noggs' patience was wearing dangerously thin. 'The First Battalion's in the Cape Colony, but its depot is in Brecon, where a company is maintained to provide replacements if the battalion falls understrength. I'd advise that you write to the depot commandant, Mr Dyson, to enquire the possibility of a Second Lieutenancy.' He lifted his glass and drained it slowly. 'And unless you want the same response as you had from Colonel Burnaby, I suggest you keep your fat mouth shut about "D & B", your money, and the filthy way you earn it.' He placed down his glass carefully, nodded coldly at Gay and Francis, and walked for the door.

'Damned impertinence!' Dyson snorted. 'Who the hell does he think he is?'

Gay sighed, mildly disappointed. 'Ah — a strange one, is our Noggs. A first-rate soldier — Delhi, the Northwest Frontier, and decorated by Her Majesty. If it hadn't been for the Waziri affair, he might have had his brigade by now —'

Dyson nodded. 'I've heard of his kind,' he sneered. 'The gallant, blood-stained hero with a broken sword in one hand and the regimental colours in the other, facing hopeless odds for Queen and country.' He glanced up. 'What was the Waziri affair?'

Frances interrupted for the first time. 'It happened on the North-West — somewhere near the Swat river. Noggs' company marched into an ambush, and the Pathans were armed with British-made Snider-Enfields. It was pretty bloody business, with six hours of daylight remaining before they might withdraw under cover of darkness. Noggs crawled out to bring in a wounded man, and got winged and taken by the Pathans himself. His men found him two days later, staked out, but just alive.'

There was a moment's pause, and then Frances resumed, very slowly. 'When the Pathans capture an enemy, Mr Dyson, they do some pretty sadistic things. I know. I've seen some of the results, and they made me vomit. Nobody seems to know what happened to Noggs. Obviously his men knew, but they were a lovely bunch and never talked. In fact, they got damn belligerent if anyone asked. As for Noggs, well, he hovered between life and death in Peshawur, and was eventually invalided home. He's fit enough now, but he's never been the same man — as Gay says, a strange one. He keeps to himself, has numerous acquaintances but few friends. He's usually alone, and nobody knows how he spends most of his leisure time —'

'I can guess,' Dyson said. 'I know his kind. In Birmingham we know how to handle that kind —'

CHAPTER FOUR

It had rained continuously, monotonously, during his first eight days in Ireland, during the seemingly endless journey by rickety light railway as far as Londonderry, thence by the jaunting car that also carried the mails, to Letterkenny. Beyond was the wilderness of bog and mountain, the Derryveagh, to the wild Atlantic coast that frothed under a leaden, sullen sky. He had been glad to be gone from the cheerless, wet streets of Dublin with its poverty and drunkenness, the children begging for ha'pennies, the well-fed, indifferent priests, the tramping feet of soldiers in puddled Sackville Street. He was not ignorant of the Irish problem, of the recently failed potato crops, unemployment and rising prices, and he had been warned of the growing bitterness and resentment — even of the Fenian Brotherhood — but he had not been prepared for the destitution of Donegal.

The jarvey had loaded his box, feigning he hadn't the English, and presenting a sodden, unconcerned back to Noggs for fifteen miles of rain-swept road. After several unsuccessful attempts to establish a conversation, Noggs held his peace, but at Letterkenny the jarvey, after throwing down the box into the mud, muttered, 'God save ye, sorr' — which might have been interpreted in several ways.

Letterkenny was a straggling street of dilapidated houses. There was peat-smoke flattening in the wind over the chimneys, and the windows were like hostile eyes surveying him as he stood, uncertain. Nothing moved, but opposite was a paint-peeling sign bearing the legend 'Smiley's' and 'Ales and Whiskey'. A bell jangled over the door as he entered, and a murmur of conversation died as if cut by a knife.

Inside, the air was thick with the smoke of plug tobacco mingled with the smell of damp clothing and the sour odour of beer. Four or five men were grouped about the blackened maw of a fireplace — men in muddied, corduroy breeches, home-spun stockings, and shapeless, felt hats over faces void of expression as they gazed at his entrance. Another man — presumably Smiley — stood in shirt-sleeves behind the small bar-counter. He met Noggs' demand for rum with a nod, but no comment.

The spirit flared in Noggs' throat — a damn sight more warming, he decided, than die reception he'd had in Letterkenny so far. 'The Glaziers' estate house,' he said. 'I'm told its two miles further on the Fintown road. Is there anyone with a cart or trap that I can hire?'

Smiley — if it were he — pondered over the question carefully. He was a stocky man with a putty-coloured face and eyes that did not rise to Noggs'. 'Ah,' he answered finally, 'I'd not be knowin', sorr. Ye'd better be after askin' the Constable.' He did not offer advice on the whereabouts of the Constable, and Noggs' annoyance was rising, but he drank his rum slowly, ignoring the battery of stares from the fireplace. The door jangled again as he left and, behind him, someone hawked and spat.

He found the 'Constable' — or, more accurately, Sergeant Michael Cooley of the Royal Irish Constabulary — in the small, white-washed station-house at the further end of Letterkenny. Cooley was large, bovine, with ruddy features that might often have been creased into a grin. Today he did not grin, but he was, at least, civil.

'Captain Norris-Newman, sorr — aye. I've been expecting ye. Sit ye down by the stove, sorr, and I'll hot ye some tea. Shure, it's graveyard weather we've been having, an' no mistake. Aye, I've a dog-cart that's used for hauling the drunks — they're rare bhoyos for the poteen — but I'll take ye to the Glaziers', sure enough.'

Cooley talked — about Irish weather, the condition of the roads, the railway that was promised for Letterkenny, his earlier service in the Fusiliers. By degrees his grin reasserted itself, but disappeared immediately Noggs referred to the Glaziers' estate and his own appointment. The sergeant sighed. 'Captain, sorr, ye're the fourth agent in three years. Two o' the others threw in the towel after a few months. Shure, they had judgement, Captain — an' likely they're still alive. The last one, Campbell, stayed nearly two years.' He paused. 'A hard man, was Campbell. He was a Scot, as big as meself, and wi' fists like steam-hammers. No "bluidy bog-Irishmen" were goin' to frighten him, he said — an' nor they didn't. The Devil himself wouldn't have put fear into Campbell.'

Noggs lifted his eyes from his scalding, bitter-sweet tea. 'And — ?'

Cooley had turned away, his bulk almost filling the window that overlooked the wet Letterkenny street. 'He had an accident — cleaning a gun. Death through misadventure, the Coroner said,' He turned to face Noggs, then shrugged. 'Mind ye, Doctor Ternan's an auld man —'

'You mean,' Noggs asked, 'that it wasn't an accident?'

'Ah — I didn't say that, Captain, sorr. And ye didn't hear me say it.'

Noggs frowned. 'You implied that the Coroner might have been mistaken —'

'Shure, an' he might not. I'm no doctor meself.' He struck a match on the stove to light his pipe. 'But it's likely the auld doctor hadn't seen many men killed by gunshot, either. Because the gun was found within hand's reach of Campbell's body, it don't mean that the shot was fired from the same distance — or by Campbell —'

Noggs was silent for several moments, then, 'So things are as bad as that?'

'Aye, Captain — and it'll likely get worse. It's been building up fer a long time — bad crops, and then the cheap wheat an' bacon from America that's sent prices down. The rents demanded fer the holdings are sheer blackmail, Captain. Shure, some o' the land, wi' out the labour the cottier gives to it, wouldn't be worth a shillin' an acre, an' if the cottier sweats to improve it, then the rent's raised. If he can't pay the rent, he's thrown out. So, in the end, the cottier jes' scratches the soil, enough to live hand ter mouth — praties an' goats' milk. Ha' ye seen the goats, Captain? Ye'll not get a pint a day from one of they starvin' bastes. And the pigs — the gentlemen who pay the rrent' — share the home wi' the "Christians". The cottiers don't eat meat, Captain, 'cept likely at Christmas.' He paused. 'I've seen a choild eatin' *earth*, Captain, ter satisfy the pain in its belly!'

His pipe had died, and he struck another match. 'There are people wi' black hate in their hearts, Captain, an' there's others who see to it that the English are always blamed — whether or not the landlord's English. The Irish Revolutionary Brotherhood — the Fenians.' He drew thoughtfully on his pipe. 'Shure, it's a bad business, and there's innocent blood will be spilled, or me name's not Cooley. There's bad English landlords, right enough — though as often it's a bad agent — but the cottiers are blamin' the black-mouthed Protestant English fer all their troubles — bad weather, blight, bad crops that follow their own poor farmin', food prices and, most of all, the rents.'

Beyond the window the rain had not ceased, with the sky as grey and foreboding as the Sergeant's voice. The man was probably embroidering, Noggs decided, for reasons of his own — perhaps to exaggerate his own problems in maintaining law and order. Noggs' employers, the Worshipful Company of Glaziers, in London, could hardly be accused of oppressing the Irish peasantry. All cottiers on the Glaziers' land, they had told him, had fixity of tenure, and were entitled to compensation for improvements if they gave up their holdings. There could be no evictions without reference to London.

Still, he'd not question the Sergeant's opinions at such short acquaintance. 'Are there any Fenians in Letterkenny?'

'Shure, they don't wear a badge in their hats, Captain, but I have my eye on a few, so I have. The names won't mean anythin' to ye now, but ye can bear in mind Casey, Lynch, Whelan, Rice, Mc'Doon and Mitchell — and they spend as much time in Smiley's bar as they do in diggin' praties. Poteen's cheaper 'n tea, so it is.' He paused. 'Rice is a cashiered officer — "Her Majesty having no further use fer his services", — but the bhoyo to watch is Thomas Whelan, Captain. He's a sly blackguard, and his holding's nearest to the Glaziers' estate house. If ye're looking fer the perpetrator o' any mischief, ye can start wi' Whelan.'

Noggs thrust out a lower lip, 'Ireland's not the only damn place to experience civil unrest, Sergeant. It's not much better in England.' He shrugged. 'Don't you think you're looking for trouble where it doesn't exist?'

'Aye, I'm looking fer trouble, sorr,' Cooley sniffed, 'every bloddy morning that I get out o' bed. That's why there's twelve thousand military in Ireland, an' the Constabulary's been armed. Do ye have infantry an' bayonets patrolling the streets o' London and Manchester? Or flying columns an' artillery ready to march at an hour's notice?' He shook his head. 'No, Captain — but I'll tell ye. One more harvest like the last one, and there'll be a million starvin' — an' the Devil himself wouldn't be houldin' down a million starvin' people —'

Noggs rose to his feet. He shared the sentiments of his predecessor: no 'bluidy bog-Irishmen' were going to frighten him either. If the cottiers were planning to make trouble, they'd find that a man who had pitted his wits against frontier Pathans, and hunted down the professional thieves of the Punjab, might be more than a match for a few drunken farm-hands. Tonight he'd clean and load his old Adams' pistol, just in case.

'The rain's almost stopped, Sergeant,' he said. 'If you'll oblige with that dog-cart —'

* * *

He'd arranged for a woman, Cooley confided on the road to the Glaziers' estate house, to come in daily — and then added, to Noggs' mild surprise, that the woman was Mrs Whelan. Noggs made no comment, and the Sergeant added, almost apologetically, 'Shure, it's likely her man won't be after causing mischief that'll lose wages.' Then, incomprehensibly, he said, 'She's got red hair.'

The house lay lower than the road, grey-walled and grey-roofed, surrounded by a dry-stone wall and overgrown grass that should have had a scythe to it a month before. The neglected drive proceeded beyond the house to terminate in a cobbled yard, littered with dead, sodden leaves and enclosed by outbuildings. He could see a dusty gig resting on its shafts, broken bales of hay and an upturned cattle-trough. Even allowing for the depressing influence of the rain, Noggs mused, there was nothing very elegant about the Glaziers' estate house.

He didn't need a house of such size, and now, with dusk falling, he did not intend to explore every corner. It could wait until tomorrow. There was a fire burning in the gloomy hall and another in a bedroom, with a bed turned down and oil lamps prominently placed with matches at hand. On the dining-room table waited a meal of cold meat and pickles, bread, cheese and milk — and a bill from a Letterkenny grocer. Mrs Whelan, then, had already begun her duties, and he was not ungrateful.

'We-ell,' Cooley said reluctantly, 'I'll be leavin' ye, sorr.' He hesitated. 'It's a damp 'oul place, Captain, and ye'd best not sleep wi' any windows open. Ye'd not want ter catch ye' death on ye' first night, would ye now?' He grinned, a little sheepishly, as he turned the dog-cart away.

Tomorrow, Noggs decided, he must arrange for more supplies to be sent from Letterkenny — but the woman could advise on that. Tomorrow, too, he must begin an inspection of the estate. In addition to the tenants' holdings, there were twelve hundred acres of Glaziers' land, and there'd been no agent since March. That meant a lot of neglect to mend. The warnings he'd received in London, followed by Cooley's pessimism, suggested that labour might be difficult to obtain, but other agents, he knew, had imported labour from Tyrone and Armagh and, with difficulty, had managed.

He'd need a couple of horses. And he'd have to write back to London for a manservant — preferably an old soldier who could put his hand to anything in the house and stables. He had never had a woman servant before but, if she were only in the house during the day — when he would most likely be absent — there could be no inconvenience in the arrangement. The Irish sense of decorum was unlikely to be very different from that of the English. A bachelor might have as many women as he wished in his house by day, but never, under any circumstances, one woman by night.

The rain, thank God, had paused. The fire in the bedroom was only a dull, red glow and, extinguishing the oil lamp at the bedside, he was gratified to see moonlight through breaks in the heavy cloud beyond the window. If it did not rain tomorrow, and with a few days of good, drying wind —

There was a splintering crash, and something stung his cheek. Noggs whirled, cursing, flinging himself to all fours. Christ! Cold, night air was streaming through a jagged hole in the window above him, and the floor was scattered with glass slivers. A yard away, in a pool of moonlight, lay the missile — a stone as big as a man's fist. Noggs cursed again. His pistol was still unloaded, at the bottom of his box, and he might have paid a sorry price for his stupidity. He'd become soft and forgetful since India — but then, in India there'd have been no second chance. The Waziris didn't waste time in tossing stones.

Put yourself in the enemy's place, he remembered. Think like he's thinking, and then out-think him. Noggs listened. There was not the faintest sound to interrupt an utter silence. All right, then. The unknown visitor had thrown the stone, and then had done one of two things. He had either fled, in which case it would be profitless to pursue him in the darkness and a completely unfamiliar locality — or the stone-thrower was still waiting, hoping that Noggs would be lured into leaving the house.

Ah no, my friend, Noggs mused. He'd choose his own ground and his own time, dammit, and he'd not be provoked into anything until he was ready. Starting with tomorrow's dawn, then — and sooner or later, perhaps, the enemy would get a little over-confident —

And if the stone-thrower was still waiting out there, well, it was a cold, wet night, and Noggs wished him well of it. He, Noggs, wasn't going to lose a good night's sleep.

* * *

Climbing from his bed at dawn, he felt mildly ashamed of his fears of the previous night. One broken window hardly meant a civil uprising and, dammit, this was Ireland, not the Shahur Tangi. Still, as he walked from room to room, he found himself unconsciously preparing a defensive position — a section here with a field of fire thus, another here, and a Gatling or a Nordenfelt at each corner of the dry-stone sangar. It was really all nonsense, but there was no harm in amusing himself.

He emerged into the open. There was no rain, but everything was wet, sodden. A few rooks circled the nearest trees, but nothing else moved. The stone-thrower of last night must have been within yards of the house, waiting for the oil-lamp to be extinguished. Then, sooner or later, he *must* have made a retreat through the surrounding, knee-high grass — unless he had wings. Noggs walked the edge of the drive slowly, and then grunted with satisfaction. He'd been right, Goddam. Through the high, soaked grass was a narrow, trampled furrow, running erratically north-eastward. That, Noggs congratulated himself, was a start.

Returning to the house, he unfolded the ground-plan of the estate that he had brought from London. North-eastward from the house — his finger moved across the paper, and he grunted again. There was only one north-eastward holding within three miles. Whelan's.

He'd have to meet this fellow Whelan. Mind, the trampled grass was no real evidence. The stone-thrower might have moved in a circle beyond the wall, but Noggs didn't credit Irish peasants with any sense of tactics. Besides, if he was looking for the perpetrator of any mischief. Sergeant Cooley had said, he could start with Whelan.

He lifted his head. From the direction of the distant kitchen he could hear the clatter of dishes. In the dining-room the table was laid for breakfast, and he could smell bacon. Then, as he stood, hesitant, a woman entered.

She was red-haired, as Cooley had oddly said — hair that might have fallen lower than her waist had it not been plaited and coiled at her neck.

She wasn't beautiful, Noggs decided — no, not beautiful, but she had an immediate, natural grace, a rustic comeliness, that amply compensated for any lack of classical refinement. She wore an ill-cut dress of drab, grey winsey, with clumsy, worn shoes, and there was a tiny crucifix at her throat. Her eyes, startled, met his, and she flushed.

'You must be Mrs Whelan,' Noggs said.

She made an inexpert attempt at a curtsey. 'Yes, yer honour.' There was nothing very sinister about Mrs Whelan, at least, Noggs mused — a simple, wholesome woman, not unattractive. He hoped her cooking was as promising. He smiled. 'I'm not sure that I warrant the "honourable" title, Mrs Whelan — but how did you get in? I didn't think I'd left a door unlocked?' Indeed, how had she entered the house before his arrival yesterday?

'Shure, an' I've got a key, yer honour.' She held it up to show him. 'I did the house fer Mr Campbell, before ye, an' it was himself that gave it to me.' She turned away to the sideboard, to set down a pot of coffee and uncover a dish of bacon, kidneys and eggs. 'I took the liberty, sorr, of orderin' groceries. If there's anything special ye'd be likin'?'

He nodded absently, seating himself. Hell and damnation. After the window-breaking incident of last night he'd slept like an innocent, content that he was behind locked doors — and all the time Whelan's wife had a key!

'No salt beef, choke-dog biscuits, or hard-boiled peas, Mrs Whelan,' he smiled, 'otherwise I've no particular likes or dislikes. The trades people can send in their bills weekly, and I'll give you an additional allowance to cover any other housekeeping expenses. Perhaps you'll keep a rough account?'

She nodded quickly, apparently satisfied, but seeming anxious to leave him alone with his breakfast. When he rose, she had not returned and, still with several questions unanswered, Noggs waited. Was she deliberately delaying her reappearance? Was she in the kitchen, listening for his departure? She came at last, almost reluctantly, gazing at the floor. Noggs lit a cheroot.

'Are you a native of these parts, Mrs Whelan?' His voice was casual, almost as if he did not care about an answer. She was off guard. 'No, sorr, but my husband is. I come from Galway.'

'Ah, Galway,' he nodded, then, 'Did your husband get home late last night, Mrs Whelan?'

She was not taken by surprise, but continued gathering the dishes from the sideboard. Then she turned to face him. 'Shure, he often gets home late, sorr — if he takes a drop in Letterkenny. A hard-working man needs a drop, sorr.' There was a hint of defiance in her voice.

'And having had his "drop" last night,' he persisted, 'he didn't take a walk in the dark — in this direction?'

A hand went to the crucifix at her throat. 'It's always Tom Whelan, sorr, that's blamed fer anythin'. If orl the cows in Donegal ran dry, shure the Constable wid be questionin' Tom Whelan. Can a man niver escape the black name that's given him fer no reason?'

She was right, of course, and he shouldn't be interrogating her. If anyone at all, it should be Whelan himself, and Noggs had no real proof that Whelan was responsible for what was, after all a trivial thing — a broken window. He left Mrs Whelan to her dishes, returning to the bedroom to don a stouter pair of boots in anticipation of a tramp to Letterkenny. The bed had already been remade, and the scattered glass swept from the floor. Mrs Whelan, then, had known the reason for his questioning, and she'd been prepared.

When he descended again, Mrs Whelan stood in the hall. This time there was anxiety in her face. 'Ye'll be goin' to Letterkenny, sorr, to lay charges wi' the Constable?'

Noggs frowned. 'I'm going to Letterkenny, Mrs Whelan, but I hadn't considered laying any charges.' He paused, then added, 'Not yet, that is.' She couldn't be more than twenty-four or five, he estimated, but her hands were already work-worn and he wondered if she could read and write — and what discomposure had he caused by his request for a rough account of housekeeping expenditure? Still, even if uneducated, there was no suggestion of stupidity in her manner, which conveyed an impression of maturity and experience without loss of essential innocence. Mrs Whelan would be submissive, and she might bend, but she would not break.

But now she was pleading. 'Tom Whelan's a good man at heart, sorr, an' he'd be foin with the holdin' if he'd had a fair chance — but what wi' the blight, an' the rent, an' the black luck of it all —' She gave a little shrug. 'An' it's the company he keeps, sorr. When the drink's in him, wi' the swearin' an' boastin' —'

Noggs made a gesture of mild impatience. 'If your husband's getting himself involved with Land Leagues and Fenian Brotherhoods, Mrs Whelan, he can't blame "black luck" if he finds himself under constant suspicion — but I've no particular views about him or any other tenant.' He had already scanned the Glaziers' rent list. Tenants might be exploited in other localities, but not here. For the acreage he held, Whelan's rent was modest and had not been raised for years. If the man was in difficulties, there must be other reasons.

And he found the reason when, on the Letterkenny road, he looked down on what his ground-plan told him was the Whelan holding. There was little evidence of serious cultivation; most of the land within sight was weed-infested and had obviously not received the attention of a plough for several seasons. Hollows were filled with water, and a small area had been planted with potatoes which, unattended, rotted in the mud among nettles and thistles. A few gaunt, disconsolate goats were tethered to stakes, eyeing him sadly. The heavy scattering of dung suggested that they had not been moved to fresh grazing for weeks.

Noggs pressed a heel into the ground. It was yielding, waterlogged, but he'd seen worse yielding a crop, and sustaining cattle. This holding couldn't be earning a penny in revenue. It would probably never earn a fortune but, with hard work and careful husbandry, it would give a man and his wife a reasonable living. This man, Whelan, just hadn't been trying. If he ever had, he'd surrendered to laziness or frustration. Give an Irishman a pick or a shovel, he'd been told, and supervise him, and you've got the best labourer in the world. But leave him to work and fend for himself, and he'll share his time equally between drinking, brawling, sleeping, and complaining continuously of his 'black luck'. The unseen Whelan, Noggs calculated, was typical of his breed

He could see a roof of broken slates, and he pushed his way towards it, the mud rising to his ankles. He was at liberty to inspect any holding, and now was as good a time as any. The slates sagged over the walls of a cottage, windowless and leprous with peeling patches of old white-wash — little more than a hovel, a single room-space enclosed by damp brick. Inside, Noggs guessed, there'd be a floor of beaten earth that would seep wetness in the winter, an open hearth over-spilling with peat smoke, and a few rickety pieces of furniture. It must be a miserable sanctuary from the bleak Atlantic winds. The mud huts of an Indian village, he mused, were scarcely poorer — with the advantage of sun and warmth.

Noggs looked at his watch. It was barely ten o'clock, and Whelan wasn't here. The cottage was silent and, in the desolation surrounding him, only the goats followed his movements with dejected eyes. He turned, to retrace his steps to the road, and at that moment the bullet struck the cottage wall, three feet from his head.

He heard the familiar crack of a distant gun almost simultaneously and, instinctively, he crouched. There was no cover and, above him, the splintered gouge in the wall gave no indication of the direction from which the shot had come. But he couldn't stay here, dammit. He'd been shot at too often to experience any fear, but he was angry. He straightened and began to trot towards the road, weaving, with the tethered goats tugging away as he splashed among them. It was too late to look for gun-smoke; the wind that rustled the wet grass would have dispersed it in seconds — and he wasn't going to attempt stalking a hidden marksman who could pick him off at leisure. He reached the road, panting, and then halted to survey the soaked grassland behind him.

A smashed window was one thing — a display of petulance, ill-humour — but a gunshot was attempted murder. He was damn angry. Whoever had fired must be well acquainted with the terrain, and might still be watching Noggs over his gun-sight at this moment, unavoidably lying flat — and soaked to his skin. The road in both directions was deserted and the distant goats had resumed their meagre grazing. Noggs turned his back on the Whelan holding and walked on towards Letterkenny. He wasn't going to give anyone the satisfaction of seeing him run.

Still, he was glad, twenty-five minutes later, to reach the shabby houses of Letterkenny. With the rain ceased, there were people in the main street, a few carts, with gossiping groups at doorways, bare-foot children and old women with clay pipes clenched between wrinkled lips. They couldn't all be conspiring against him, Noggs decided, but he knew that eyes followed him. Well, there was probably curiosity towards the appearance of any stranger in a place like Letterkenny, and it meant nothing. He did not pause until he reached Smiley's.

As he pushed open the jangling door he was met by the same smell of tobacco smoke and stale beer; and there were four men at the fireplace, although he could not have identified them as those who had occupied the bar-room yesterday. Noggs ordered a brandy.

'Brandy?' Smiley considered. 'Sure, there's no brandy, sorr. There's no call fer it. I couldn't sell ye a brandy if ye offered a poun' a glass, sorr.'

'Then I'll take whisky. Scotch.'

'No Scotch whisky, sorr. Irish. Or there's ale or porter.'

Noggs nodded. 'Irish whisky.' Behind the bar counter there were several bottles whose labels blatantly indicated both brandy and Scotch, but he was not going to be baited into controversy. The colourless liquid that Smiley poured had an earthy, oily flavour, and boiled in his throat. It was only with an effort that he refrained from coughing. He pushed the emptied glass towards Smiley. 'I'll take another,' he said, and had the satisfaction of seeing a flicker of disappointment in the other's eyes.

Noggs turned his attention to the other occupants of the bar-room. It was just possible that the sniper at Whelan's holding had reached Letterkenny before himself, but with insufficient time to change soaked and muddied clothes. The corduroy breeches and clumsy stockings of the men he gazed at were dirt-stained, but none showed signs of a crawl in a bog during the past hour. 'Which one of you,' Noggs asked, 'is Whelan?'

The man who edged forward was totally unlike the mental picture of Whelan that Noggs had vaguely formulated. He was short, narrow-shouldered, almost weasel-like, with black eyes in a thin face that had not had the attention of a razor for several days. He wiped the palms of his hands on the front of his shabby coat. 'I'm Whelan, sorr.' His eyes met Noggs' momentarily, truculently, and then dropped to the floor. Behind him, one of his companions sniffed loudly, and Whelan thrust out a lower lip.

'It's probably unnecessary to tell you that I'm Norris-Newman, agent for the affairs of the Glazier's Company, and responsible for estate management, the observance of tenants' rights — and rents.' He paused. 'I've just come from your holding, Whelan.' There was a quarter's rent owed by all tenants from the last day of September — a week since — but he was unwilling to discuss that here, even though it was a matter of some urgency. Never let them get into arrears, they'd warned in London.

If they've got rent money in their hands that you've not collected, they'll spend it, as sure as fate — and once they've spent it, they'll never recover it. Unpaid rents can only be countered by evictions, and evictions mean trouble — civil disorders, sometimes involvement of the military, and even questions in the House —

He was aware that Whelan had received a nudge from a man behind him. 'If it's the rent ye'll be after collectin',' Whelan retorted, 'it's robbery fer a bit o' bloody land like that, so 'tis. Have you heard the prices in Derry? Not thirty shillin' fer a hunner'd-poun' pig, nor eight poun' fer a prime heifer. An' that stinkin' land won't grow nothin', sorr. It's a damn' thafe that wants rent fer it, from people that's starvin' —'

'I've seen poorer land worked,' Noggs said quietly, 'and that's what your land needs, Whelan — work. I'll give odds that you've got no blisters from a spade-handle this year, and you'll not find the rent in a Letterkenny bar.'

'Shure,' Whelan spat, 'an' it's always the bloddy poor workers that's expected ter give their sweat fer the dirty rich, so 'tis. It's exploitation o' the masses by the privileged few — the division o' society, the manifestation o' conflict between falsely opposed finalities —'

Noggs stared. 'Falsely opposed *what*?'

'Falsely opposed finalities. The Glaziers, is it? An' would they be demandin' the rent if bloddy Red Hugh O'Neill hadn't betrayed Ulster ter the English — an' ye' filthy London livery companies? Shure, an' the Irish kin go ter hell or the mountains o' Donegal, an' pay rent, an' watch their children starve, But the time will come when the enslaved an' disinherited will rise up —'

'Aye, the Irish have nothin' to lose but their chains,' someone else added. 'Have ye not heerd o' Charles Stewart Parnell?'

'Where in blazes did you learn that quibbling drivel?' Noggs barked. His eyes flickered beyond Whelan. 'Are these men Glaziers' tenants?'

'Casey is — and Mitchell,' Whelan nodded. 'Not Mc'Doon — but, shure, he thinks the same.'

Noggs gazed from man to man. None of them, he'd swear, had sufficient political education to contrive phrases like 'exploitation of the masses' and 'manifestation of conflict' — and Parnell, the Home Ruler, would hardly have voiced such claptrap. Noggs sucked in his breath. 'That sort of talk will get you nowhere, Whelan, and talk's cheap.

Another thing — it doesn't need a damn hero to hide in the dark and throw stones through windows.' He paused. 'But a gun is different. There's only one reason for a gun, and it's called murder. That means the Assizes, a black cap, and a hanging.'

He had expected that his words would provoke at least a fleeting reaction — a flicker of guilt, fear, or even amused satisfaction, but he was disappointed. They eyed him blankly, and in silence. It was odd, but perhaps he'd failed to make his point clearly. 'I'll not have,' he went on slowly, 'anyone prowling about the estate house after dark, and nobody is going to shoot at me without getting a bullet back. After today I'll be carrying a loaded gun, and I'll be mounted. I'm accounted a good marksman, a fair horseman, and I've a more than useful experience in dealing with aspiring assassins.' He paused. 'And I shall take particular care not to suffer an "accident".'

The four men at the fireplace continued to contemplate Noggs with expressions that indicated nothing but incomprehension. Smiley, a yard away, began to wipe the bar counter with a beer-sodden cloth, whistling softly between his teeth, and Noggs' irritation was increasing. 'You'll not persuade me that the leprechauns have taken to carrying fire-arms — any more than it'll be the "little folk" who'll tear up your damn floorboards if I hear one more gunshot.'

'It's the bloddy sojers, is it?' Whelan challenged. 'Are ye not satisfied wi' takin' the bread out o' children's mouths wi'out bringing bayonets to do murder wi'? Shure, ye've already got the blood o' Cromwell's butchery on ye' hands, but ye'll not be finished until every bloddy Irishman's been buried under the stones or driven ter America! Mother o' God — !'

* * *

Ten minutes later in the station house, Sergeant Cooley was scratching his head.

'Whelan, Casey, Mitchell and Mc'Doon, ye say — an' ye don't think it was any of them? Whelan's got an auld shotgun, but I doubt he has the money fer powder an' shot —'

'It was a rifle,' Noggs said.

Cooley nodded. 'Aye — and when I said that Whelan was ye' man fer mischief, I wasn't thinkin' o' murder. Stone-throwing, likely, or firin' a hayrick or a barn, laming a horse — anything like that, now. But murder

—' He shrugged. 'Shure, he's got plenty o' blather, but no belly fer killin' —'

'Well, somebody has, dammit. And there's something else. Whelan is talking a lot of cheap gibberish, straight out of Marx's Manifesto, and he didn't learn it from his cronies in Smiley's bar. It's the sort of talk that can make simple-minded men, with cheap liquor inside them, do some damn stupid things. It was the same twisted talk that sparked off the Sepoy Revolt.' He paused, then laughed. 'Dammit, I'm beginning to talk nonsense myself.' As he'd told himself that morning, this was Ireland, not the Shahur Tangi. A few penniless smallholders muttering half-cock Communism didn't amount to blood-hungry mobs and barricades in the streets of Dublin and Derry. Still —

He glanced up at Cooley. 'You mentioned some other names yesterday, Lynch — ?'

'Lynch an' Rice. Well, Lynch isn't ye' man either, sorr, because last night he was dead drunk, an' he snored like a hog in the cell here until I kicked him out this morning — an' still seein' double. He couldn't hev been at Whelan's holding and, even if he was, he couldn't hev hit the side o' Sackville Street Post Office at ten feet.'

'That leaves Rice.'

Cooley frowned. 'Well, sorr, it leaves everyone in Donegal except six — but, if ye like, it leaves Rice.'

Rice. The name had a vaguely familiar ring. A cashiered officer, Cooley had said — and then Noggs did remember. There'd been a young infantry Captain named Rice during the Aldershot manoeuvres of 1871, whose company of Fusiliers had made the fashionable 10th Hussars look foolish in front of an ambushed Prince of Wales. There, Noggs had mentally predicted, was a future corps commander — and had then promptly forgotten. Four years later an officer named Rice had been charged and found guilty in a civil court — something to do with an indecent assault on a young lady in a railway carriage. Noggs had never known the full details — he'd been covering die insurrection in Bosnia in' seventy-five — but Captain Rice, following a brief prison sentence, had been cashiered and had then disappeared from polite society.

And there was something else. 'Weren't you telling me yesterday, Sergeant, that you served in the 7th — the Fusiliers?'

Cooley's eyes jerked towards Noggs, surprised. There was a moment of silence, then he nodded. 'Aye, sorr, an' ye needn't ask the other question.' His voice was resigned. 'I served under Rice, an' I saw him broken, so I did. An' if ever a man were rooked, sorr, it were Captain Rice. Shure, he had an eye fer the ladies, but not a cheap little tart like this one, and it weren't twelve months later that she were picked up fer accosting,' — he sniffed — 'in a railway carriage, like Captain Rice claimed in the dock. "Five pounds," she sez, "or I'll scream I've been indecently assaulted".' He pulled a wry face. 'Well, that were the end fer Rice, so it was — and he turned sour in prison. I didn't know he were in Ireland until I joined the Constabulary an' came to Letterkenny.'

It was possible, Noggs mused — an embittered man, with a grudge against the society that had expelled him, justifiably or otherwise, inciting a deprived, disgruntle peasantry into disorderly behaviour towards authority. Far-fetched, perhaps, but possible. 'Does Rice have a gun?' he asked.

The Sergeant frowned again. 'Ter spake the truth, sorr, I don't know. His holding's towards Kilmacrenan, outside my responsibility, an' besides' — he grinned apologetically — 'it's difficult fer a man like me to be a guardian o' the law towards a man who was his commanding officer —'specially knowing what I do, an' all —'

'Good God, man — if you've got suspicions about him or anyone else, you've always got the magistrates or your own superiors to consult, haven't you? What about the Campbell business? You're a police sergeant, not a damn guardroom orderly!'

Cooley agreed. 'Shure, an' ye're right, sorr. I'll not deny it. But when Mister Campbell had his accident, I didn't think o' Captain Rice. If it *wasn't* an accident, I reckoned — He was choosing his words carefully. 'If it *wasn't* an accident, it would more likely be because o' Mrs Whelan.'

'Mrs Whelan?' Noggs was finding it difficult to reorientate his thoughts. 'You mean that' — he hesitated — 'if it *wasn't* an accident, Mrs Whelan —'

'Well, sorr,' Cooley said slowly, 'she's got red hair.'

Noggs was baffled. He stared at the Sergeant. 'You told me that yesterday. What in hell's name has red hair got to do with it?'

Cooley drew a deep breath and fumbled in a pocket for his pipe. 'Well, now, sorr — bein' English, an' all, it's likely ye wouldn't know. In Ireland, wi' country folk, people don't marry who they like. Ah, no. Marriages are arranged by parents an' match-makers — sometimes the priest — wi' the dowry argued over a bottle or two o' poteen. It might seem an outlandish custom to ye, but it's surprisin' how it usually works out well.

'Mary Whelan was a Galway girl — wi' red hair.' He held up a hand to forestall Noggs' protest. 'In Ireland, red hair's a curse. Shure, it's tolerated in men, but red-haired women are considered omens o' misfortune. I've known farmers, sorr, drivin' cattle to a fair, seein' a red-haired woman, an' straightaway turning the cattle home again — swearin' they'd have no luck wi' sellin' the bastes that day. That's why the matchmakers couldn't find Mary Whelan a husband in Galway, sorr, an' why she came ter Letterkenny. In the end she married Tom Whelan, who was no prize fer any woman, an' a lot below Mary's breedin'.'

Noggs considered. 'All right. I understand that, Sergeant — so far. Mary Whelan was an Irish wallflower, and married below her. What's that to do with Rice?'

'Nothin', sorr — but wi' Campbell. Mary Whelan did the house fer him, and he were a Scot wi' no objection to red hair. D'ye see, sorr?'

Noggs was beginning to see. He nodded cautiously. 'Campbell made advances to Mrs Whelan, and she — er — responded?'

'So quick, it weren't dacent, sorr.'

That, Noggs decided, was the biggest surprise of all. Mrs Whelan was about the last person he would have associated with infidelity. Brief as his acquaintanceship with her had been, it had been her air of inviolability that had most impressed him. It just showed how deceptive appearances could be.

'What persuaded her? Money?'

'Ah, I reckon not, sorr. Mary Whelan's not the kind that can be bought, jes' like that, now. But fer a woman that's had better things, an' living wi' a drink-sodden loafer like Whelan in the pig-sty ye've seen —' He shrugged, 'Shure, Campbell were a foin figure ev a man, an' educated. Likely Mary Whelan were curious ter know what it were like ter be bedded on clean sheets by a man that washed — instead of a beer-stinkin' lout on a pile o' sacks. Ye kin niver tell wi' women, sorr.'

'You can't, indeed,' Noggs agreed. 'And did Whelan find out?'

The Sergeant sucked on his pipe. 'Aye, Whelan found out, so he did — but *when* he found out, I'd not be knowin'. It weren't difficult fer Mary Whelan, wi' her husband spendin' all of his time, an' most of her wages, in Smiley's bar. Shure, everyone in Letterkenny seemed ter know except Whelan.' He sucked on his pipe again. 'It's my guess, sorr, that he was *pretending* not ter know. It's a sad day, so 'tis, when a man will tolerate his wife's whorin' fer the sake o' the drink-money she earns.

'But, in time, there was so much dirty whisperin' he couldn't ignore it any longer, fer the shame of it. So he filled himself ter the gills wi' Smiley's brew an' lurched off ter the Glaziers' estate house, shoutin' blue murder —'

'Ah!' Noggs murmured, but Cooley shook his head. 'No, sorr. When Whelan came back, he had a smashed mouth an' a handful o' sovereighs. Like I said, Campbell had fists like steam-hammers, but he always paid fer what he had, so he did. Whelan an' his cronies were as drunk as McGinty's bitch fer a week.' He shook his head again. 'No, sorr. After that, Whelan had no cause fer wantin' Campbell dead.'

CHAPTER FIVE

By the following day the activities of Whelan and Rice were becoming of less concern to Noggs as he acquired an increasing awareness of the primary, almost insuperable problems which would underline his every attempt to improve, or even maintain at present levels, the quality of the estate under his charge. He had been totally unprepared for the poverty of Donegal, of which every hour presented more incredible evidence. Squalor he had seen in India and China, but he had not conceived that there might be worse in Ireland, that thousands of the Queen's subjects possessed nothing but the rags they wore, and lived like animals in holes dug in the earth and roofed by sticks and turf, unemployed and unwanted, dependent upon charity soup, or boiled cabbage leaves, nettles and weeds. Nobody had mentioned that in London, and nobody had mentioned the detested 'gombeen men' — the money-lenders to whom thousands of people had mortgaged their meagre earnings for a lifetime ahead, or the families of five or six totally sustained by the produce of 1½ acres of bog, or men tramping ten miles to and from a day's labour on the road for tenpence. Noggs had been unprepared.

He knew a little of the Great Hunger of the years between 1845 and 1849 — when the potato crops had failed — as a result of which one and a half million Irish people had died of starvation, typhus, dysentery and famine dropsy, and another million had fled to Canada and the USA, and swarmed hungrily into England — but that had been thirty years ago, and he had thought the wounds had been healed and forgotten. They were not; they were still suppurating, and they were not forgotten.

He was new to Ireland, and as yet had seen only one small part of it, but he did not understand the Irish. Dammit, how could a man like Whelan allow his acres to lie rotting in idleness when every year there were apprehensions of crop failures? And why did the Irish stubbornly stick to growing potatoes, a crop notoriously prone to blight and similarly devastating diseases? Would they never learn? True, the potato would grow almost anywhere, and it provided a higher yield than almost anything else, when everything went well — and six people would never survive on an acre and a half of wheat or barley — but by the beginning of October, when the last gleanings of other vegetables had disappeared, nothing remained but the potato stocks to maintain them through a long winter. Nothing. And through the winters the Irish sat in their hovels, crouched over peat fires, cursing the landlords and the rent, and sinking still deeper into the apathy that characterised them in the eyes of all Englishmen.

And Noggs, dammit, was English. Being so, he shared the opinion of all his countrymen that Ireland's difficulties were self-imposed or, more accurately, were sustained only because of an inherent laziness, a reluctance to work if charity was available, to look no further than today's full belly, and to spend every possible ha'penny on alcohol. Millions of pounds of English money had been poured into the bottomless pit of Ireland, in the provision of vast relief programmes, seed for farmers, public works for unemployed, but England's generosity, it seemed, had achieved nothing except encourage Irish sloth and lawlessness.

Well, lawlessness at least was one thing that the English were capable of dealing with. There were, thank God, infantry companies in Derry, Enniskillen and Ballyshannon, dragoons in Donegal Town and Omagh, and forces of armed constables everywhere — a half dozen in little barracks behind Sergeant Cooley's station house, and an Inspector and twenty more in Strabane. Even if a third of the Army and all of the police were themselves Irish, experience had shown that the people were incapable of organising a serious insurrection. The last armed rising, born in 1848 with shouts, threats and grandiose boasting, had quickly disintegrated following a pathetic scuffle with a handful of constables. No, insurrection wasn't likely. The Irish, blast them, wouldn't fight for what they claimed were their liberties. They preferred to waylay and murder landlords and agents on lonely roads, hamstring horses, club dogs to death, drive cattle over cliffs, and burn down stables, barns and hayricks — acts of spiteful ingratitude that did not engender sympathy from either the Irish gentry or the English tax-payer. This was the last quarter of the nineteenth century. Britain was prosperous, powerful, civilised, but Ireland insisted upon being an embarrassment.

There were plans for a new provocation, Cooley told him, in County Mayo. Uncompromising landlords or agents were to be 'isolated from their kind as if they had been lepers of old' — with local people ostracizing them and their families, refusing to work and harvest for them, or sell them food or supplies, and terrorizing all others into doing the same. 'Mind ye,' the Sergeant added, almost apologetically, 'Mayo don't mean anythin' ter people hungry in Tyrone an' Antrim. Shure, there'll be labourers cornin' from Ulster, and soldiers to guard thin. Ye'll niver see the Irish standin' together.'

It was difficult to understand what the Irish tenantry hoped to achieve other than increased discomfiture — but who could understand the Irish? Home Rule, for certain, was unthinkable. An Ireland governed by Irish would explode into chaos and anarchy within weeks. He was himself already aware of the veiled hostility of Letterkenny tradespeople towards him. He had made purchases, but only with the accompaniment of doubts and delays, and prices were high. The horse he had hired from a Letterkenny dealer was a poor animal, but Cooley had advised hiring rather than the purchase of a better animal which might be discovered pouring its blood into the stable floor on any morning. He was not annoyed that the few local gentry who refrained from being permanent absentees from their properties did not seek an acquaintanceship with him. A land agent, it seemed, was neither gentry nor commoner, and was accepted by neither.

There was a great deal to be done, and not much time before winter began in earnest. Noggs would have to recruit labour, but first there were the rents of a dozen tenants remaining unpaid. In cases of inability to pay, he was at liberty to seize crops or livestock in lieu, and the recent harvest, he knew, had been a bad one. Any additional depletion of stocks could mean extreme hardship — and what did one do with a man like Whelan, who seemed to have neither rent money nor chattels other than a few scrawny goats? The prospect of evicting anyone, with winter coming, was abhorrent. He would need authority from London, and the help of the Constabulary, 'crow-bar men', and perhaps even soldiers. He hoped, b'God, that it never came to that.

Sergeant Cooley and old Doctor Obadiah Ternan, of the Medical Hall, Enniskillen — making his weekly visit to Letterkenny as Medical Officer to the Board of Guardians — confirmed the opinion earlier expressed by the Worshipful Company of Glaziers. 'If you fail to extract rent from a tenant at the end of a quarter,' Ternan nodded, 'you're only aiding and abetting an eviction in the end, because he'll never achieve twice the sum in a further three months — unless he goes to the gombeen man, and that's only delaying the inevitable and putting him still deeper in debt. You must use every means, every threat, to squeeze the rent out of him somehow. It's like surgery without anaesthetic — cruel, but damn necessary if the patient's going to survive at all. The tenant may have a hungry winter — a million Irish are at starvation level every year — but he'll still have his holding. If there's absolutely no hope of getting rent' — he paused and shrugged — 'then evict.'

'Ye'll need a warrant o' removal,' Cooley added, 'signed by two magistrates.'

The Glaziers, Noggs knew, would be sending him a sharp reminder if he did not take some action soon. It would have to be tomorrow, one way or the other. He spent the remainder of the day in the stable, fixing a trip-wire which, if someone entered, would jostle an old bell in the rafters. It would have been as simple to rig a spring-gun — a device he had employed with success against night-crawling intruders in India — but it was a drastic measure for defending a stable in Ireland.

On his knees on the straw-scattered floor, he had glanced up to see Mrs Whelan, standing silently and watching. He climbed to his feet. 'Ye' supper's sorved, sorr,' she said quietly. 'Ye'll not be wantin' it cauld.' Her eyes fell to the trip-wire, then rose again. 'Ye'll be wishin' I hadn't seen that, sorr, wi' ye' suspicions o' Tom Whelan.'

Noggs considered. 'No, Mrs Whelan. If someone does take a knife to the horse without disturbing the wire, then I'll know exactly who to send the police for — assuming that you're not in the habit of mutilating horses and cattle yourself. Besides, there are a few other things here that an uninvited visitor will find a lot more unpleasant than a tin bell.' It wouldn't be a bad thing, he decided, to encourage a rumour to circulate that the Glaziers' estate house was a nest of armed snares. But there was something more immediate. 'Tomorrow morning, Mrs Whelan, I'll be making my last circuit for rents. Perhaps you'll tell your husband that I'll be at your holding before nine.'

It was only rarely that he had been able to penetrate the almost trance-like calm with which she always moved and spoke, but this was one of those occasions. He saw a flush rise into her face, and then she rubbed one ankle against the other, shaking her head. 'Yer honour, sorr — ye'll as likely get rent from Tom Whelan as a bucket o' water in hell. He's nothin' put by, not even seed fer nex' year, sorr, an' not a stick of anythin' in the house worth a shillin'.' She paused, watching him gather his few tools. 'Mr Campbell, sorr, niver asked fer rent.'

He responded without thinking, naively. 'He didn't? You mean he allowed you the tenancy for nothing?'

'Not nothin', sorr. Mr Campbell niver allowed anythin' for nothin'.'

He could have bitten off his own tongue. 'I've a rent roll to maintain, Mrs Whelan. That's what I'm here for.' He did not look at her, but walked away, leaving her motionless. Goddammit, had she been about to offer herself to him in lieu of her husband's rent? The whole thing was developing into one of those ludicrous playhouse melodramas with himself roled as the unscrupulous landowner, and Mrs Whelan bravely sacrificing her chastity to save an impoverished husband from ruin. Only it wasn't quite like that. Mrs Whelan, for all her Mona Lisa serenity, appeared to have no qualms, and her husband was a not unwilling accomplice.

Mrs Whelan, however, was evidently not convinced that she had made her offer sufficiently clear. As she served his supper she broached the subject again. 'Tom Whelan don't mind me stayin' late, sorr, or orl night, an' the rent's not much fer a gentleman like yerself, now.' She spoke with the composure of a woman making a purchase in a grocer's shop. 'Shure, ye'd pay a foin price in Dublin or London fer the same, sorr, an' niver know whit ye were gettin' fer ye' money. Ye'd shiver, sorr, if ye knew some o' the diseases thim wimmin have got, sorr —'

Noggs winced, then pushed aside an untouched supper. 'Mrs Whelan — attractive though the prospect may be, I am not anxious to continue the arrangement you had with Mr Campbell. I'm a land agent, and my primary duty is to collect rents. If every tenant's wife transacted a similar exchange, all landlords would be bankrupt and every damn agent on his knees —'

He laughed, then decided to drop his bombshell. 'In any case, there's going to be a change. In two weeks I've a man-servant arriving from London — William Sutton, an old soldier. Most of my life's been spent in men's company, Mrs Whelan, and although I've no complaints about you? housekeeping — I'll write a reference saying so — I'll be more at ease with a man.' He paused, then continued apologetically. 'When

Sutton comes, I'm afraid I must dispense with your services.' He had no desire to see the effect of his words, but as he pushed back his chair he was aware that Mrs Whelan's eyes had widened, that she flinched as if she had been struck before, with an effort, she gained control of her feelings and nodded. 'Aye, sorr, I see,' she whispered, then turned and was gone.

* * *

He saddled his horse at dawn, before the knee-high ground mist had dispersed, and before Mrs Whelan had arrived to kindle the kitchen stove for his breakfast and hot water. Noggs didn't want to meet her — not, at least, until he had first talked with her husband. He'd reached a decision which probably demonstrated that he was the most ill-qualified land agent in Ireland and a soft fool, but he could think of nothing else.

Mrs Whelan's, offer, made with such incredible unconcern, had abruptly decided him against maintaining her in employment in addition to the man from London. He'd been reluctant to deprive the woman of wages that apparently formed the Whelans' sole income, but his good intention had turned sour. And if Whelan could not meet his obligation this morning, Noggs would have to set in motion the process of eviction. Certainly the Whelans would have to relinquish their holding, but there was one thing he could do. He could pay their expenses of emigration. In Belfast there was a shipping company which undertook to transport emigrants to Quebec, supplying 7lb of provisions weekly and three quarts of water daily, at a cost of £12 per head. In Canada the Whelans would have no reason to complain of land unfit for farming; there were millions of acres to choose from, and nothing to prevent them crossing the border into the USA, where there were endless opportunities for a man prepared to work hard. And Whelan would have to work, dammit. He'd find that neither Canadians nor Americans would take kindly to his whining of black luck and exploitation. In America a man had to make his own luck.

Besides their fare money, the pair would need additional food for the passage — a pound of porridge stir-about a day was starvation fare — and a small sum to feed and shelter them during their initial week or two in Canada. A total of £35 should be sufficient, and it was about as much as he could muster. As for the Glaziers, and the Whelans' vacated holding, well, he'd cross that bridge when he came to it.

The Letterkenny road was deserted, as it always seemed to be, potholed and puddled, surrounded by a landscape as dreary as any he'd seen in four continents. Whelan's goats had gone from their grazing, and were nowhere in sight, but Whelan himself stood at his cottage door, watching Noggs' approach.

'If it's the rent ye want, sorr,' Whelan said sullenly, 'there ain't nothin'. I told ye before, it's sick land, so 'tis — an' it's a black crime ter ask rent fer land that's not worth a streak o' spit —'

Noggs dismounted. 'I see you've moved off your goats.'

'Aye. Ye're not gettin' thim, ye're not. Ye might think ye'll drive us out loik bloddy rats, wi' the sojers an' the polis ter help ye, but ye'll not be gettin' thim goats, I'm tellin' ye —' Beyond Whelan, Noggs could see a few feet into the unlit interior of the cottage, an earth floor into which old sacking had been trodden and mud-cemented to hardness, a small, gimcrack table supporting an oil lamp, a miscellany of soiled crocks and, half wrapped in crumpled newspaper, a fist-sized remnant of bacon that, he guessed, had come from his own larder. He had already suspected that the groceries he paid for were more than necessary for the needs of himself and Mrs Whelan, but he had not been disposed to dispute the matter.

He waved the other to silence. 'For God's sake, man, stop whining. I don't want the damn goats, and I've no intention — if I can avoid it — of evicting anyone. There's a solution, if you and your wife will co-operate —'

Whelan swallowed, then wiped his mouth with the back of a dirty hand. 'Jasus!' he spat. 'Ye don't ask a man ter bloddy *co-operate* in givin' ye his wife ter pig wi', do ye? A man's not ter blame if his wife's a whore, an' too good fer the loiks ave me, an' sniffin' aroun' the breeches o' the gentry loik a bitch on hate — becos she's been ter a bloddy Galway board-school! It's co-operation ye want, is ut? Whit's the worth ev a man's wife, thet he's took before a priest, an' worked an' sweated fer?' His speech was angrily incoherent. 'A man's wife, naked in ye' bed, in exchange fer the rent o' this stinkin' houldin', is ut? Shure, an' whit am I paid fer the black shame ev ut? An' fer hiding the scandal from reachin' ye' bloddy Glaziers' Company in London?' The indignation in his voice suddenly disappeared. 'Five poun', now, sorr —' He was almost wheedling. 'Five poun' a month, an' there'll be no trouble, sorr — no trouble at orl. I kin tell ye' — he winked confidingly — 'she's a hot little handful, so she is, when ye've got her goin', sorr. Shure, she'll give ye as good as ye want. The last agent didn't complain, sorr, an' he were built loik a bull, wi' the appetite ev a buck rabbit —'

Noggs was already replacing a foot into a stirrup. 'I had a different proposal, Whelan,' he said disgustedly, 'but it didn't allow you the opportunity to pimp on your wife's behalf and live on her dirty earnings. It meant you had to work, Whelan — and that, I'm beginning to realise, is a forlorn prospect, blast it.' He lifted himself into the saddle. 'It'll be eviction, then, as soon as I get authority from London.' The words were out before he could stop them, and it was too late.

'And what, exactly, was the "different proposal" you had in mind, Captain?' A man emerged from the door behind Whelan — a tall, slim man with dark eyes over a well-trimmed imperial, and clothes which, if threadbare at cuffs and elbows, had once been cut by a London tailor. In the crook of an arm he held a long-barrelled gun, its muzzle lowered, but his lips smiled. 'Mr Whelan's offer, now, is a generous one, Captain. What greater love can a man have for his land, than he give his wife to retain it?' He cocked his head quizzically. 'And the lady, I'll be bound, has already offered herself, choking back her sobs of shame, eh? You've not been so ungallant as to refuse?'

'You,' Noggs said, 'must be Rice. I was beginning to wonder when you'd show yourself.' He paused. 'Rice of the Ninth, if I remember correctly?'

'Rice, at your service, Captain,' the other nodded, still smiling, 'and, as you say once of the Ninth.' He raised his eyebrows. 'Has Sergeant Cooley been gossiping? No, I shouldn't think so. He has an odd sense of propriety, has our Sergeant.' He laughed softly. 'Do you know that Cooley was once a drunken, brawling terror? That every pay-night it took four men to drag him from the barracks canteen, and that he had more lashes than anyone else in the Fusiliers — until someone decided that, instead of repeatedly flogging the spirit out of him, they'd promote him? The result was a transformation that you'd never credit, Captain — and I inherited one of the finest sergeants *in* the British Army.'

'Do you always carry a gun?' Noggs asked.

'Ah,' Rice laughed again. 'Just for the occasional pheasant, y'know.'

'Pheasant? Here?' Noggs gazed around at the treeless bog-land. 'That's optimism, if you like. And a rifle too?'

Rice assumed an expression of mock dejection. 'You're right, of course, Captain. It's just the ritual of a gentleman in reduced circumstances, who likes to pretend he's still strolling the Berkshire spinneys with a Purdey twelve-bore on his arm. This' — he raised the gun nonchalantly, until it pointed at Noggs' chest — 'is only an old Remington rolling-block. Not at all the thing for pheasant but, on balance, preferable to a percussion Adams from the Sepoy Revolt, eh, Captain?'

'Better,' Noggs agreed, 'at six hundred yards' — he glanced around again — 'which would be the distance of the nearest cover from here.' He shrugged. 'Not that the Fusiliers ever had a reputation for marksmanship. In the 60th a rifleman's expected to hit a six-foot target five times out of five at that range — bog or no bog.' Below him, Whelan was gazing at both men in turn, uncomprehending.

'There's the matter of the eviction,' Rice reminded Noggs, and Whelan nodded, anxious to be involved. 'Shure, the eviction. It's only a bloddy thafe that'd ask rent fer land thet won't grow nothin' —'

'Whelan and your predecessor had a sort of — Rice grinned — 'understanding, Captain, which Campbell seemed to find quite acceptable. It's a lonely life for a bachelor agent in Donegal and, in any case, the Letterkenny gossips will put Mrs Whelan into your bed whether you like it or not — so, like inevitable rape, you may as well lie back and enjoy it. Why involve yourself in all the sordid business of eviction, police and troops, and the ill-feeling it'll rouse? Do you suppose the Worshipful Company of Glaziers will send you a medal — or curse you for getting their name blacked?'

'I'm not tempted,' Noggs answered. 'Odd though it may seem, I don't want a woman in my bed. Any woman. I don't even want one in my house. And at this moment the one woman I never want to see or hear about again is Mrs Whelan. That, I hope, is quite clear.' The gun muzzle below him had not moved, but he went on. 'Security of tenure under the Land Act doesn't mean rent-free tenancy, and you know it. I'm not anxious to go running to the magistrates, but no rent — or saleable goods to the same value — mean no tenancy.'

'I sympathise on one point, Captain. Any man who disclaims any desire for a handsome woman is damn odd, or a liar. The conventions of society demand it, don't you know? It's always the man who's a ravening seducer, and nobody will believe otherwise. Any pasty-faced kitchen maid could put the Bishop of London into the dock just by unbuttoning her bodice and screaming atrocity.' His smile had not disappeared, but his eyes had hardened. 'For you, Captain, the choice is clear-cut. In exchange for a modest financial arrangement you can have the complete freedom of Mrs Whelan's services, in or out of bed, without the slightest danger of repercussion.' He glanced at his companion. 'Isn't that right, Whelan?'

Whelan sniffed, nodding. 'Shure, an' no questions arst.'

'The alternative is horrible to relate,' Rice grimaced. 'First of all, gossip. Then the anonymous letters to the Glaziers, and the newspapers. Then the magistrates. Simple, innocent woman — married, too — compelled to submit to agent's lust, threats of eviction and husband frantic with anguish. Do you remember the scandal of the Manchester mill-girls? The public's not forgotten that yet. And when Sergeant Cooley is sent to investigate, he'll find Mrs Whelan suitably unclad and distraught. Whatever his private feelings, he'll have to report what he saw. Worse, it might be the Inspector from Strabane, who's a Methodist and a Sunday School man who hangs a curtain around his dining-room table to hide the legs from the children —'

Noggs snorted impatiently. 'Godammit, Rice, I haven't time to listen to this clap-trap. Coming from Whelan, I might have understood it, but I gave you credit for better sense.' He began to turn his horse. 'When Mrs Whelan leaves the estate house today, she needn't return. There's a man joining me from London in a fortnight, and I'll manage alone until then. In the meantime I'm applying for a warrant of removal, and you can go to hell.'

'That's what Campbell said.' The muzzle of the gun had followed Noggs' movement. 'Only his language was obscene.'

'An' ye know whit happened ter Campbell, an' all,' Whelan sneered.

Noggs checked the horse. 'No, I don't. What happened to Campbell?' He had seen a flicker of annoyance in Rice's face as Whelan spoke. The man had been momentarily discomfited — but the moment had gone, and Rice grinned again. 'Ah,' he said, 'Campbell decided to change the rules of the game, Captain. If he hadn't lost his temper and taken down his gun, he wouldn't have had to clean it, and so wouldn't have had an accident.'

'Shure, that's right,' Whelan agreed.

Noggs had the sudden, instinctive feeling that the attitudes of Rice and Whelan did not share the same motive. Whelan, with an inherent resentment towards landlords, could see little further than a prospect of easy money. Much of Rice's conversation was beyond his comprehension, but he was agreeing, regardless. And Rice was using Whelan for reasons other than the mere evasion of a smallholder's rent. Rice, with his smile, was far more dangerous than any number of disgruntled peasant farmers, and he wanted Noggs enmeshed in a sordid altercation which would aggravate still further the hostility between tenants and landlords, increase the embarrassment of the authorities, and incense local trouble-makers. If necessary, Rice would see him dead. Like Campbell.

But, Noggs calculated, Rice wouldn't shoot him here — in the open, with his own gun and with the unreliable Whelan as witness. When it happened, Rice would be unseen and the death bullet untraceable. Or an accident, as with Campbell.

'You're a damn fool, Whelan,' Noggs said. 'A puppet — if you know what that means. Ask Rice what he's getting out of this, and why he's so concerned about your welfare — then ask yourself why it's your wife and your holding that's being staked.' He pulled his horse around and kicked it into a walk, presenting his back to Rice's gun, and listening for the click that would tell him of the Remington being cocked. There was a tingle in his scalp he'd known before. The Remington's .50 calibre shell would smash his spine and tear a hole in his chest as big as a fist. Involuntarily he tensed, but nothing happened.

But would he know of it? A bullet travelled faster than its own sound, about twice as fast — and he knew this was a stupid calculation he'd made many times, with his belly squirming and the sweat running into his eyes. Would he even feel the bullet strike? And would his brain react sufficiently quickly to tell him, in that infinitesimal fraction of time, that he was dead? He'd fall forward from his saddle, but probably never know that he'd hit the ground. Mind, there were French doctors who claimed that a human head separated from its body by the guillotine, could see, hear and be fully sensible of all that happened around it for up to thirty seconds after decapitation. If Rice pulled his trigger now —

But these were panic thoughts — the kind that broke a man's self-control and sent him running wildly, helpless in fear. He'd seen men reduced to sobbing incoherence because they'd thought too much about death and the nothingness that came after. Far better to think of mundane things, like the hooves of his horse sinking into the boggy pasture below him — mingling, he noted, with its own foot-prints in the reverse direction. More than one animal had trodden this way. Rice, then, had a horse, and had tethered it behind the cottage, out of sight. Perhaps the goats were there also.

Nothing happened. At a hundred yards, he knew, he would be beyond the sight of Rice and Whelan, but the distance seemed endless, and he had an overwhelming urge to hammer his heels into his horse's flanks; but that wouldn't do, and he'd be damned if he'd look over his shoulder. The horse tugged up the last slope to the road, and he reined, angry that the palms of his hands were sweating. He'd grown damn soft, blast it.

What now? He had a dozen tenants to find, but he might be wiser to first ride into Letterkenny, to Sergeant Cooley. Festering hell! What could he tell Cooley? Neither Rice nor Whelan had committed any crime. They had merely made a few unpleasant suggestions which could be either refuted or shrugged aside as jokes. Noggs, they would say, had no sense of humour. They were damn right.

First, he would return to the estate house, pay Mrs Whelan a week's wages, and send her packing. That, at least, would deprive Rice and Whelan of their bargaining position. Then he'd telegraph London regarding the Whelans' eviction, and he could see the magistrates tomorrow. As for Rice, well, he'd have to think. First he'd dispose of Mrs Whelan.

He wished, b'God, that he'd never come to this brutish place. He had been bored by London, but never repelled. He should never have come to Donegal, that was certain. In London, tonight, he might have dined at the Bristol, then strolled to see Jenny Lind at the Trocadero or Champagne Charlie Leybourne at the Pavilion, or Bessie Bellwood, MacDermott or Chevalier, a late supper of poached rabbit at Weston's and a cab to a quiet bed in St John's Wood. When he had told Willie Mudford, the editor of the *Standard*, of his appointment in Ireland, that gentleman had looked over his steel-rimmed glasses and said, 'I'll give you three months, dear boy. By spring the Russians will be at the gates of Constantinople, and the Fleet will be in the Aegean, so don't throw away your fur-lined boots and your sleeping bag. You'll never keep yourself away.' Noggs had laughed.

Still, by now Gay and Francis would be in Plevna. Whom would the *Standard* send? George Henty, or Cameron. They were both sound men. Then there'd be Forbes of the *Daily News*, Fripps of the *Graphic*, and Melton Prior of the *Illustrated* — a tough, intrepid breed of men who braved dust-storms or snow-blizzards, flooded trenches or searing heat, bullets and disease, just to be first with that vital photograph that would set the eager news-boy screeching in Fleet Street and the lights burning late at Westminster. Noggs recalled the tangy taste of success when, numbed with weariness in some remote telegraph office, his cold fingers had scribbled frantically as the operator's key chattered his hard-won news to distant, sleeping London, knowing himself a priceless hour ahead of his nearest rivals and with only his own dispatch reaching the hungry presses tomorrow. 'From our own Special Correspondent,' the *Standard* could gloat, 'an exclusive despatch from the beleaguered Turkish headquarters at Tashkessan —'

But the Special Correspondent, Charles Leonard Norris-Newman, wasn't in Tashkessan, watching through the swirling snowflakes for the massed battalions of the Russian Imperial Guard on the Sofia-Plevna road. He was in Donegal, damn and blast it, involved in the sordid business of rents and evictions, a tenant pimping for his wife, and the possibility of a hole in his head from a murderer's gun.

The estate house stood in chilling silence, above it the sky overcast and leaden. It would rain later. Goddam — he'd never known a place for so much rain. From the rutted drive he could see the broken window of his bedroom, and the stableyard still littered with dead leaves, the gig with its lowered shafts, and the old cattle trough on its side in the dust. Other men before him had gazed at the house, like this, and cursed it. There was no warmth here, nothing to provoke that sense of home-coming that anyone could feel for even a tent of ragged blankets in a wilderness. Many had come to the Glaziers' estate house, but it had never been a home, never embraced the loves and tears of a family, the shouts and clatter of children, a cat in the hearth, happy laughter on sunlit mornings, slippers chewed by puppy dogs, singing kettles and chestnuts on the hob, soiled babies, and all the other things that made a house a living entity. This house was like an unwanted old spinster, coldly virginal, and grown bitter and hostile with the long years of emptiness and unfulfilment.

Noggs stabled the horse, carefully replacing the trip-wire, and entered the house through the kitchen. He entertained no enthusiasm for his task; he could order a malcontent soldier to be flogged without qualms, take a crop to a *syce* for ruining a horse's mouth, hang a captured hillman with his own hands — but he had never been able to handle a woman firmly. The kitchen was empty, and so was the dining-room.

Ah, there had been women. Before. How many? There were several of whom he could remember nothing but the occasions — at Simla, for instance, where women who for years had been paragons of wifely virtue suddenly became shameless libertines as soon as their husbands were an hour away. And the Sudder Bazaar at Meerut, and Delhi, and Benares. He could recall occasions, the eager guilt immediately before and, afterwards, emerging into the blinding sun-glare, walking quickly to put the place as far behind him as possible, wanting to forget. Those had been the brief, physical experiences, but there had been others, vivid memory pictures as if they were only of yesterday. The very first.

It had been the year of the Great Exhibition, when he had been seventeen and she a year younger — a country cousin awed by the first visit to London and innocently credulous. She was plump, blonde-haired, pink-cheeked, and it was her trusting naivety that had inspired his first vague speculations. Boyishly, it was her breasts beneath the pearl buttons of her blouse, pouting and full, that repeatedly captured his attention and made him swallow at a drying throat. Once she had enquired, 'What are you looking at, Charles? My brooch?' But her eyes had been guileless. Then, at the Exhibition, strolling ahead of their parents among the palms, they had been confronted by the marble Adonis, whitely naked and prominently masculine. It was something from which well-bred young ladies would normally lower their eyes and pass on demurely, but she had halted at his side, uncertain, too inexperienced to ignore the embarrassment, and he had not helped her. Her chatter stopped. There was a long moment of silence, and then her eyes turned to his, and she flushed. Terrified to speak, he shrugged, and she suddenly giggled, as if sharing with him the naughtiness of it. It was stiflingly warm under the vast, glass canopy. He was sweating, and he thought that he might choke, but his hand was over a breast, squeezing gently, and she did not move. Her eyes were still wide, apprehensively but not offended. From beyond the nearest palms came the sound of approaching voices. He squeezed again, gently, urgently, and her lips parted. In the next moment they had moved apart and were walking on.

As a result, it had been so easy that, looking back, he felt almost ashamed. She had been utterly ignorant of sexual matters, and he knew very little. In the doubtful security of her bedroom he was content, at first, to merely kiss her and be kissed, and to unbutton her blouse. She was compliant, from curiosity rather than desire, and did not resist when he inexpertly embarked upon his final experiment, but splayed her plump legs obligingly, and seemed more concerned over his subsequent exhaustion than her own involvement. That had been twenty-six years ago. Noggs mused, but he remembered every impetuous second of it. He had not seen her again until his return from India, by which time she had become the wife of a baronet, fat and whale-boned, with three sons and two daughters. Her eyes had twinkled as he bowed over her hand. 'The Exhibition,' she nodded, 'and Adonis. London was full of surprising things for a country girl that year.'

He found Mary Whelan where an odd premonition told him he might find her — in his bedroom. As Noggs entered, she rose to her knees on the bed, naked except for the sheet over her legs. Her red hair was unbound, and she brushed it back from her face so that it fell over her shoulders in a cascade crimped by recent plaiting, to the upturned soles of her feet, 'Mr Campbell always loiked me waitin', sorr,' she said, 'Ye'll have spoke wi' Tom Whelan?'

Noggs extracted a sovereign from a waistcoat pocket and placed it on a marble-topped wash-stand. 'You can get yourself dressed before you catch cold, Mrs Whelan. And you can leave immediately.' She had a good body, he noted involuntarily, of that delicate whiteness common to all red-haired women. Her shoulders were hunched, as if in modesty, so that her breasts were pushed together between her upper arms. She was thin-flanked, but a few months of good food would make a handsome woman of her. He wasn't surprised at Campbell's interest, only at Whelan's indifference. 'I've spoken to your husband,' he nodded, 'and I'm not buying.'

She stared at him. 'Faith, then I'll have his fists in me face, so I will. And he tellin' me it wud all be agreed wi' ye, an' I was ter be waitin' and ready.' There was mild surprise in her voice, but no other emotion. She eyed the small pile of her clothing on the floor, then looked up at him. 'Shure, ye don't know the trouble ye'll be causin' — an' ye're not even giving it a try? I'll tell ye somethin', sorr. It'll cost ye nothin' ter try me paces She twisted her legs from under her and swung them from the bed, then leaned back on her hands to expose herself to him. 'I'm arsking ye, sorr, so I am. Ye'll not be wantin' me ter shame meself wi' begging ye? But I'll beg, sorr, if ye loik. If ye don't, I'll be raw from Tom Whelan's belt-buckle, an' he's a cruel man wi' his fists when the black humour's in him —' She saw Noggs frown, and hurried on. 'If I kin tell him ye tried me, sorr, it won't be my fault — jes' once, an' ye kin do what ye loik She lay back on her elbows. 'Shure, I'll shut me eyes, an' ye kin do what ye loik —'

Noggs grimaced, stooped to take up the bundled clothes on the floor, and tossed them towards her. 'Dammit, woman, doesn't anyone understand plain English? I'll tell you once more — and that's all. No. I'm not interested. In fact, I'm getting bloody angry. Get yourself decent, and get out of the house. Your husband's black humours aren't my business. You married him, Mrs Whelan — although, b'God, marriage doesn't seem to mean much in this damn country.' He paused grimly. 'You'll be out of this house in ten minutes, and I don't want you back. I don't want you on Glazier property, either — and I'll see that you're not, within the next few days.'

He had turned to leave, but she was not finished. 'Captain, sorr — ye don't know the half of it! Shure I know it's not ye' business if Tom Whelan thrashes the spew out o' me. He's done it often enough, so he has. If it's not his belt or his fists, it's his boots. Mother o' God, there's times I've been near to dead, an' crawlin' on me knees for a bucket o' water ter wash the blood from me. Ye've not seen a bigger man than Mr Campbell, sorr — an' he had the madness in him when he took hould ev me, but that were nothin' to Tom Whelan's leatherin'.' She stopped, then, 'But that's not ye' business, sorr — an' it ain't ye' business if we've no rent money, an' nothin' 'cepting a few praties stinkin' wi rottenness, an' Tom Whelan waitin' on every ha'penny I earn ter spend on Smiley's brew. That's not ye' business, sorr.' She paused again. 'But if he's driven into a corner, sorr, there's no knowin' what wickedness he'll be intendin for ye. Mr. Campbell —'

Nogg's voice was quiet, void of emotion. 'Mrs Whelan, nothing you're saying can make the slightest difference. If you were the Comtesse de Castiglione or Giulia Barucci, with perfumed ermine and free champagne, I'd be incapable of complying. *Incapable*, do you understand? It's something that your husband, and Rice, didn't know about, and it's why any fabricated accusations regarding my relationship with you or any other woman wouldn't hold a cupful of water in a court of law — even if the jury were all members of the Ladies' White Cross Army and full-blooded Fenians to boot. And that, Mrs Whelan, is why the dirty little scheme that was so successful with Campbell can't possibly begin to work with me.' He shrugged. 'So if you've no other reason for occupying my bed in a state of dishabille, you may as well put on your shift, take your sovereign, and take the news to your anxious collaborators.'

Mary Whelan reached for a threadbare stocking, with her eyes, uncertain, on Noggs. 'Incapable? Faith, an' who d'ye suppose wid believe a man thet sez he's incapable? Widn't I be swearin' thet you did it? An' widn't Tom Whelan be a witness?'

She tossed her head. 'Shure an' the moon's made o' green cheese, so 'tis. Nobody'd believe ye. Incapable, is it? Tell that in Green Street Courthouse an' it'll get ye no further than Kilmainham Gaol, so it will.'

He was silent for several moments, contemplating the tall china jug, decorated with trailing red roses, that stood in its matching basin on the wash-stand. Then he sighed. Twelve — thirteen years ago, Mrs Whelan — in India — I had the misfortune to be captured by hostile tribesmen on the North-West Frontier.' He paused, deliberating on his words. The Pathans are a damn nasty breed, Mrs Whelan. Compared with them your Fenian Brotherhood yahoos are innocent lambs — beginners. Give a Pathan a knife, and he'll do things that'd make the Devil himself sick to his guts — do you understand?' He paused again. 'Well — they did things to me with a knife.' Her face showed indecision for a further few seconds, and then her eyes widened as comprehension came to her. Noggs nodded. 'That's right, Mrs Whelan — with a knife.'

He remembered the moment. The confused jumble of years behind him was divided into two distinct groups — before and after. Immediately before, he'd been certain of death and, being certain, resigned. *By my troth I care not A man can die hut once; we owe God a death. And let it go which way it will, he that dies this year is quit for the next* His eyes were clenched fast against the blinding glare of the sky, and then there had been die moment, with the scream in his throat, the searing, racking agony of it, and he could hear men laughing...

Mary Whelan was laughing, with her hand over her mouth and her head flung back. 'Did ye ever hear ev it? Shure, an' there's Tom Whelan wid orl his foin plans — five poun' a month, an' no rrent, wid himself the squire o' Smiley's, standin' treat fer every bloddy scrounger in Letterkenny — an' Captain Rice, an' all, talkin' auld bull about human moralities! There's nothin' easier, sez he — an' meself, bedad, naked on ye bed an' showin' meself loik a shameless Jezebel —' She choked on her words. 'An' orl the time ye was *incapable*!'

If she thought it amusing, Noggs considered, then the irony of his own confession was just laughable. For thirteen years he had lived with the secret of his humiliation, walking in loneliness to hide the knowledge of it from others and, deliberately, never remaining in a social environment long enough to establish more than fleeting acquaintanceships. His evasiveness had often been mistaken for churlishness; he was an odd fellow, and men shrugged when his name was mentioned. A man who carried an empty sleeve or stumped on a wooden foot could wear his disability like a military decoration, but this was different. There were things a man could hide, the surgeon-major had said. What he'd really meant was that there were things a man didn't *have* to hide, didn't have to feel shame for. Women whispering over tea-cups could send him flying from a drawing-room and a casual conversation on Afghan border incidents would have the sweat cold on his face. Now, after thirteen years of furtiveness, he had confessed himself to an unprincipled slut of an Irishwoman —

There was a distant bell jangling, like the bell that jangled over the door of Smiley's bar — and then, distinctly, the shriek of a horse, shocked and terrified. Mary Whelan jolted upright, her face suddenly aghast, and Noggs sprang for the dressing-table where his pistol lay. 'Christ!' he spat. 'The stable!'

'No!' she shouted at him, desperately, scrabbling for her scattered clothes. 'Captain, sorr — they'll be watching fer ye! I kin tell ye —

they'll be waitin'!' But he had snatched up the gun and, quickly checking that it was loaded and capped, flung himself from the room. Mary Whelan's mouth twisted. 'Holy Mary, Mother o' God —'

He descended the stairs in three bounds, then halted. He had almost made a damn fool of himself. Put yourself in the enemy's place, blast it. Think like he's thinking — and then out-think him. Who was the enemy? Rice or Whelan — or both? Rice had a Remington rifle. Noggs' own old Adams' percussion revolver was obsolete, but at short range it would stop a running man dead in his tracks or put a standing one flat on his back. At short range, Rice's Remington was more accurate, and it would probably be fired from behind cover, but it was a single-shot weapon. Moreover, it fired black-powder cartridges that smoked — and that made a difference. The stable-yard was thirty-five feet square. That meant that Rice could fire one shot but, assuming he missed, he'd never reload before Noggs had reached him and put three bullets into him. Assuming he missed — and that wasn't counting Whelan.

Rice was probably expecting him to emerge from the rear door of the kitchen, and had his gun aimed. Or perhaps not.

Rice was a tactician — a damn good one. He, too, might credit Noggs with sufficient acumen to avoid the obvious. There were only two doors, the front and the rear. Noggs would use neither.

Without too closely approaching the window of the dining-room, he could see a little of the stable-yard, but most was hidden from view by the out-jutting bulk of the kitchen. He could see the open door of the stable — and something beyond, darker than the shadows, that moved. It was the horse, outflung on the straw and kicking out its last few moments of life. If Rice waited in the gloom of the stable, watching, then Noggs would never get through the window. He lifted the window-latch quietly.

Behind him, however, there was a flurry of footsteps, and he whirled with his pistol raised. Mary Whelan was running from the stairs towards the kitchen, half stooped, and holding up the skirt of her grubby, shapeless shift. One foot was stockinged, the other bare, and her mouth was wide in a white face. 'Holy Mary!'

'Mrs Whelan!' he roared, but he was too late. She sped the length of the kitchen, reached the rear door, and wrenched it open. 'Tom Whelan! Will ye be listenin' ter me?'

Noggs heard the rifle-shot, followed by a distant, unintelligible shout, and then Mary Whelan spun, her features contorted and ugly with stupefaction. She fell forward, towards him, but he could not reach her before she struck the tiled floor in an inelegant dishevel of crumpled linen, pallid legs and splayed, red hair. He dropped to his knees, turning her so that she lay on her back and with her sagging head cradled in his arms. Her hair fell untidily over her face, and there was a widening, crimson stain between her breasts. Mary Whelan was dead.

Beyond the open door there was a clatter of iron-shod boots on the cobbles of the stable-yard. Glancing up, Noggs could see Tom Whelan running — not towards the kitchen but in the direction of the old gig between the hay-bales and the cattle-trough. He was carrying a shot-gun, and he shouted.

'Ye treacherous, murderin' divil — ye butcherin' savage! A bit o' sport ter frighten the bloddy agent, was it? Intimidatin' the bourgeoisie, ye sez — an' ye shoot down a man's wife wid ye first filthy bullet!' He halted, feet apart and shot-gun unsteadily raised. 'B'Gud, an' if ye show ye dirty carcass from behind that cart, I'll shoot the schemin' black heart out ev it I'

Rice emerged from behind the gig. He was thumbing a cartridge into the block-breech of his rifle, ignoring Whelan and eyeing the door of the kitchen. 'Don't be a damn fool, man.' His voice was strained, but level. 'It was an accident, blast it — and I'm sorry, but who'd expect your wife to come screeching out of that door?' He snapped his gun-breech shut. 'I've never seen you display any conjugal sentiment before, Whelan — but that bloody Englishman's got to be finished now, or it's both our necks.'

In the kitchen, Noggs levelled his pistol over a crook of an elbow, but in that moment Whelan, only a yard from Rice, fired. Rice's face was suddenly a mangled, red-drenched horror in a shroud of black powder-smoke. The blast of the gun jerked his head backwards grotesquely, and he staggered two wild paces before crashing into the broken bales of hay behind him. Whelan flung his shot-gun to the ground.

He was still standing, motionless, with his back to the kitchen, when Noggs approached. 'Your wife's dead, Whelan,' Noggs said quietly. Whelan remained silent, and Noggs added, 'Do you want to see her?' Whelan continued his study of the clotted leaves that scattered the cobbles at his feet, but lifted his head at last. 'No, sorr.' He paused. 'Shure, an' it's not thet I don't care. I'm jes' not bloddy man enough — an' that's the trut' I'm tellin' ye.' He glanced at Nogg's pistol. 'Ye'll be savin' the Quane's justice a bit ev trouble if ye shoot me in self-defence an' finish wid it.'

It was beginning to rain, and north-westward, over the Derryveagh Mountains, the sky was like charcoal. A dozen or more white gulls were circling over the flat blogland's beyond the Fintown road. Noggs drew a deep breath. 'I'm not a judge or an executioner, Whelan. I'm going to Letterkenny to fetch Sergeant Cooley. If you're not here when we return, I suppose he'll organise a search — and probably report to the Inspector at Strabane. I don't know. Anyway, you've got at least an hour.'

Whelan contemplated Noggs with narrowed eyes. 'I've got a brother in Killybags, wid a fishin' boat —'

'I don't want to know,' Noggs interrupted quickly. 'I don't care whether you're taken or not, but if you are, I'll give evidence against you. If you get clear, and I ever see you again, I'll have you arrested for murder. There'll be no second damn chance. I don't want to know the road you're travelling, or if you're taking Rice's horse, or who's likely to help you — but the first time we meet again will be the last. I'll see you hang.' Noggs turned on his heel and began walking towards the Letterkenny road.

CHAPTER SIX

'I knew it, dear boy. I gave you three months, didn't I?' William Mudford peered over the top of his glasses. 'You simply can't put an old gun-mule out to graze with the cows, I tell you.' Beyond the window was the constant rumble of wheels on Ludgate Hill, the shouts of newsboys, the faint, tinny junketing of a mechanical piano. Mudford examined his ink-smudged fingers and smiled. 'But I'm delighted, Noggs, Something's about to happen — and there isn't a war correspondent worth an old boot left in Fleet Street. They're all in the Balkans or Afghanistan. Except you, dear boy.'

Noggs had guessed it. Willie Mudford didn't telegraph unless he smelled headlines. 'What's about to happen?' he asked. 'And where?'

'Africa, my dear Noggs. Africa.' Mudford leaned back in his chair, and Noggs knew what to expect. 'During the next twenty years we shall witness the final dissection and complete colonisation of that dark continent by the powers of Europe. The ignorant black men are at last to enjoy the full benefits of our civilisation — prisons, orphanages, workhouses, brothels, lunatic asylums — the hallmarks of social progress. Africa is to be neatly parcelled up, and nobody intends to be left out. France is sniffing at the Ivory Coast, Tunis, Morocco and Madagascar. Bismarck has marked out the Cameroon, the South-West Territories and Tanganyika. Leopold will have the Congo Basin, and Italy will probably settle for Libya and Abyssinia.'

'And us?'

'Ah, yes — Britain.' The editor nodded. 'It's odd, isn't it, how we've always managed to get the plums without really trying? If you look at a map of Africa, dear fellow, you'll see that most of the more valuable areas are already painted red. Wolseley has recently scooped up the Gold Coast, and the Niger territories are secure, but the gem is that vast green hinterland that stretches from the Transvaal clear to lake Nyasa and the southern Congo — and beginning with Zululand.' He smiled again. 'As I said, my dear Noggs, we're not greedy. We don't want ail of Africa. Only the best parts. The French Republic is welcome to three million square miles of Sahara Desert, and the Italians can dig up all the Roman ruins they want in Libya. All the diamonds, gold, copper, most of the ivory — and the rich, black soil that grows tobacco, tea, coffee, cotton, and flax — are being painted red.'

Noggs sighed. 'Dammit, Willie — now that you've decided on your editorial and I've had my geography lesson — what's this about? You mentioned Zululand. Is there something in the wind?'

'Very much in the wind, dear boy. I've been smelling it for months. In short, a rat.' He paused weightily. 'You'll know the political climate at the Cape. The Governor-General, Sir Bartle Frere, is obsessed with confederation, and he'd like to achieve it before this chap Kruger whips the Transvaal Boers into defying Crown authority. The border Boers want more land — Zulu land. Frere wants confederation, which is impossible with an independent Zululand.' He paused again. 'Ergo, Frere must annexe Zululand.'

Noggs shrugged. 'Frere has no business to annexe anything. It's a matter for Westminster. This is 1878, and we're not damn buccaneers. Anyway, I doubt whether Frere has sufficient military strength to achieve it. The Zulus aren't going to be knocked over by one battalion of Imperial troops and a rag-tag collection of Boers and volunteer militia. He'd need more regulars — and he'll not get them from Whitehall without damn good reason.'

'He's got them, my dear Noggs,' Mudford triumphed. 'Frere and Company have been experiencing a lot of Kaffir unrest — nothing to do with the Zulus, mark you — and the Imperial battalion, the 1st Battalion of the 24th Regiment, has been at full stretch, flushing out bands of stubborn blacks who won't fight in a civilised manner. You'll know the sort of thing, Noggs — and it's damn frustrating work for drilled troops. It's Frere's ready-made excuse for asking for reinforcements — and Whitehall has swallowed it. The 2nd Battalion of the 24th, at Chatham, is ordered to the Cape, and will sail in the *Himalaya* from Portsmouth in a few days. That's for a start.' He beamed at Noggs. 'At the same time, Lieutenant-General the Honourable Sir Frederic Thesiger has been despatched to the same place to assume command of all British troops in the Colony. That's the fuse, dear lad. We can rely upon Frere and his cronies to supply the match.'

'He wouldn't dare, b'God!' Noggs snorted. Imperial troops are intended for defence, not for invading inoffensive and independent neighbouring territories — and, as far as I recall, the king of the Zulus — Cetshwayo? — has always taken damn good care not to antagonise our people.' But he was uneasy. He remembered General Thesiger in India; a conscientious and competent man, but lacking the verve and temper that attracted the approval of the Horse Guards and the public, and perhaps feeling outshone by the more colourful performances of Wolseley, Roberts and Gordon. Such a man, in his fifty-second year, might well be tempted to seize a last opportunity to gain the adulation afforded to his younger colleagues and, in so doing, abandon his customary caution. 'A bloody bad mixture,' Noggs nodded reluctantly. 'An unfulfilled general and an ambitious governor.' He glanced at Mudford. 'And you think, between them, that they'll establish a *casus belli*?'

'Nothing could be easier.' William Mudford smoothed back his thinning hair. 'There must be dozens of minor border incidents that can be used as excuses for punitive action — and the line between punitive and offensive operations is damn hazy. Ah, Frere will telegraph some vaguely-worded justification to London, a few hours before he makes his final move, but by the time it reaches the Colonial Office, been pored over by a lot of nervous old men, and a prohibition formulated and telegraphed back to the Cape, it will be too late, Noggs. Thesiger, with Frere's blessing, will be in Zululand with horse, foot and artillery.'

It was beginning to make sense. William Mudford usually did. 'Nobody else in Fleet Street has smelled it yet, dear boy. If we're lucky, the *Standard* will be the only rag with a correspondent on the spot when hell breaks loose. The others are going to have a knotty problem in getting their best men from Sofia and Kabul to the Cape.' He chuckled, then reached for a paper at his elbow. 'Passage has been booked for you on the National Line *Egypt*, sailing from Southampton on Tuesday next. You'd best be aboard on Monday, dear lad. She makes Simon's Bay in twenty-eight days, East London in thirty-five, but we've arranged to have you put down off Durban — in a boat, I understand, through the surf. Ostensibly' — he grinned — 'you're going to work for the Cape Town *Standard & Mail* and the *Times of Natal*, but that's just to fool the opposition. When the Army starts moving, just remember that your last telegraph office is in a place called Pieter Maritzburgh, with a line to

Cape Town. After that, there's nothing except a black man with a cleft stick, or something.' He took up a small, brass hand-bell. 'Will you take tea, dear boy?'

CHAPTER SEVEN

There was very little in Birmingham that young Edwin Dyson had been reluctant to leave behind him. He had always disliked the baroque monstrosity of a house that his father had built at Aston Manor, and even more the warehouse that stood among the slums of Thomas Street and Lichfield Street, whose sagging roofs and tottering chimneys, broken windows and damp, rough pavements represented the worst aspects of the midlands city. It was true, however, that where there was muck there was brass, and there was plenty of brass in Birmingham, including his father's. 'Norman ancestors and a London voice don't mean anything without money, boy,' George Dyson was fond of telling him, 'and it's commerce that mints money, not fox-hunting and grouse-shooting.' But George Dyson, his son noted, was a member of the Schools Board, the Gas Committee, the Health Committee, the Estates Committee, and the Improvement Scheme of the Mayor, Mr Joseph Chamberlain. He was at pains to attend every Music Festival, where he might rub shoulders with, and offer entertainment to, titled gentry who considered commerce a necessary but degrading occupation. George Dyson's most treasured possession was a large, sepia photograph, ornately framed in the smoke room, in which his paunchy figure — one of a hundred — posed at the laying of the foundations of Birmingham's new Council House, another monstrosity of stained glass and frescoes, beneath a sculptured group depicting Britannia rewarding the Birmingham manufacturers.

Then there was his mother and, not least, Roxanne Beatrice Paton.

Mrs Martha Dyson, born Martha Toogood, was of humble origin, and her husband did not allow her to forget it. George Dyson bitterly regretted his marriage to a woman incapable of accompanying his ascent of the social ladder. Martha was a simple woman, insignificant and retiring, happier with her hands in a bowl of flour, or darning a holed sock, than with playing hostess before the critical eyes of pseudo-genteel ladies. On such occasions she dressed badly, used cosmetics crudely, and suffered the indignity of disparaging asides from her husband in her own drawing-room. George Dyson sneered when she put a ladle of coal on the fire instead of ringing for the maid, sneered again when she addressed the gardener as 'Mr Brook' instead of just 'Brook', and was angry when she paid cash to tradesmen instead of making them wait for a month, or better, two months or three.

Edwin's regard for his mother was undermined. She had long abandoned any serious interest in his activities or ambitions, her unvarying comment being, 'I'm sure that will be very nice, dear, but have you asked your father?'

If he was indifferent towards his mother, however, she did not represent a positive problem. Roxanne Beatrice Paton did. She was the daughter of Sir Digby Paton, Justice of the Peace, Master of Foxhounds, unchallenged doyen of Aston Manor's better people. The Patons did have Norman ancestors and, if they did not have a great deal of brass, the better people acknowledged them respectfully. Roxanne, George Dyson considered, could provide an excellent link with an illustrious family. Few doors would be closed to Roxanne Paton-Dyson or, by association, her father-in-law.

But Roxanne had scarcely a single attribute that Edwin found attractive. She was tall, thin and angular, talked of horses loudly and incessantly, and rode better than most men. Normal female pursuits — embroidery, sketching, visiting the poor — never claimed her attention, and she preferred the smells of liniment and saddle soap to those of perfume and toilet waters. Roxanne's suitors were few and of brief attendance, and Edwin was not surprised. He was, as yet, only mildly interested in the opposite sex, and the prospect of the masculine Roxanne becoming his lifetime consort, as his father desired, was worse than uncomfortable.

Edwin might not have confessed, however, even to himself, that his antipathy towards Birmingham was really centred upon his father. Life with George Dyson was a series of embarrassments, beginning with childhood and continuing through adolescence, when a number of college bursars in Cambridge and Oxford had coldly declined George Dyson's imperious demands for a place for his son. Edwin had attended Birmingham's Mason College. He would have preferred Oxford, if only because he would have been free of his dominating overseer and, in Oxford, the name 'D & B' would have been unknown.

His feelings towards the company, Dyson & Bradley, were mixed. Unlike others — Chamberlain's screw foundry, for instance — no manufacturing was carried out, unless one counted repairs to gun-locks and springs, the splicing of new stocks, the erasure of makers' marks. But there was always an air of conspiracy surrounding the activities of the 'D & B' warehouse. Its visitors were widely varied, from distinguished-looking gentlemen who alighted from closed carriages to dark-skinned, shabby aliens, sea-captains and colonial traders. There had been many Americans, from both Washington and Richmond, and departing wagons laden with crates marked 'Agricultural Tools- Jamaica'.

Only the guns intrigued young Edwin. He hated the warehouse, and yet, in its gloomy depths he could walk the narrow alleyways walled by racks of thousands of military weapons, of Bakers, Brunswicks, Whitworths, Enfield-Pritchitts, stacked piles of dusty Tower muskets fit only for the African trade and, more recently, breech-loading Sniders. What stories, he mused, could these silent guns of half a century tell? How many, in the sweating hands of blaspheming redcoats, had torn down Ney's cavalry at Waterloo, charged the Russians at Inkerman, or defied the onslaught on the Lucknow Residence? Occasionally, alone in the gloom, he would take down a weapon at random, press the cold walnut of its butt against his cheek, and reflect that, somewhere, sometime, another had done this, with the sting of powder smoke in his nostrils and death in the air, the Queen's enemies before him and, behind, the flag that he served for a pittance. What manner of man had he been? A slum-reared Englishman, a Highlander, a Dublin Jackeen? Had his belly knotted with fear as his company's ranks were shredded by canister, with his officer dead and the sergeants white-faced? Had the engagement been successful, or had he stumbled away in gut-raking defeat? Perhaps he had fallen, to be survived only by this thing of black steel, wet with his blood. How would he, Edwin, feel if this silent, dank warehouse were suddenly a shot-torn battlefield, and he standing thus, with gun levelled, hard against his cheek, as a thousand Cossacks thundered towards him, blood-lusting?

George Dyson entertained no such romanticism. It was the old story of supply and demand. When people wanted guns, they usually wanted them urgently, and were prepared to pay in gold. 'In this business,' he told Edwin, 'you never trust letters of credit or promises written on paper. Nobody pays a loser's creditors, and one side always loses. Besides, written contracts can be damning. The winning side might also be a customer, present or future. It's cash on consignment, before loading shipboard, and in gold — British, American, Austrian, Spanish, it doesn't matter.'

But George Dyson adhered to another law. The guns he supplied were reliable. Others might, and did, sell gimcrack rubbish — often specially manufactured — that could blow off an owner's face when the trigger was pulled. The customers of 'D & B' paid a high price, but their purchases were all government surplus weapons, all examined and, if necessary, repaired before being offered for sale.

For this purpose, 'D & B' employed four aged armourers, who hammered and filed in a small, filthy workshop, the floor of which was littered with debris: old springs, screws, lock-plates, ramrods, butt-caps, flash-pan covers, sawdust and metal filings. There was a small forge, with anvils, bullet moulds and grinders, wad cutters, nipple keys and prickers — and the old armourers had a language of their own, of which young Edwin strove to achieve an understanding. They were an exclusive people, these four old men, who sniffed and spat, and could take up a battered, nondescript gun, and say, 'German Dreyse, breech-loader,' sixty-three, corroded bore, sprained bolt, no pin, no fusée spring, no bleedin' good.'

Daily, George Dyson applied himself to the colonial and foreign affairs columns of *The Times* for news of threatened insurrections, border incidents, and diplomatic contention, which might be his first warning that, in two or three weeks, he must have available two thousand Sharps for Mexico, fifty Gatlings for Chile, Remingtons and ammunition for onward routeing from Macao, muskets and powder for the Hudson's Bay Company. George Dyson had a particular reason for seeking potential markets in advance of competitors. The British Army was in the process of replacing its Snider-Enfield rifles with the Martini-Henry, but to many armed forces the Snider was still a highly desirable acquisition and indeed, would continue to be carried by some British regiments for a number of years to come. If Dyson could purchase the Army's surplus stocks cheaply, there could be buyers from five continents beating a path to Birmingham, cash in hand.

It was no more than a further step in the fulfilment of George Dyson's ambitions. Next he would consider artillery and heavy calibre ammunition. Then why not warships and naval armaments? In the Balkans and South America almost annual revolutions provided lucrative opportunities. Japan was reorganizing her army and navy on European lines. There were war-lords in China, quarrelsome Egyptians and rebellious Sudanese, even Americans willing to sell to their own Indians. But Indians and Fuzzy-Wuzzies were small fry. Dyson had his sights on massive contracts from established governments, which would make the name 'D & B' a byeword in half the chancelleries of the world and George Dyson a man to be reckoned with. He could snap his fingers at the arrogant blue blood of the country. Goddam — a whisper from 'D & B' could have the Commander-in-Chief himself shivering in his polished boots. And Joseph Chamberlain might not be the most brilliant star rising from the smoking chimneys of Birmingham.

That his son would remain with 'D & B' he never for a moment doubted. In due course, perhaps, the company title could become 'Dyson, Son & Bradley', implying family tradition and stability. Young Edwin had his bread well buttered.

Unfortunately, young Edwin Dyson had long been aware that he had no desire to follow his father into 'D & B'. He had always subconsciously rebelled against the prospect, but only recently had his antipathy become stark and unconfused. Now, having determined upon a course of action, the years of morose anticipation, of an office stool and bills of lading, Birmingham's grimy factories, nails, screws, pen-nibs, the Assembly Rooms and die Sparbrook Club, the *Birmingham Mail*, and a nouveau riche society with its veneer of culture belied by a steel-works accent and a passion for pigs' trotters, all were thrust away. Above all, he resolved, he would never play stable-boy to Roxanne Beatrice Paton.

But then, having decided, what was the alternative? When he came to consider, it seemed he had less choice than any factory hand. He had no income of his own that was not derived from his father, no future that his father did not approve of. Still —

He chose his moment carefully. 'I think, sir,' he ventured, steeling himself, 'I should like to go into the Army.'

He had expected an explosion, and George Dyson exploded. Edwin held his ground sullenly. The Army, Dyson retorted, was composed of drunken, dissolute gutter-scum commanded by incompetent fools in plumes and tassels who'd not make counter-clerks in a Smethwick draper's shop. Soldiers were wasters of public money, unwilling or incapable of working for a living like honest men. Stamping up and down in a red tunic, or trotting a troop through St James's Park gratified nobody except small boys and nursemaids. Why the Army, anyway? If 'D & B' wasn't damn good enough, then, he, Edwin, could be found a place in another Birmingham company — Chamberlain's, Avery's, Boulton & Watt's, Cadbury's. It would be a disappointing arrangement, but anything was better than the confounded Army.

George Dyson's vociferous disapproval continued, unabated, for a week, and then, quite suddenly, ceased. George Dyson, as he did before any commitment, had been undertaking a little research, the results of which gave him considerable food for thought.

It might not be too bad, he had mentally calculated, if his son was an officer of a fashionable regiment, say of the Household Brigade. Indeed, an elegant figure in the gold-braided, blue patrols of the Royal Horse Guards would cause a stir in the smoke-room of the Grand Hotel — perhaps even outshine the teenage Austen Chamberlain, the son of the local industrialist for whom much was predicted. Then followed another satisfying discovery. Eighty-two Members of the House of Lords, and forty-one Members of the Commons, were either serving or past officers of the Household Brigade.

George Dyson was nothing if not speculative. He was a confirmed Whig, and a Horse Guards officer could only stand as a Tory, but that was a bridge to be crossed later. Birmingham was a Whig stronghold with its seats firmly held by three Liberal giants: Chamberlain, Muntz and Bright. Edwin, then, would be unwise to fight a Birmingham election but, again, there were easier seats elsewhere. The final fact was one to be savoured. One of the three Tory candidates to contest Birmingham in the coming election — though the result was a foregone conclusion — was Lieutenant-Colonel Frederick Gustavus Burnaby, Commanding Officer of the Royal Horse Guards.

The more George Dyson thought about it, the more lucrative horizons revealed themselves. A son in the Royal Horse Guards and a Member of Parliament, with brass behind him to entertain at the United Services, the Naval & Military, White's and Romano's, a pair of good horses, perhaps a tactful bestowal of mess silver, a box at Ascot and Covent Garden, an under-secretaryship — all these could mean the attention of the Duke of Cambridge, the Prince of Wales, the Select Committee on Ordnance, foreign embassies, possibly even a visit to Windsor. Many an officer had achieved high rank and influence with no other qualifications than a generous allowance and a good marriage. The prospects of 'D & B', George Dyson had decided, were suddenly scintillating. He was only surprised that he had never thought of it before.

The first target, of course, was Colonel Burnaby. If the man wanted to make any impression on the voters of Birmingham, he'd better learn that the advice and support of George Dyson would be invaluable. Not that Burnaby, or any other Tory, seriously threatened the Liberal fortress, but that was not Dyson's concern. Nor did he consider it necessary to confide in Edwin. He took train to London, to Gunter's Hotel, thence by hansom to Regent's Park Barracks.

George Dyson returned to Aston Park two days later. His mood was somewhat subdued, and he confined himself to his library, lined by books purchased by the yard, for several hours. His absence from Birmingham had meant nothing to Edwin except a measure of relief.

CHAPTER EIGHT

'If the Russians cross the Bosphorus,' George Dyson's finger stabbed at *The Times* editorial, 'it could mean the signal for a blood-bath in the Ottoman Empire — with Bosnians, Croats, Serbs and Greeks all at the Turks' throats.' It was an intriguing possibility. 'There could be half a million pounds for the taking — likely three quarters — if we have stock ready and crated.' He pondered, then glanced up at his son. 'This afternoon you can go to Theobald's at Bilston. Offer fifty pounds for a six-weeks option on making up two hundred crates, each to hold fifty rifles — say four-feet-six by two — unplanned deal, screwed and rope-handled. Then you can go to Hughes and do the same. Myself' — he dragged his watch from a waistcoat pocket — 'I'll go to the Buller Line's agent to look at sailings for the Eastern Mediterranean. A sovereign spent now can be worth fifty in a month's time.'

With Russia and Turkey again at war, and the Czar's armies at the gates of Constantinople, the British Government was reluctantly deciding to intercede, urged on by a bellicose little Queen at Windsor, who protested to the Prime Minister: 'Oh, if the Queen were a man, she would like to go and give those Russians, whose word one cannot believe, such a beating!' It was not so much Constantinople that the British were concerned for, but the road to India. In February 1878, the Royal Navy entered the Sea of Marmora and an additional six million pounds were voted for armaments.

Thousands of time-expired soldiers, and not a few still serving who did not enjoy the detached security of a Windsor or Westminster, choked back the nausea in their throats at the prospect of another Crimea, but there was a new generation of fire-eaters who insisted on fighting the Bear, who sang patriotic songs in music-halls and talked incoherently of 'national honour'. The command of a military expeditionary force was given to Sir Robert Napier. In Birmingham, George Dyson engaged another armourer and a further two carts.

'Bulgars and Serbs, sir?' Edwin rose from the breakfast table. 'You mean you'll supply arms for use *against* the Turks? That's not much different to supplying them to Russia, is it?' He paused, frowning at his newspaper. 'The Fleet has been ordered to Besika Bay, at the head of the Dardanelles. We're likely to be at war with Russia at any moment. That means —'

'It means nothing, boy,' George Dyson snorted. 'There's a lot of responsible people including Mr Gladstone, who would rather be supporting Holy Russia against the filthy Bashi-Bazouks who've been massacring and burning alive thousands of Christians in the Turkish provinces. Now the Turkish government has repudiated its loans — and *that* means that the British taxpayer has been bilked of one hundred million pounds! Britain doesn't owe Turkey anything! There are also people who swear we were on the wrong side in the Crimea, and would like to see Turkey thrown out of Europe once and for all, bag and baggage.'

'Dammit, sir, Russia's up to her old tricks — pushing for the Mediterranean and threatening our communications with India. Constantinople is the key to India. Perhaps the Turks don't all smell of violets but they do happen to be our allies. If British regiments man the lines before Constantinople, and you supply guns to be used against their rear —'

George Dyson flung his own newspaper to the table. 'All this talk of a Russian threat to India is just political drivel, boy, invented by humbugging Tories like Disraeli and Derby before every election. If the Russians do have designs on India, they don't need to fight a way through half of Asia. From Kazakhstan it's only a few miles' march through Afghanistan to the North-West Frontier, where there's precious few British to stop them.' He wagged a finger. 'If you're going to follow me into this business, boy, you'll need to develop a few new distinctions and forget a lot of others.'

Edwin was silent, then, 'I've thought about it for more years than I can remember,' he said. 'And I can't stay with "D & B", sir. I simply can't sell guns and ammunition without knowing exactly how they're going to be used. It's even worse selling guns and *knowing* they're probably to be used against British troops, or those of a friendly power. In Burma, Perak — and, for God's sake, times enough on the North-West Frontier — it can't be a coincidence that our men have found themselves faced by European weapons. And Magdala? Where did the Abyssinians' percussion muskets come from? Perhaps not "D & B" — but a few thousand Maria Theresa dollars found their way into some arms broker's pocket, and thirty-five British soldiers died. If you could guarantee sir, that not a single *gun* in that Thomas Street warehouse will ever be fired at a British soldier, colonial official, a British settler or trader, then I'd sit at that office desk and write pro-formas and bills of lading for the rest of my life.' He paused. 'I've decided to go into the Army, sir, and I'd like to go with your approval. But, if necessary, I shall go without it. I've got a foolish notion that I'd be repaying a little — a little of the bloody sin of companies like "D & B".' He paused again, shrugging. 'And then, sir, the next time you sell a thousand Sniders to the Amir of Afghanistan, you might bear in mind that one of the redcoats of the Peshawur garrison is Private Edwin Dyson.'

George Dyson stood with his back to the fireplace, his thumbs anchored in his waistcoat pockets and his eyes angrily on Edwin. 'You're an ungrateful puppy and a damn fool. If you believe that either God, Queen or Country will ever do anything for you, or be even aware of your existence, unless you put cash on the table, then you're mightily mistaken.' He waved aside Edwin's attempted interruption. 'All right, it'll be the Army — but I'll wager that within six months you'll be crying to come home, and you'll have swallowed some of those fine principles. There's one thing.' He thrust out a lower lip. 'I'll not have a son of mine enlist as a common soldier —'

The War Office Act, the Army Establishment Act, the Localisation Act, all initiated by Viscount Cardwell, had already done much to rationalise the structure of the Army and to abolish the purchase of commissions, but there were loopholes still, carefully outlined to Dyson by a half-pay Captain of the 6th Regiment. In another two years, when the Cardwell reforms would begin to bite irrevocably, it would be too late.

George Dyson left nothing to chance. He had made contingency arrangements. Get your son a commission now, the half-pay Captain had urged, as he drank Dyson's brandy. Any regiment will do. Later, with money, a transfer to something more fashionable would be easy enough — but don't wait for these lunatic Cardwell regulations to clamp tight.

'I've decided,' Dyson said, 'to decline a commission in the Royal Horse Guards.' Edwin had never for a moment considered the Royal

Horse Guards; he had never considered anything. He was not even convinced, at this moment, that he really wanted to enter the Army. It had been the only thing he could think of in a moment of frustration, 'There are a number of fine line regiments,' his father expanded, 'with excellent records. I've spoken to several influential people, and have written to Lieutenant-Colonel Pulleine of the 24th Regiment.' He went to a bureau, opened a drawer, and extracted a sheaf of papers. 'Subject to certain conditions, you may offer yourself for a Second-Lieutenancy in the 1st Battalion of the Warwickshires, which is now at the Cape, but which maintains the Dering Lines Depot at Brecon. You'll need an account with a military tailor.'

And the tailor, Dyson resolved, would supply only one equipping of 24th Regiment scarlet. Thereafter it would be the blue and gold of the Horse Guards. He'd see to it.

* * *

Events, however, had already overtaken both George Dyson and Edwin. In Berlin, Russia and Turkey had reached a reluctant compromise and, despite the Queen's threats of abdication, British fire-eaters were silenced. Sir Robert Napier's regiments tramped back to their barracks at Aldershot, Shorncliffe, Colchester and the Curragh. 'D & B' would have twenty-three thousand Snider rifles, gleefully sold by the War Office, but with nobody beating a path to Birmingham, cash in hand.

Well, there would be time for Snider-Enfield rifles; they represented a tangible asset, but Dyson's plans for his son were invalid even before Edwin reached the depot town of Brecon. A telegraphic despatch from Whitehall had reached the 2nd Battalion of the 24th Regiment, in barracks in Chatham. It was January, the furlough season, and the officers were scattered, but the despatch was emphatic.

On 1 February 1878, the 2nd Battalion entrained for Portsmouth to embark in the *Himalaya* — 24 officers, 8 staff sergeants, 39 sergeants, 40 corporals and 746 men. Two days later the troopship nosed into the foggy Channel, bound for Simon's Bay and East London. Only a few miles across the shrouded Solent, Charles Norris-Newman shivered on the boat-deck of the *Egypt* as she turned out of Southampton Water — Willie Mudford had been right, damn him, and the white surf of Durban was only five weeks away.

Ten days later, yet a third steamship threshed, smoke-belching, across the Solent into the mud-coloured Channel, bound for Cape Town. On board was Frederick Augustus Thesiger, Lieutenant-General, with several of his staff. Thesiger's feelings towards his appointment were less than enthusiastic. He was considered by Whitehall to be a 'reliable' commander, which was another way of saying that he was a mediocre plodder who could be relied upon not to embarrass his superiors. Whitehall did not want a fire-brand soldier in southern Africa, only a copybook, cautious officer who would effectively dampen the territorial aspirations of colonial speculators. But Thesiger was in his fifties, already behind in the popularity league of the Army's commanders. A campaign against uneducated, black bushmen, armed only with spears, was poor fare — but it was probably his last opportunity.

* * *

North of the White Umfolozi, across the vast, undulating veldt, the herds of zebra and wildebeeste grazed among the scattered, yellow-green grass, and plunging springbok raised scurries of dust that the distant lion and hyena watched speculatively. Solemn groups of massive elephants browsed, lazily stripping the new, green growth from the stunted trees, and ostrich strutted.

Among the kraals of the amaZulu the smoke of crowding fires hazed the beehive roofs and the evening insects clouded over the cattle pens. Laden women chattered, laughing, as they came gracefully down from the mealie-fields, and the men, for whom there were no menial tasks, sat in the *kgotla*, drinking beer and talking men's talk. The Great King, Cetshwayo, was at Ulundi, and the medicine men predicted an abundant harvest. It was a fair and fruitful land, wanting for nothing, and there was no threat of any kind to darken the sun.

CHAPTER NINE

'Ye're a bloddy dishgrace ter the Ridgement, Whelan,' Sergeant Gamble snarled. 'Look at ye — a sack o' praties tied up wid string. Hev ye niver stood straight in ye loif? Holy St Michael! Ef we're recruitin' bloddy Kilkenny bog-peasants thet's niver walked upright loik *men*, thet don't know the diff'rence ev left an' roight, an' niver washes below their chins — whit's the future ev die British Arrmy?' Sergeant Gamble positively bristled. 'Hev ye *seen* yeself? *Hev* ye?' He wheeled, his immaculate boots crashing, his face puce. 'Look et him!' He invited the attention of the platoon of recruits and awkward men. 'Hev ye heerd ev *Homo Saypeens*?' They had not. 'Ef ye read books — *ef* ye kin read — *Homo Saypeens* es the *ultimate* en the development o' mankind.' He leaned forward, his face inches from Whelan's. 'But theer's some craytchers thet's niver developed, bedad. They're called *missin' links*!' He paused. 'Ye're a bloddy *missin' link*, Whelan! Jasus, I'd not be surprised ef ye wuz covered wid hair under thet *dishgustin'* uniform. And thet' — he pointed — 'es a Martini-Henry rifle, the foinest infantry weapon en the worrld — *not* a bloddy pitch-fork!' He strode three paces, then whirled again. 'Theer's ridgements thet recruits missin' links, loik the Dublins en the Connaughts, see? This' — he roared —'es the 24th Redgement o' Foot! Howard's Greens, the Bengal Tigers! The jewel o' the British Army!' He slumped dramatically. 'An' we hev *things* loik Private Whelan!'

Sergeant Gamble was an Irishman in a regiment drawn predominantly from Wales and the northern midlands of England. The names on the battalion's muster-roll were those of the Rhonda, Merthyr Tydfil and Abergavenny — names like Griffiths, Jones, Morgan, Owens and Williams. If there was such a thing as an average British soldier, then these men could be said, in terms of morals, to be better than average. Many were the sons of mining villages where Chapel elders firmly regulated local behaviour, or of Sheffield cutleries where employees were bound by fraternal trade union loyalties.

Sergeant Gamble made no secret of his Irish origins, but he was also a good soldier, and he was coldly incensed when faced with the inadequacy of a recruit from the Emerald Isle. It was painful but true that, compared with the Welshmen, these uncouth, illiterate products of rural Ireland were an embarrassment. No Irish recruit to the 1st Battalion of the 24th Regiment could expect concessions from Sergeant Gamble.

And Private Whelan was a disappointing specimen of Irish manhood. He was an insignificant, weasel-lie man, round-shouldered, awkwardly elbowed, with a dark-skinned face from which no amount of shaving would remove a slate-coloured shadow. No tailor would have measured such a frame with confidence — least of all a quartermaster-sergeant, accustomed to a swift glance at a recruit, then shouting, Tunic three, breeches five, boots eight, helmet seven!' Most men broadly speaking, were of similar shape. Private Whelan was not. His cuffs fell to his knuckles, his breeches cascaded over incredibly large boots, and his crowning glory — his helmet embellished by the brass Sphinx of the 24th — sat solidly on his outsplayed ears.

'Ye're a bloddy tragedy, Whelan,' Gamble resumed remorselessly. 'A dishgrace ter the country thet's bred the greatest sodgers en history, a dishgrace ter a ridgement thet *Kings en Princes* wud be proud ter sorve en.' His moustache quivered. 'Jasus, why did ye choose the 24th? Ef I knew the recruitin' sergeant thet gave ye the shillin', faith. I'd batter him senseless wid me own fists, so I wud!'

Whelan recalled the recruiting sergeant at Beggars' Bush. That had been after he, Whelan, had flogged Rice's horse from the Glaziers' estate house — not for Killybags, or for Belfast or Derry, as the Inspector at Strabane would calculate, but across country to Dublin. He'd had not a ha'penny in his pocket, and he had offered the horse for sale to a livery stable in Lucan, but the proprietor, following a glance at the mud-spattered horse and a dishevelled Whelan, had sent a boy for the Constable. Whelan had run for it, sick in the gut, straight into the arms of the recruiting sergeant who had not signed a man for a week, who shrugged and spat, aware that it was not he, but the Surgeon-Lieutenant, who would qualify a man fit for the Queen's service. In barracks, Whelan had his first hot meal for four days, was sluiced with icy water, had his hair cropped and four teeth viciously extracted. After that, there was Sergeant Gamble.

Within seconds of their first meeting, Whelan suspected that he was going to dislike Sergeant Gamble. Within twenty-four hours Whelan detested him and the regiment in which he had enlisted, of which he had previously known not even the title. He was sick of the endless hours spent in drilling, marching and counter-marching, in applying pipe clay and metal-polish, of meticulously folding his blankets, of standing straight with thumbs to trouser-seams when spoken to by an NCO. And he was contemptuous of the stocky Welshmen who adapted to the disciplined routine so much more easily and who, between themselves, often conversed in their native language, which left him an outsider, and resentful. They needed only the slightest encouragement to burst into choir-like song — and Whelan had no ear for singing. He was not one of them, and they knew it. He was an unwashed lazy Mick, content to sprawl on his bed when others were burnishing buttons or blackballing the toes of their boots. He was an odd man out, and most of the Welshmen would have agreed with Sergeant Gamble on the subject of Private Whelan.

Mind, the depot provided the recruits with two cooked meals per day which, if the Welshmen wrinkled their noses, were better than Whelan had experienced. He had never eaten meat daily, even if of poor quality and carelessly cooked, never tasted kippers, or jam other than wild blackberry. Nor had he used eating utensils other than a spoon and his fingers, and Whelan's shortcomings at the mess-table were yet another source of irritation to his companions who, if far from genteel themselves, did not hesitate to criticise the crudities of an ignorant clod of a Jackeen.

'Look you,' said Private John David Hughes. 'What haf we that walks on two legs, belches like a pump-engine, iss blacker than an Abergwynfi check-weighter, and eats his porridge with both feet, indeed?' But Private John David Hughes was a giant with the huge scarred fists of a Rhonda miner, and Whelan held his peace, seething.

It was several weeks before Whelan achieved the privilege of walking out on short furlough, and Brecon — a three-quarter-mile walk from the Dering Lines — was totally different from Letterkenny. Neat, white-washed houses clustered on the northern bank of the Usk among green trees and meadows, grazed by sleek dairy cattle. There were immaculate, white doorsteps and gleaming brass door-knockers, gay curtains and clambering wisteria. Whelan bitterly resented Brecon. There was little sign of poverty here. Coal-mining was a flourishing industry and, it was said smugly, there were households with an income of twelve pounds weekly. Twelve pounds! Holy Mary, it was unbelievable!

And the people of Brecon were as well-fed and sleek as their cattle — men with silver jingling in their pockets, women and wenches well-fleshed, rosy-cheeked and laughing, with shoes to their feet and good mutton in the pot — and they were devoted to music and Chapel, neither of which aroused the slightest enthusiasm in Private Whelan. Singing and sermons, it seemed, were the two obsessions among the Welsh, Almost every tiny cottage had its harmonium, often a piano too, and there was hardly, a person who was not a member of a choir. For their preachers they were prepared to pay good money, and a forceful minister could bargain with his deacons, 'For one guinea I will preach you a ferry good sermon. For two guineas I will bring tears to the eyes of the women and children. But for three guineas I will preach you a sermon which will *knock the dust out of the cushions*, look you!'

For all that, there were plenty of beer-houses — but, Whelan discovered, no potheen or porter. The Welshman drank ale in large quantities and, sooner or later, broke into song. Whelan cursed the black luck that had brought him to a town of hymn-singers, gospel-mongers and ale-swillers, to a regiment of foreigners and, most of all, to a horse-breaker like Sergeant Gamble.

Something would have to be done about Sergeant Gamble, but not yet. Whelan had no desire to draw the slightest attention to himself until the business of Rice had blown over. In Dublin, when it was too late, he had realised with horror that he had given his own name to his attestation. Faith, there were plenty of Whelans in Ireland, but it had been a stupid oversight. Weeks had passed and nothing had happened, nor had there been news — although it was unlikely that news of an obscure affair in Donegal would reach Brecon in Wales. What had the land agent said? 'The first time I see you again will be the last. I'll see you hang.' With time to think, Whelan did not see the justice in hanging a man for killing the murderer of his wife — but, like the Sergeant, there was no justice for a man with the black luck of a Whelan.

And Gamble wuz bloddy persecution, so he wuz. The Sergeant derived a satanic pleasure from parading a scapegoat before the eyes of watchers

— of recent weeks the three newly-joined subalterns, whom Gamble addressed as 'Mr Dyson, sir — Mr Franklin, sir, — Mr Weallens, sir', or, collectively, 'Gentlemen —' with a sniff. The Sergeant stood, ramrod stiff, his cane under arm and wooden-faced as the young officers' hesitant voices drilled an equally inexperienced squad. 'Theer's some recruits, gentlemen,' Gamble opined, 'that ye kin make sodgers ev — given toim en *infinite patience*. En theer's some — loik thet misbegotten Whelan — thet the Divil himself wid throw out ev hell fer an *insubordinate malingerer*. Ye'll nayd ter watch Whelan, gentlemen, so ye will.' Whelan felt the subalterns' surprised gaze fasten on him, and seethed again. B'Jasus, he gritted, but his time would come.

Gamble was a black-mouthed Protestant, that was it. The truth came to Whelan in a sudden moment of inspiration. Gamble was a festerin' Protestant — like that other English-loving bastard, Cooley of Letterkenny. Gamble, with his taunting and bullying, his fatigues and extra drills, intended to goad him, Whelan, into retaliation. That would mean vicious punishment and likely the rogues' march, discharge with disgrace and then the unwelcome attention of the civil police. Whelan didn't want to attract that sort of attention. Well, Sergeant Gamble wasn't going to be his persecutor for ever. Gamble was a depot drill-sergeant, and as soon as the battalion at the Cape called for a draft of recruits, Whelan and his companions would be gone from Brecon — and Gamble.

But Whelan was wrong on several counts. The first was that Gamble harboured any spite towards Irish Catholics. He did not — only against Irish recruits who humiliated the 'auld country' by their slovenliness. It was unfortunate for Whelan that, in the 24th, his companions were largely from communities of which the adult males resorted frequently to a tub of soapy water in removing the grime of the pit from their bodies — except for their backs, which were considered to be weakened by the application of water. Whelan had already stood nakedly on the frosted cobbles of the bath-house yard, under Gamble's disgusted gaze, as bucket after bucket of freezing water deluged his shocked, shrinking flesh — and that was enough for any man, bedad, for a year. Jasus, water was for cattle.

Whelan was wrong, too, in his anticipation that, very soon, he would be beyond die reach of the detested Sergeant.

* * *

'The Second Battalion o' the 24th,' Sergeant Gamble sourly informed his squad, '"es been ordered ter the Cape ter reinforce the Ridgement!' To the Sergeant the 'Ridgement' was the 1st Battalion, which had never met, and had little communication with, the later raised 2nd, quartered at Chatham. It was one of the hotly resented aspects of Cardwell's military reforms — that hitherto unrelated regiments should be forced into marriage, with old identities and traditions tossed into an administrative melting pot. It made a man want to spit.

'An' thet's not all, my buckos,' Gamble fumed. 'This lot — *this lot* —' He pointed a finger at the recruits facing him. 'You tangle-footed, degenerate *objecks* — you soddin', incompetent bloddy cattle He paused, then whirled, his boots exploding. 'An' Whelan! Holy St Michael!' Behind him stood two more new subalterns, Second-Lieutenants Phipps and Curll, uncomfortable in their stiff-creased regimentals. '*This* lot — an' Whelan — es ordered ter join the Ridgement! Wid yer belayve ut?'

Second-Lieutenants Phipps and Curll studied the chimney of the distant guardhouse. 'Theer's not one ev yez thet's fired a bloddy shot,' Gamble snorted. 'None ev yez worn the shine arf ye soddin' hob-nails — an' they're sending yer ter a fightin' Ridgement!' Phipps and Curll gazed at the sky. They had been at Brecon for two days, the castigated recruits for several weeks. Gamble, however, was only echoing, in a cruder fashion, the sentiments of General Thesiger, who was already complaining to Whitehall that the men being scraped from the depots to bring the Imperial battalions at the Cape up to strength were all recruits still in training, of whom none had undergone the intensive musketry course that made all the difference between a fumbling novice and a passable rifleman. All of them would have to complete their training in the field, a burden and a hazard to the seasoned troops, who themselves were hard put to adapt to conditions incompatible with the Army Manual. The Army's almost unbroken history of success against more numerous colonial insurgents had been based upon discipline and co-ordinated fire-power — and the British soldier's inherent gift for improvisation. The recipe had worked so far, but there had been a number of near-run affairs, and there must come a time when brute discipline would not be enough. The thin red line was becoming stretched, and thinner. One day — one disastrous day — a British square was going to be broken.

'But ye've got thray more wakes in depot.' Gamble's voice was like gun-wheels on gravel. 'An' in thim thray wakes ye're goin' ter lorn how ter load an' fire the Martini-Henry, see? Lying, standin', knaylin', runnin', walkin', and settin' on ye' arrses. In thray wakes ye'll be draymin' en ye slape about braych-blocks an' firin' pins. Ye'll wake en a cauld sweat, scraymin', an' thumbin' cartridges up ye nose, an' ye'll be firing dummy-ball all day'til et's too dark ter see ye fore-sights. In thray wakes, me buckos, y'll know the pants o' the Martini-Henry loik you'll niver know ye woif s, b'Jasus.

'And theer's another thing.' Gamble had saved the most horrifying part until last. 'Ye're all filled wid misery et the thought ev being out ev me gentle hands en thray wakes.' He eyed the recruits with a mirthless grin. 'Well, ye kin rest aisy, because I'm coming wid ye — all the way ter the bloody Cape!'

* * *

The Martini-Henry, of .45 calibre and sighted up to 1,450 yards, weighed 8½ pounds. It was a single-shot weapon, and lowering a lever behind the trigger guard automatically opened the breech, worked the ejector, and cocked the firing pin, with the centre-fire cartridge pushed home by the thumb. With older soldiers it had not achieved popularity because of its vicious recoil, and was thus unfavourably compared with its predecessor, the Snider-Enfield, which was a muzzle-loader converted to breech-loading, still widely issued, and a pleasanter weapon to fire. The Martini-Henry was simple and robust, but it had two other shortcomings. One was that its deep, square-cut rifling grooves became quickly fouled, the other was that grit was liable to jam its mechanism — a serious hazard for troops constantly employed in colonial, sandy terrain.

The cartridge was the successful Boxer modification, with a case of coiled brass that housed 83 grains of powder, detonator and a nosed, lead bullet. Dummy cartridges were used in training. They had a concave base, but were otherwise of similar appearance and weight to ball cartridges, for which, at a glance by a recruit, they might be mistaken.

* * *

'Et the command "load", ye holds ye' 'Teeny en ye left hand, et the point o' balance, so.' Gamble demonstrated. 'Wid ye right hand ye lowers the cocking lever, an' *widout lookin' down* ye takes a cartridge from ye pouch, pushes et into the chamber, an' then slams back ye cocking lever, see? Et the command "present", ye brings the butt ter the shoulder, hard in till et hurrts. Ye close ye left eye.' He paused. 'D'y know which es ye *left eye* Whelan? Et's the same side es ye left foot, see? Ye aim low fer the gut, orl except Whelan, who'd better aim fer the bloody knees. Whin ye gits the command "fire", ye squeeze gently — an' I mean *gently*, Whelan —'

Whelan's self-control, never a notable quality, was approaching the point of complete exhaustion. He had made strenuous efforts to improve in every aspect, but as he did so his comrades were always ahead of him; he remained the fumbling, least expert part of every undertaking. Gamble's incessant derision on the drill-ground was followed by the unfeeling ostracism of his fellow recruits. He experienced no consoling back-slaps, no good-humoured banter, and there was nobody with whom to share a fortifying quart of ale.

'Theer's a hundredweight o' Irish praties ter be payled en the cookhouse,' said Sergeant Gamble thoughtfully. He scanned the recruits, weary at the conclusion of a long day of drilling. 'Who d'ye suppose es *exparienced* wid Irish praties?'

There was a concerted, relieved response. 'Whelan, Sar'nt!'

'B'Jasus, an' I'm thinkin' ye're roight! *Exparience* es a foin thing, so'tis.' He pondered. 'By unanimous agrayment, then, et's Whelan.' He turned to his sullen countryman. 'An' ye'll payl thim praties bloody thin, Whelan. Ef ye don't, shure, I'll hev ye paylin' the payl!'

But it was on the drill-ground that Whelan suffered most, and it was on the drill-ground that the Sergeant's bullying rhetoric suffered its first check, from a surprising quarter and with little benefit to Whelan.

Gamble was involved in his favourite subject — the Martini-Henry rifle. Adroitly, he snapped open a breech. 'This parrt es the barrel — d'ye see, Whelan? Ye'd better listen, becos ef ye can't repeat whit I'm tellin' ye, I'll hev ye doublin' fer an

104

hour wid ye rifle over ye head.' He paused. 'The barrel ev the 'Teeny has foive grooves, see, givin' a full turrn en four feet —'

The interruption came from behind him. 'You're wrong, Sergeant,' said young Mr Dyson, quietly. 'That's the Mark 1 Martini-Henry you're holding — and you're confusing it with the Enfield. The Martini has seven grooves with a right-hand turn of one in twenty-two inches, the depth of groove progressive for the first eleven inches, then of uniform depth to the muzzle.' Mr Dyson shrugged. 'I suggest you learn your subject, Sergeant, before you attempt to teach it to others.'

It was a mistake. It was unwritten law that no officer should censure an NCO in the hearing of his subordinates, and for a man of Gamble's experience to be bluntly belittled by a subaltern of only a few weeks' service was unforgivable. He choked, reddening, knowing the recruits' eyes to be on him, secretly exulting.

'Shure, an' yer roight, Mr Dyson, sir,' Gamble gritted, incensed. 'Et wuz a slip o' me tongue, so it wuz.' He spun back to his squad. 'Did yer heer whit the officer said, ye misbegotten rabble?' he roared. '*Sivin grooves*, wid a full turrn en twenty-two inches — an' theer's not one ev ye wid the sense ter know the festerin' diff'rence! Theer's not one ev ye kin tell a fore-sight from a bloddy firin' pin!' But it was too late. The damage was done. Gamble might bluster for the next three weeks but, suddenly, he had feet of clay.

Later, in the security of the barrack-room, the Sergeant's deflation was a subject for gloating discussion. '*Seffen* grooves, look you,' chortled Private John David Hughes, 'and the auld Sergeant grindin' his teeth like the Refferend Jenkins when he found his daughter in the organ-loft — and Owen Lewis between her legs, whateffer!' He punched his straw-filled mattress delightedly. 'I sutchest you learn your supject, Sergeant' — he mimed Dyson — 'before you attempt to teach it to others!' He guffawed.

But the rejoicing of Private John David Hughes and his fellows was premature. Mr Dyson's ill-judged comment had done them no service, as the following day would prove. Gamble was too old a soldier to contemplate a vengeful battle of attrition against an officer however junior, but the recruits were a different matter. It was ironic that recruits did not need to know the intricacies of a rifle's barrel-grooves, and the Sergeant's error of explanation was, as he had said, a genuine slip of the tongue. He had demonstrated the Enfield for twenty years, the Martini-Henry for only four, and he could have kicked himself when reminded that he was speaking of the wrong gun. It was not his moment of error, however, that infuriated Gamble, but the fact that it had been exposed before a platoon of smirking recruits — and Whelan, b'Jasus, that misshapen clod of an Irisher. Mother o' God, but he'd wipe the grin from Whelan's black mouth.

CHAPTER TEN

On the drill-ground they were divided into pairs, of which one man lay, legs splayed and rifle to shoulder. The other, also prone, faced him, a few feet distant, holding to one eye a small target-painted disc of which the exact centre was a pea-hole. The recruit with the rifle aped the motions of cocking, ejecting, reloading and sighting, then snapped the trigger of his empty weapon. Peering through the target-like disc at the aimed gun-sights, his companion would comment on the degree of steadiness and jerk. The disc was a poor substitute for ball-cartridges firing at even the novices' 300 yards, but it was better than sod-all. It was unlikely that the 24th's recruits would be accorded more than one full day at the butts before they embarked for the Cape.

There was always an odd man, and it was always Whelan. Nobody wanted to be partnered with Whelan.

'Ye're a bloddy leper, Whelan,' Gamble spat. 'But thet's no excuse fer malingerin' see? Git down there, an' *I'll* judge how ye kin insult a foin weapon. Ef thet rifle cud spayke, bedad, it'd be scraymin' fer mercy.'

Outspread, Whelan hugged his rifle-butt to his cheek, squinting through its sights. Twelve inches from his muzzle was Gamble's face, partly obscured by the disc held to one eye. Indifferently, Whelan cocked his empty Martini as, yards away, the other guns of the platoon rattled like hail on a tin roof.

'Ye're a black-hearted Donegal bastard, Whelan,' Gamble said softly, 'an' ye're all yaller. I'm guessin' the polis' es waitin' fer yez. Did ye cut ye auld mother's throat fer her rent money? Or wuz ye rapin' ye sister?'

Whelan's rifle clicked, and he cocked again, unspeaking.

'Shure,' the Sergeant taunted, 'ye bloddy bog-peasants ez all the festerin' same — filled wid wind en piss whin the potheen's in ye, an' crawlin' curs whin ye're sober. Ye're a soddin' animal, Whelan — a soddin' animal. Ye ain't fit ter mix wid *men*. Ye shud hev been pole-axed et birth, see? They shud hev pushed a bloody peat-clod into ye mouth es soon es they saw yez —'

Whelan's rifle clicked. Then he re-cocked, silently.

'Are ye listening. Whelan ye bastard?' enquired Gamble. 'An' ye're a bastard, o' course. Ye' mother wuz a 'Derry prostitute, poxed ter the eyebrows, an' ye father wuz a rot-gutted Liverpool ponce. She niver even saw him — et wuz too dark en thet alleyway —'

Whelan's rifle clicked.

'I'm goin' ter drive ye, Whelan — every minute o' every bloddy day. I'm goin' ter drive yer till ye weep, ye bastard. Ye'll remember the name Gamble, an' ye'll call the Black Curse on it, Whelan, becos whin I've finished wid ye, b'Jasus, ye'll detest the shit-faced swine thet spawned ye an' the pox-eyed whore thet spewed ye. An' ye'll curse the day ye tuk the shillin' fer the 24th.'

There was a hesitation, and then Whelan's rifle clicked.

'Wid yer loik ter see me dead, Whelan?' Gamble sneered. 'Shure, ye bloddy wid. But wid ye have the gut ter do et yerself, ye bastard? Bedad, ye moight, ef ye hed the chanst ter shoot me en the back from the firin' line, *ef* ye wuzn't runnin' fer ye soddin' life, which es more loikly. I know ye festerin' Fenian gutter-scum. Ye're brave bhoys en hamstringing a horse, or burning a hay-rick, or shootin' a land-agent en the darrk, but the nex' momin' ye're orl "Holy-Mary-Mother-ev-God, hev-mercy -on-this-poor-sinner", drippin' wid holy medals, an' crossin' yeselves, an' moanin' gibberish Latin thet ye don't bloddy understand. Jasus, ye can't even wroit ye own soddin' name. Then, whin ye sins es washed whoit by the blodd ev the Lamb, et's a drop ev the harrd stuff, ye knock sivin kinds ev shit out ev ye woif, an' then ye're blatherin' about the Sons ev Ireland, orl ev ye descended from Kings an' Princes, an' not one of yez seen a bar ev soap fer a twelve-month.'

Whelan spoke at last. 'Shure, I'd loik ter see ye dead, Gamble — an' I'd swing fer ye, b' Gud. Ef I hed a bullet en this gun roight now, I'd put et between ye bloddy eys, ye black-hearted sod, an' I'd not be concerned ef they shot me the nex' minute. I'd go laughin', knowin' ye'd be bumin' en hell before me — an' I'd enjoy the stink ev ye roastin' carcass, ye rot-guttin' Protestant bastard —'

He had risen to Gamble's bait, and Gamble jibed. 'A bullet, es ut?' He chuckled. 'Thim's foin worrds, me bucko, whin ye're houldin' an empty rifle. Bedad, ef I gave ye a cartridge, an' offered ye the chanst, ye'd be shiverin' wid bloddy terror, ye gutter-rat.' He fumbled in a pocket, laughing softly, then withdrew a cartridge and held it between finger and thumb before Whelan's eyes. 'Ye hevn't the gut, Whelan — an' ye know ut.'

Their low-voiced exchange had attracted no attention among the other recruits, industriously manipulating their cocking levers. Whelan's teeth had drawn back over his teeth. 'Ye widn't dare.'

For reply, Gamble tossed the cartridge with a twist of his wrist. It fell at Whelan's elbow. 'Dare?' Gamble snorted. 'Put ut in ye gun, Whelan — an' ye kin use me roight eye es a target.'

Their stares locked for several long seconds, and then Whelan reached for the cartridge, fed it into his breech, and rapped it shut. His eyes, narrowed, had not left Gamble's face. The Sergeant grinned. 'Now all ye do es pull the bloddy trigger, ye scab. Not even a sorry bastard loik you cud miss from theer. But ye've not the courage ev a starrved rabbit, Whelan — an' I'm guessin' ye're fillin' ye breeks wid stink.' He raised the perforated disc to his face. 'Whin ye fire, ye'll be spattered wid me brains, an' theer'll be a hole en the back ev me head es big es ye fists. I'll not see ut, but they'll drag ye away en irons, an' then they'll hang ye, kickin' en fartin', an' cryin' fer the whore thet wuz yer mother.'

Flushed with hatred, Whelan glared at the red, sneering face of the Sergeant, inches away from his gun muzzle. He could feel the gravel of the drill-ground biting into his elbows, and his hands were sweating. He had only to crook a forefinger and the detested face with its mouth spewing insult would shatter into crimson fragments.

Did Gamble consider him, Whelan, so contemptuously white-livered that he could give him a cartridge with such confidence? If he fired, to be sure, he would hang — but Gamble would be dead. Whelan was by no means certain that he was secure from arrest for his killing of Rice, and a man could only be hanged once. The taunting, foul-minded Sergeant did not know that.

And if Whelan did not fire — if he confirmed Gamble's despising opinion of him — he could expect nothing but increased insult and humiliation, to be further goaded until either life would be impossible or he reacted like a cornered animal. In either event, it must end in the same way.

Whelan's finger tightened on the trigger.

It would be now. He remembered the cobbled stable-yard of the Glazier's estate house, littered with wet leaves, and Rice walking towards him, reloading his Remington. Rice was talking, jeering, and then Whelan had fired, had felt the shot-gun jolt in his hands. Rice's face was a grotesque thing of bloody shreds that bounced on a rolling neck —

Whelan lowered his gun-muzzle to the ground.

Gamble guffawed. 'What did I bloody tell ye, ye gutless little runt!' This time, his voice was sufficiently loud to reach the ears of the other recruits, and the rattle of empty rifles ceased, expectantly. 'Wit did I bloddy tell ye? Ye hevn't the backbone ev one ev ye own stinkin' lice, Whelan. Ye're somethin' thet crawled out ev a Donegal dunghill. Ye've got a yaller strake down ye back es wide es me bloddy arm!' He glanced around at his squad, raising themselves on their elbows. 'Look et him! Theer's a cartridge en his braych, wid me orderin' him ter fire. Thet's refusal ter obey an order, Whelan, see? But I'm not goin' ter put ye on a charrge. Every man en this platoon hes a belt wid a brass buckle, an' every man es goin' ter lay ten strokes across ye arrse, wid ye tied ter ye bed. An' after every ten, ye kin say, "Holy-Mary-Mother-ev-God, hev mercy-on-this-poor-sinner." '

'A cartridge, look?' whispered Private John David Hughes. 'Whelan's got a real cartridge in his gun?'

Whelan turned his head. 'Shure, the Donegal gutter-rat's got a loaded gun. He can't rayd or soddin' wroit. He don't wash ivery day wi' soap en wather, en he shudn't be bloddy mixin' wid men. Thet natcherly manes he's a white-livered, spunkless bastard thet anyone kin spit on.' He paused. 'Thet's whit ye belayve, becuz a big-mouthed Sergeant sez — only the Sergeant wuz wrong, see? He's been wrong before, but this es the laast toim —'

Whelan raised his rifle, then pulled the trigger.

'It takes a ferry brave man to face a rifle tha' he *knows* iss loaded wi' dummy-ball, look,' observed Private David Hughes later. 'It's a pluddy dare-devil that auld Sergeant is, eh? An' pelt-buckles, was it indeed?' He spat. 'Wi' the flat o' my auld spade I'd make a black puddin' of his pluddy arse, I tell you.' He glanced at Whelan, seated morosely on his bed. 'If you can put up wit some Welsh singing, Whelan bach, there iss seventeen men here that iss waitin' to buy you a quart, look you —'

CHAPTER ELEVEN

The crossing of the Buffalo into Zululand, at Rorke's Drift, had been a noisy, confused business and, although the opposing bank seemed deserted of life, Noggs had no doubt that hidden eyes had watched every clumsy phase of the prolonged operation. If this were the North-West Frontier, he had mused, hundreds would have been picked off by sniper-fire before a single man had wet his feet, but the Zulus, it seemed, were content to watch and wait. Unlike the Pathans, they preferred a man-to-man confrontation.

The leisurely pace of the crossing had annoyed Noggs. True, it was a cumbersome column, almost unmanageable, with 220 Cape wagons, 82 carts, six 7-pounder guns and two rocket batteries still struggling up from Helpmakaar, on the Natal side, in addition to 12 companies of Imperial infantry and the locally recruited auxiliaries — the latter varying in quality from the superb Edendale Horse to the downright time-serving Kaffir vagrants of the Natal Native Contingent. As well as the troop and battery horses, there were forty-nine draught horses, 67 mules and 1,507 oxen. The column's strength, including conductors, drivers and voorloopers, was 4,659.

Still, Noggs fumed, speed was an essential element of this initial thrust into Zululand. Hours, even minutes, could be vital in a campaign against an enemy who fought afoot, but was capable of running a horse into the ground. Noggs had never fought in Africa, but neither had General Thesiger, and almost nobody had fought Zulus on their own ground. To Noggs the whole thing seemed too damn casual, too much like a gigantic shooting party — the officers with their sporting guns, with native beaters and redcoat ghillies. Put yourself in the enemy's place, Noggs had always ruled. Think like he's thinking, and then out-think him. But during a dozen staff durbars that Noggs had attended, nobody had discussed Zulu tactics. It seemed that the black-skinned warriors of Cetshwayo were only waiting to be flushed out and shot down.

And his first view of Zululand was disappointing. The skies were drizzling chilly rain through scattered mist, with visibility, at best, reduced to less than a mile. The Buffalo river swirled and chuckled, and the NNC vedettes kicked their horses ashore, deploying, the red rags about their battered hats like blood-splashes against the greeny-dun of the surrounding, sodden terrain.

Noggs, also, had tied a red rag around his wide-awake. He felt more comfortable in the company of the colonial levies, despite their cavalierly discipline, than with the Imperial officers. Not that the 'red jobs' were bad chaps. They weren't — and the predominantly Welsh rank and file were as fine a bunch as he'd seen anywhere. They had the *esprit de corps* of men drawn from a specific community. They were Welshmen, were proud of it, and showed it. And they sang. B'God, how they sang! It required only the merest suggestion of a middle C for hundreds of men to soar into thunderous harmony. They sang as they marched, when they halted, as they worked, and especially when they drank. No, there was nothing wrong with the 24th. Even the latterly arrived 'recruits' from England, suffering from their first sunburn, had been enveloped in parental, regimental arms, and they now sweated and swore like veterans, indistinguishable.

No, it wasn't the Imperials. The Imperials — the 24th, the Artillery, the Engineers — these were predictable. They would stand, as they had been taught to stand, and fight to the last round and the last man. There was no alternative offered by the Army Manual, and no alternative had been considered for a moment. The Achilles heel was the locally-recruited men — Boers, riff-raff Kaffirs, gin-soaked hangers-on. And they were numerous.

He had no doubt that both officers and men of the 24th would give a good account of themselves under any circumstances. He only hoped, b'God, that such good material would not be abused by incompetent command. It had happened before.

It had happened to the 24th, at Chillianwallah in 1849, when the regiment had been ordered into an impossible assault in an enemy position, and had been shot to bloody rags. Noggs, only a few days earlier, in Helpmakaar, had joined a social gathering of officers from both the 1st and 2nd Battalions. The date had been sufficiently near to the anniversary of the Chillianwallah for Captain Degacher and Lieutenant Porteous to propose a toast: 'That we shall not get into such a mess, and have better luck this time.' It was unfortunate. The mention of the earlier disaster had imposed an oddly pessimistic air on the gathering of young officers, and the humour that followed was forced. It was damn silly, Noggs decided, but he had left early. 'Blast it,' Degacher was snorting. 'Zulus ain't Sikhs — no artillery, no fire-power worth mentioning, I fancy. All we need is to get'em into the open space, and if the Kaffirs and the local riff-raff don't get in the way, it'll be like cock-shying at a fairground. So m'Lord will have to choose his ground.' M'Lord was General Thesiger, who had become the Second Baron Chelmsford following the recent death of his father.

Well, Thesiger-cum-Chelmsford had seen service in the Crimea, in the latter period of the Sepoy Revolt, and during the Abyssinian campaign, at all times adequately but scarcely with distinction. He was a teetotaller, but was also courteous and considerate towards subordinates, and mindful of the comfort of his men. His tall, well-built figure, semi-military attired in a dark Norfolk jacket, topee, cord breeches and tanned, spurred boots, was seldom absent from the troops' drill sessions, and he had already ordered that the intervals between files in attack formations were to be doubled. As a result, there had been murmurings of doubt from the more experienced men of the 1st Battalion. Wider spaces were asking for trouble against Zulus who were reputed to charge in mass with the stabbing assegai. Sod it, Chelmsford had better not let them blacks get too bleedin' close.

Still, no British regiment allowed an enemy horde to get too close. There was the Martini-Henry rifle, for a start, and every redcoat would stand in line with fifty cartridges in his pouch. Multiply fifty by the eight hundred men of a battalion-It was a comforting thought.

There was, however, a minor, nagging factor that, so far, had involved only the quarter-masters. If any military action became prolonged, the. men's pouches would be replenished from the regimental ammunition reserves. There were ample reserves, but they were packed in heavy wooden boxes, each in turn secured by copper bands and nine iron screws that were often rusted into immovability. While still at Greytown, the 2nd Battalion had requested screwdrivers, or similar implements, that would simplify the task of opening the boxes, but a reply from the ordnance stores had revealed that no such implements were available, further observing that, 'However useful and necessary such appliances may be in European warfare, it is not expected that they will be required in a war such as the troops are about to enter upon.'

Camp health was good, with all men of less than 15 years' service ordered to run a thousand yards before breakfast. Food was well cooked in field ovens, and fresh bread baked daily. True, at the Helpmakaar bivouac, a storm had blown down tents and flooded the site, but there had been no serious damage and the troops remained cheerful. It was still raining steadily on New Year's Day 1879, and on 10 January, the eve of the crossing at Rorke's Drift. At dusk, the vedettes had reported seeing a group of mounted Zulus watching from the opposite bank, out of range, who had turned to vanish into the rain haze.

Noggs had never been an armchair strategist. An army commander seldom revealed all the cards in his hand, least of all to a newspaper correspondent. All the same, Noggs considered, the force that Chelmsford was about to lead into Zululand seemed too small to advance through hostile territory, protect its camps, to keep open its rear and send forward strong reconnaissance parties, while simultaneously maintaining an effective main body. It might have been different if Chelmsford had intended a rapid dash for the Zulu capital, followed by an equally rapid withdrawal, but Chelmsford obviously did not — and a number of obvious precautions were going to be stretched dangerously thin.

Willie Mudford had been right, damn him, and now Noggs was committed — the only correspondent with the invading column. Behind him, 12 miles into Natal over a muddy hunting track, was the tiny Boer settlement of Helpmakaar, and a hundred miles southward of Helpmakaar was Pieter Maritzburgh, his nearest telegraphic link with Capetown and the outside world. It was going to be bloody tricky getting a story back to London, but London now knew of the impending invasion of Zululand, and Mudford's last communication had told of the frantic efforts of Fleet Street to send reporters — Archibald Forbes of the *Daily News*, Francis Frances of *The Times*, Philip Robinson and Capel Miers of the *Telegraph*, Fripp of the *Graphic*, Melton Prior of the *Illustrated* and, from Paris, Paul Delage of *Figaro*.

But they'd never get here until it was all over, Noggs knew. And perhaps they were the lucky ones.

* * *

The first brush with the enemy had been a minor affair. The mud track that climbed the wet ridge beyond the river fell again to the Bashee, a diminutive stream flanked by swampy pastureland in which the heavy wagons would quickly founder. The track would have to be reinforced before the train could proceed to the firmer veldt beyond, and since the track to Ulundi, the Zulu capital, was also barred by a sizeable native kraal, there offered an opportunity to blood the two Imperial battalions in co-ordinated tactics while the roadwork was carried out by sappers and pioneers.

The kraal was that of the local chief, Sirayo. It was a natural fortress, spread over a rocky knoll, in turn surrounded by table-topped hills with steeply cut sides, and the ravine that comprised its only approach offered excellent cover for a defending force.

And it was hot work while it lasted. The Imperial troops, supported by Kaffir irregulars, scrambled up the sides of the rock-strewn knoll in the face of fierce but ill-directed small-arms fire from hidden Zulus. The Kaffirs had quickly lost enthusiasm, but the bayonets of the 24th prodded them on. There was a final flurry of flung spears and boulders, an untidy melee of stabbing redcoats among the caves and gullies of the hillside, and then the Zulus broke and ran, vanishing into the ravine and the mist-wreathed slopes beyond. Except for twenty dead, and the abandoned cattle, die kraal was deserted.

Captured weaponry was negligible — an assortment of spears, a half dozen battered Tower muskets. More surprisingly, however, there were several hundred packets of nitrated paper cartridges.

'Cartridges?' Captain Cavaye, commanding A Company of the 1st Battalion, broke the sealing wax of a packet and spilled the contents into the palm of a hand. 'If they've got cartridges, it's likely they've got damn breech-loaders. Why else would they have cartridges?' He glanced up. What d'ye make of'em, young Dyson?'

His subordinate took up a cartridge. 'Terry cartridges — capping breech-loaders — for either the Terry carbine or the Westley-Richards.' He pursed his lips. 'A bit out-dated, the Westley-Richards, but a useful gun — still issued to our own Yeomanry, and good enough for the Portuguese Army.'

'Westley-Richards?' Cavaye whistled. 'Damme, I thought the blacks only had a few gimcrack muskets. Where in hell would they get Westley-Richards carbines?' He frowned, then, 'Bloody gun-traffickers?'

Around them men were beginning to fire the huts, but the rain-sodden thatch burned badly, enveloping everyone in acrid, throat-choking smoke.

Dyson shrugged. 'It's possible, I'd say, sir — perhaps the odd gun or two from further north, Mozambique. On the other hand, the Natal Kaffirs have carbines, and it's not unlikely that a few have trickled through to the Zulus.'

Cavaye's eyes were smarting. He coughed, then hailed the appearance of a third man through the swirling smoke. 'Noggs! If it's a story you want for that rag of yours, then here's something to make your gentle readers choke over their toasted teacakes! "Unsuspecting soldiers faced by Zulu' breech-loading carbines! Savage enemy equipped with British weapons by Mozambique gun-runners!" ' He snorted. 'That ought to get a question asked in the House. It's high bloody time these Judas gun-merchants were nailed, once and for all.'

Dyson protested. 'A few cap-cartridges are hardly evidence of an organised gun trade, sir. It's just as likely that these Terrys have been foisted on the Zulus by some trader as convenient packets of powder and ball for their muskets. Being paper, they can be tom open and emptied into the muzzle —'

Cavaye chuckled. 'All right, young Dyson, I'll take your word for it. All the same, blast it, I'd welcome any chance of putting a knife into those gun-peddling jackals.' He raised reddened eyes to Noggs. 'Noggs, old son, if you ever want to know anything about guns, ask Dyson here. He might be the greenest bloody subaltern in the Army, but he knows more about small-arms than the select Committee on Ordnance *and* the Musketry Manual put together. Every damn Sergeant-Instructor in the Regiment starts to shiver in his boots when Second-Lieutenant Dyson's within earshot.' He laughed. 'And you, young Dyson, can listen to Noggs here. He'll spin you a few yams about the other side o' the coin — what happens when native hostiles are supplied by arms brokers with modem weapons. It can be a bloody business.'

Dyson? And arms brokers? Noggs wiped a sweat-streaming face with his bandana. 'Yams are for die mess,' he grinned, 'with the port.' They moved down the slope of the knoll, away from the smoke. 'Dyson? Would you be from Birmingham, Mr. Dyson?'

The other shot him a glance, startled. 'Yes, sir.'

Noggs took his time, then, T) & B? Dyson & Bradley? There's no Bradley of course, but two names are always better than one. More solid, y'know.'

Above them the thorny cattle enclosures exploded into spitting incandescence, and they could feel the heat even at this distance. They lowered their heads from the deluging sparks. 'That's right,' Dyson said, slowly. 'D & B, of Birmingham. Does it give you a story, sir?'

Noggs pressed his bandana to nose and mouth. 'It could give me a damn good story, Mr Dyson.' For three or four seconds they stood, staring at each other, with the soot swirling.

'If I had one of those gun-running bastards at arm's length,' Cavaye gritted, 'I'd use a bloody bull-whip.' He glanced up. 'Dyson and what? Bradley? Who's Dyson & Bradley?'

'My father's company, sir.' The defiance in Dyson's voice was emphatic, and Cavaye's eyebrows rose. He shrugged. 'Slow up, young Dyson. I'm not one of those chaps that look down their patrician bloody noses at the mention of commerce. My father was a flour-miller, and my mother came from a long line of market gardeners. Mind you,' he conceded, 'market gardeners might be described as landed gentry — except that there was precious little land, and my maternal grandfather certainly wasn't bloody gentry, b'god. I'm told he was too damn idle to go to the bucket outside after dark, and pissed on the fire, which' — he grinned — 'either put the fire out, or made a Goddam awful stink. Probably both.' He guffawed. 'So? I'm Cavaye o' the 24th, and that's all that matters, see?' He paused. 'So — who's D & B, young fellow? White slave traders? Abortionists? Or something really sordid — like bloody trade unionists?'

'Grocery, Charlie,' Noggs said. 'Wholesale grocery. There's not a soul in Birmingham, under three years, that's not heard of D & B. That right, Mr Dyson? Fine English hams and imported luxuries, bacon, salted herrings, cheesemongery. Nestles milk, Pear's soap, and Oriental botanical preparations for beautifying the complextion. I fancy Mr Dyson thinks it's not much of a military background for an ambitious young officer.'

'*Grocery*,' Cavaye snorted. 'Hang it, Dyson, grocery's nothing to be ashamed of. You've got respectability oozing out of your damn ears, even if they are still wet. If you'd said politics, now, or the Church, I might have had ye blackballed.' He considered. The next time you get a parcel from home, young Dyson, I'm fond o' smoked salmon, tinned sweetbreads, and chicken in aspic.'

From the high kranz above the kraal, the men of the 1st Battalion were hurling loud but good-natured jeers at the efforts of the sweating redcoats of the 2nd, in the lower knoll. With the brief fighting finished, tensions were relaxed, and there was a general air of joviality. It had hardly been a battle; a few score ill-armed Zulus had been flushed from a position by a vastly superior number of trained troops. Still, it was a good beginning.

'Aye, a good beginning,' Cavaye nodded. 'Good for morale. Any moment, now, and they'll starting singing about the land of their fathers.' Noggs knew that Dyson's eyes were on him, but he refused to meet them.

CHAPTER TWELVE

The oxen-drawn Cape wagons were the dragging anchor of the column. Massively built of timber, bound with iron, each weighed between three and four tons and was hauled by a span of twelve to eighteen animals.

Under the most favourable conditions of load and terrain, a wagon might be expected to achieve 15 miles in a day, but the conditions of Chelmsford's march were the reverse of ideal. Everything, from the beginning, was wrong.

First, many of the vehicles were grossly over-loaded. Hired wagoners' rates of haulage were five to six shillings per hundredweight from Pieteh Maritzburgh to Greytown, rising to six to eight shillings from Greytown to Helpmakaar. In consequence every Boer owner loaded his wagon to the last possible pound, regardless of the effect this would have on speed but aware that compensation would be paid for any draught animals dying.

Secondly, the terrain over which the wagons were required to travel was execrable. Routes marked on maps were never better than the merest tracks, pitted and rock-strewn — but more usually indicated the least forbidding of near-impossible alternatives. Now, the recent rains had turned every surface into a river of glue that reached to axle-trees. Repeatedly, at every mile, the over-laden vehicles foundered. A half day could be consumed in coaxing a single team over a ditch that a man could jump in a second, and a broken wheel might bring the entire column of 300 wagons and carts to a standstill while the casualty was unloaded, repaired, and loaded again.

'There's nice for you,' said Private John David Hughes, observing a kaffir's cooking fire under a wagon loaded with ammunition. 'It reminds me of Dai Jenkins, who lit a candle to look at his dead canary when the damp was bad at Number Five Level. Afterwards, look, we found the candle and the canary, but we neffer found Dai Jenkins.'

'That wasn't Dai Jenkins, Hughie bach,' corrected Private William Morgan. 'That was Dayfid Watkins, look, that fell in the auld rain butt and broke his knee, when he was trying to see Megan Griffiths undressed in the wash-tub.' He considered. 'No, that wasn't Megan Griffiths, see. It was Gwyneth Morris, who was courting Edwards the Milk. That was Caradoc Edwards, look, not Edward Edwards who had the shop in Tonypandy.'

'It's right you are, Willie bach,' nodded Private John David Hughes. 'And wasn't it Dayfid Watkins that got pluddy drunk at the choir festival in Penarth, and was sick in Thomas Meredith's new hat, look?'

'Aye, and the Refferend Jenkins *screeching* from the pulpit, whateffer, about the beast that lives in a bottle —'

'And all the boys with their eyes raised like angels to the organ-loft, where Owen Lewis was pumping for the Minister's daughter, Blodwyn — and all wondering who'd finish first, the Minister or Owen Lewis!'

'Not Blodwyn, Hughie bach,' frowned Private William Morgan. 'You're thinking of Blodwyn Wilkins, look you, who married auld Gareth Llewellyn of Blaengarw, after she got herself pregnant by the English tallyman from Bristol —'

'Holy St Michael!' Private Whelan spat. 'Wit sort ev a place is ut ye come from? Et's a bloddy *sink ev iniquity* so ut is.' But there was no longer rancour in their exchange. 'The Rhonda, es ut? Bedad, ut sounds loik bloddy Gomorrah!'

'It speaks!' rejoiced Private John David Hughes. 'The thing that walks like a man, look you! Bedad an' bejabers an' auld Phaynix Park! Neffer let it be said, look, that the lower orders can't be educated by *siffilised* company, see.' He paused. 'Whelan, bach, in the Rhonda there's no marrying a woman until she's been tried out in bed, look. Welshmen don't buy anythin' that's not tasted first. That's *siffilised* for you. It's *sons* a man wants, see. Since all women wants husbands, an' all fathers want to lose their daughters, there's easy it is to ask that a woman proves her *capassity*. It's nice for Johnnie Jones, look, and Gwendolyn likes it too, see?' He chuckled. 'All right then. If her little belly starts swelling, Johnnie makes it decent in Chapel — quick, look. That's why there's more six-months brats in the Rhonda Valley than anywhere in the auld world, see?' He paused again, musingly. 'There's nice, until Johnnie Jones gets three women pregnant at the same time, Whelan bach. Then it's the auld Queen's shilling, man — unless he wants a pluddy pickhandle broken over his head, see.'

* * *

It had never been seriously contemplated that the Kaffir auxiliaries would stand in a battle-line beside European regulars. As picquets, scouts, or possibly in pursuit of a broken enemy, they could be useful, for they could move more quickly over rough ground than the Europeans. However, although akin to the free-born Zulu, the Natal Kaffir was a far inferior creature, his finer qualities having disappeared during generations of association with his white overlords. He might have been more reliable if he could have been commanded by his own headman, or at least Europeans whom he recognised and trusted, but this was not so. A few of his officers had military experience, but the fact that they were now reduced to Kaffir-handling spoke little of their quality; most were complete novices.

Worse were the non-commissioned officers. Also white, they were recruited on the sole recommendation of having experienced military service — it having been determined that the Kaffirs should conform to some kind of European drill. This also was an error, since it destroyed their last remnants of natural ability, while the NCOs were degenerate, drunken, and utterly untrustworthy. They were the worst possible example of white authority, and were resentful that they must march afoot while their officers rode. Ill-conditioned for a long or rapid trekking, they were becoming a constant liability to die irregular bodies whose only claims for justification were stamina and swiftness.

And with the kaffirs travelled the two sutler-wagons of Pogo Stewart, loaded with barrels of cheap gin, known as the 'Queen's Tears' by the million of Kwini Vittori's lesser subjects, from Quebec to Hong Kong. One bottle of gin, it was said, was better than a hundred bullets.

Straggling over a dozen waterlogged miles, the column lurched into Zululand. At Rorke's Drift remained a disappointed 'B' Company of the 2nd Battalion 24th, to guard the crossing, under Lieutenant Gonville Bromhead. Three hundred yards from the mission station was Lieutenant John Chard, of the Royal Engineers, responsible for the upkeep of the crossing and, in due course, for the construction of a small defensive fort, while 'F' Company of the 1st was still on the Natal side, marching hard to overtake Chelmsford's column before the fun began. Two other companies of the 1st — 'B' and 'D' — would reach only as far as Helpmakaar, twelve miles short of the Zululand border.

'I don't know much about fighting damn Zulus, Charlie,' Noggs eyed the tents of four companies of the 2nd Battalion that guarded the engineers' road-building activities, 'but I've read *Regulations for the Field Forces in South Africa*. Aren't wagons supposed to be outspanned and in laager? And rifle pits dug, with thorn barriers if possible?' Above the tents was a precipitous kranz of Sirayo's Mountain. 'Defending this position could be a nasty business.'

Cavaye shrugged. 'It might be, against drilled troops. The trouble is that the wagons are so bloody unpredictable; we never know how many are going to be anywhere at any time, and it takes damn near a company to grapple with a three-ton wagon in these conditions. As for pits, well, the ground is either as hard as rock or, in the rains, a quagmire. So laagering or pit-digging can take hours, and so can reforming for the march next morning — and all for nothing if there's no sign of an enemy. Goddam, there's enough damn delay with the transport, without inventing more.'

Noggs was unconvinced. In Pieter Maritzburgh an old Boer had told him: 'God help you, sir, from ever seeing a camp or homestead sacked by Zulus.' Noggs was uncertain about a number of things. Several of the predictions of Willie Mudford, of the *Standard*, had already begun to unfold, but even Noggs did not know that Sir Barde Frere, the Governor-General in Capetown, had not written to the Colonial Secretary regarding his terms of ultimatum to Cetshwayo until 16 December. The despatch had arrived in London on 2 January, only nine days before hostilities were due to begin. There was no misunderstanding on Frere's part, for on 13 December — two days after his ultimatum had been presented to the Zulus — he had received a warning from the Colonial Secretary, Sir Hicks Beach, which included the underlined words: 'We cannot now have a Zulu war in addition to other greater and too possible troubles.' Frere was deliberately flying in the face of categorical instructions, gambling that a swift, cheap annexation of Zululand, and the public acclaim that followed, would compel the Government to refrain from any thoughts of censure.

There were small, scattered native settlements on the route of march, none housing more than three or four families, a dozen cattle, and surrounded by patches of melons and mealies. A few were abandoned, but most were still peopled, with the women running for the huts as the sprawling column clawed its way over the Ulundi road. And there was news in the kraals of Ulundi — gathered by what means the white men could not guess, but repeated by every headman. Two warrior impis had departed the Zulu capital and were advancing to oppose the white men's invasion. The Great King, Cetshwayo, had offered *impi embomvu* — red war — to his young men, and the spears were to be washed in blood.

What's the strength of an impi?' Noggs asked.

'There's no specific strength, or even an approximate one,' Charles Cavaye said. 'The Zulus can't communicate numbers because they've no numerical system, except by adding one, and one, and one — and so on. More usually they'll say, "as many as man has toes", which means "a few", or "as many as beans in a bean-field", which means "a hell of a lot".' He paused. 'But I'd average an impi at about two thousand.'

If the reports were true, then, Noggs considered, it was apparent that four or five thousand Zulus were approaching. Well, that number was unlikely to seriously embarrass Chelmsford's force, particularly when die dry open veldt was reached, and the troops could advance in square — and always providing the General did nothing stupid, like splintering his Imperial battalions. Noggs was mildly annoyed with his own misgivings. Goddam, he must be getting old.

The square was now the British Army's usual formation for fighting a less sophisticated but invariably more numerous enemy — not the individual regimental squares of Waterloo, but one vast complex that incorporated the entire column except possibly the cavalry screen which, however, might remain within during an attack, ready to sortie when the enemy had shot his bolt. Also within the square remained the cattle, wagons, hospital carts and similar auxiliary detachments, protected by a wall of three ranks of infantry — the first kneeling, the next standing, and the third ready to fill gaps left by fallen men. There might be field guns or multi-shot weapons at each angle to maintain a crossfire against an enemy assault. In open, hostile country, the army could march in such a square, slow and cumbersome, but ready at a bugle-call to halt and stand, bristling with guns and unchallengeable by an enemy without artillery, A British square had never been broken.

The tactical formula was well-tried and viciously successful. Threatening enemy forces would first be subjected to artillery fire to which they could not reply, but must do one of two things — retreat or attack. If they retreated, then the square advanced in slow but inexorable pursuit. If, frustrated — then or later — they attacked, they would be torn to red ruin by shrapnel and the massed fire of breech-loading rifles. The few that penetrated the blizzard of shot woud be confronted by an unbroken hedge of bayonets and the pitiless eyes of men who were the toughest soldiers in the world. One such attack was usually enough, and what remained of the shocked enemy would be swept away by a final, general advance.

Chelmsford had only to adhere to the prescribed formula, Noggs decided, and it was impossible to believe that five thousand ill-armed Zulus, however determined, could come within spear-thrust distance. Why did he, Noggs, have this stupid uneasiness?

He had met young Dyson several times since the little affair of Sirayo's kraal, but never alone, and the boy had avoided anything other than noncommittal conversation. Noggs chuckled. Captain Charlie Cavaye, a professional, no-nonsense soldier, thought well of his subordinate, although his dour, critical comments never betrayed the fact. One day, given ordinary luck, young Dyson would make a fine, conscientious officer, and Noggs, for certain, would never mar his chances with a whisper of his father's business, detested by every British soldier. He'd like to reassure the youngster about that, if he had the opportunity, and if he knew exactly how.

The night of 19 January was dry and clear, with the stars showing well, mingling with the scattering sparks of the campfires. Noggs picked his way among the tent-ropes and out-spanned wagons, skirted the horse-lines where the assorted mounts of the cavalry were tethered, patrolled by native sentries. Cavalry was a flattering description. The best were a detachment of Natal Mounted Police, and a squadron of mounted Infantry — a mixed bag of Imperial troops, indifferent horsemen, but more willing and reliable than the colonial volunteers or the mounted Kaffirs, the latter including several excellent details which were outnumbered by the completely inadequate. There was nothing in Africa, Noggs mused, that nearly matched the superb cavalry of India — the Bengal Light Horse, the Sikh Lancers, the Guides, the Scinde Horse. But, of course, India and Africa were totally different, and here he was a stranger. India, infinitely more complex, he understood. The crudities of southern Africa he did not. Only this great emptiness of the veldt he recognised. It had the same wet, earthy smell that he had known in Rajasthan after the rains, and he had walked under the same stars. Noggs lit a cheroot. Then there was a movement in the darkness, a few feet away, and he turned. It was Edwin Dyson.

Surprise was mutual, but Noggs grinned. 'Hello, young Dyson. Taking the air?'

The other nodded. 'I've not yet developed a liking for sitting in a tent with an oil lamp and a million flying insects — and the fires, with all this damp brushwood, are ten times worse. I'd give ten guineas for a hot bath. My "Patent Folding Camp Wash-basin" holds about enough water to boil an egg.' He laughed. 'A boon and a blessing to every officer in the field. I'd rather join the men in the river, but it's not the thing for a gentleman, I'm told.'

Noggs nodded sympathetically. 'Have you heard the orders for tomorrow?'

'We move off at eight for a site that's been reconnoitred, called Isandhlwana. It's a hill, a spur of the Nqutu Mountains, about nine miles away. The 1st Battalion will remain there until the wagons come up, while the 2nd will sweep up a big kraal to the south-east. The General doesn't want to leave any sizeable enemy concentration in his rear that might play old Harry with his line of communication with Rorke's Drift and Natal.'

'You mean he's splitting the Imperials?' It was the one thing he had been certain Chelmsford would avoid doing.

Dyson shrugged. 'I'm only a damn Second Lieutenant. Orders is orders. Still, it shouldn't take more than forty-eight hours. It's what is known as "a calculated risk", sir. Wellington made one at Waterloo.'

Noggs snorted. 'Damn Waterloo. That blasted battle has done more to influence British Army thinking — the wrong way — than any event in three centuries. It was Waterloo thinking that blighted the Afghan business, the Sikh War, the Crimea, and a dozen other campaigns.' He was angry. 'Wellington was damn near beaten, because he and Blücher separated, and he survived only because Bonaparte was a sick man. Since then' — he pointed a finger — 'the Wellington formula has been sacrosanct, and it's succeeded only because we've fought hordes of black men armed with spears.'

'That's ol' Indian yaller talk,' Dyson smiled. 'It's a different kind of warfare on the North-West, I fancy. A few years of fighting Pathans can make a man damn critical of set-piece campaigns like this one — not that I've much experience. I know what you're getting at, sir, but is there any different way of organising an advance into enemy territory?'

'Not according to the rule-book — but the rule-book is fifty years out of date. We adhere to it because our armchair warriors in Whitehall are too damn old to learn new tricks, and they can always righteously claim that the system has worked. So far. B'God, the Army's done bloody well, so far. But one day it's going to find itself opposed by an enemy that's equipped with something better than spears and flint-locks — men who knew their business and who aren't awed by the sight of a couple of battalions in square, marching like an Aldershot review. Then there's going to be bloody mayhem.'

'Well,' Dyson grimaced, 'that's not likely to happen in Zulu-land, is it? I'm not anxious to be one of the heroes of Chelmsford's Last Stand,'

Noggs chuckled. 'No, it's not likely, dammit. All the same —' He left the sentence unfinished.

There was silence for several moments, then Dyson said, 'I'm grateful for what you said, sir, to Captain Cavaye' — he hesitated — 'about my father's company. It could have been damn uncomfortable for me. Who'd have thought' — he was rueful — 'that I'd meet someone in *Zululand* who knew?'

Noggs chuckled again. 'If I'd been a bit faster thinking, I might have invented something better than groceries. Charlie Cavaye's expecting smoked salmon and tinned sweetbreads, so you'd better order a few hampers through Dent's. They do a good Chablis.' They both laughed.

The subject was closed, and Dyson gazed beyond the horse-lines at the scatter of camp-fires. 'Anyway, the men are in good form — or I should say in good voice. You've never known anything like it. There's abstainers, o' course.' He paused, then resumed. 'There's a man in "A" Company — Whelan — a little monkey of an Irishman.' He was talking irrelevancies only to steer the conversation away from the earlier subject. 'Private Whelan is just about the most unlikely soldier you ever saw. He's got five thumbs on each hand, and if he marches in step it's accidental. Parsons, my Sergeant, throws a choleric fit every time Whelan's name appears on the guard-detail. There's some men, I suppose' — he accepted a cheroot from Noggs — 'there's some men who were never born to be soldiers.'

'Whelan.' Noggs grunted, musingly. It was bloody odd. Whelan, in Donegal, had been a little monkey of an Irishman — but it was a common enough name, and the odd quirk of fate that had brought George Dyson's son and himself to Zululand at the same time could hardly be repeated by the presence of Whelan. Besides, the 1st Battalion of the 24th had been at the Cape since 1874.

'This Whelan,' he asked. 'How long has he served?' It just couldn't be possible.

Dyson's cheroot glowed in the darkness. 'I doubt if twenty years would make Whelan look like anything you'd recognise as a soldier, but' — he considered — 'he was drilling with the recruits' platoon when I reported to Brecon in February, which means he enlisted during the six or seven weeks before. Still, dammit, a year's enough for anyone to learn how to get his buttons into the right button-holes. I remember the depot drill-sergeant, Gamble, calling him the "bloddy Darwin Thing from Donegal"...'

If Whelan — the Letterkenny Whelan — had reached Dublin, and then enlisted, he would have been in Brecon in January 1878, and it was typical of the man that he had attested with his own name. After the double shooting at the Glaziers' estate house, Noggs had walked to Letterkenny to tell his story to Sergeant Cooley who, in turn, had ridden to Strabane. Noggs had repeated his story to a senile Doctor Ternan, the County Coroner, and the Inspector had telegraphed Whelan's description to Derry, Belfast, Enniskillen and Omagh. Then, sick to the teeth with Ireland, Noggs had returned to London, to William Mudford and the *Standard*. There had been no references in the London newspapers to the Letterkenny affair, but this was not surprising. A murder in rural Ireland, at best, justified only an inch of small print in a national daily, and would more likely pass unnoticed. And Whelan of 'A' Company was a little monkey of an Irishman. It all fitted.

No, dammit, there were thousands of Whelans, and a large percentage were probably little monkeys of Irishmen. Thomas Whelan of Letterkenny, by now, was probably hanged and buried in Kilmainham gaol's unhallowed cemetery, and his cottage battered to the ground by crowbar men. Still, the thought was intriguing.

And suppose — just suppose — that Whelan of Letterkenny was here in Zululand. What should he, Noggs, do about it? He recalled his words: 'The first time we meet again will be the last. I'll see you hang.' Bugger it, Noggs reflected, it's best left alone. I don't want to know. Let sleeping dogs lie.

'This Whelan,' he ventured. 'He was from Donegal?'

'Whelan? Hell, I don't know.' Dyson was surprised. 'If you want to write about a soldier, sir, there are plenty of better subjects than Whelan — almost anyone else in the Battalion. There's a man in the 2nd with the Victoria Cross, and several with good records against the Gcalekas last year. Whelan?' he snorted. 'Dammit, not Whelan!'

'No, it's difficult enough getting pukka copy back to Pieter Maritzburgh without pretty-pretty stuff about our gallant lads at the front. There are hacks in Fleet Street who can write that. No, it's just that I once knew a man named Whelan, in Donegal —' he shrugged. 'It's not important.'

Dyson laughed. 'You can take my word for it, sir — you've never known Private Whelan. But, if you watch "A" Company move off tomorrow morning, just look for the man that's out of step, with dirty brasses and his straps twisted, and shouldering his rifle like a hay-rake. In fact, you won't have to look. Just listen for Sergeant Parsons to shout, "Good Gawd, Whelan — d'yer want me ter draw yer a bleedin' pitcher?"'

* * *

The Kaffirs of the Natal Native Contingent went off first, straggling over the narrow track that rose from the Bashee, followed by the 2nd Battalion of the 24th, the six 7-pounder artillery pieces, the mules of the rocket battery, and then the 1st Battalion. A mile of heaving wagons, to the rear, fell progressively behind the tramping column until out of sight, but some would reach the proposed camp at Isandhlwana before nightfall. Although the terrain was noticeably less severe with every mile, the hindmost vehicles would not complete the brief march until the following day. Still, the weather was good, and the ground, drying. The worst, it seemed, was now over, and a few more days would see this whole business finished.

From a distance, as the morning bugles sounded, Noggs had watched the four companies of the 1st Battalion forming up for the march — 'A',

'C', 'E' and TT. A fifth, Captain Mostyn's 'F' Company, was still struggling up from Rorke's Drift, miles behind, and would be lucky to overtake the column before the Zulu-hunt began. Still two others, 'B' and 'D' Companies, remained fretting at Helpmakaar.

The red-tunicked soldiers, buckled with haversack, bayonet, ammunition pouches, mess-tin and canteen, jostled into dressed lines. There was a white ground mist that licked over their ankles, and the morning was chilly, but when the sun rose there would be black sweat patches seeping through every scarlet coat, and tightly-buttoned collars would rub blood from blistered necks. Feet would scald in heavy boots, and the sun-scorched metal of rifles could sear the skin from unwary fingers — but these were iron-hard, slum-reared men, and there'd be a tot of rum at midday to sweeten the spit, to encourage an appetite for years-old salt beef and choke-dog biscuit ...

The Company officers were grouped together, talking in low voices, as they waited for the sergeants to impose order. For the march, all had abandoned the swords which, designed for both cutting and thrusting, did neither effectively, and were considered by many to be unsuited for anything other than ceremonial occasions. Each, however, carried a Webley or Pryse revolver at his hip, balanced by a water-bottle. Although khaki had been issued to the Army in India for more than thirty years, no stocks of lightweight uniforms were maintained elsewhere, and troops still served in home field service dress — the traditional red and blue — with the only concession to the climate a white, dome-shaped tropical helmet.

'*Whelan*!' There came the frustrated roar of a sergeant, and Noggs turned his head. 'If yer approve, an' *if* it's bleedin' convenient, perhaps yer'll condescend ter *git fell in*! O' course yer don't need yer soddin' rifle, 'corse we ain't goin' nowhere special, jes' so long as we orl walk in the same bleedin' direction at the same time see?'

It was Whelan, sure enough — Thomas Whelan of Letterkenny, the dirty little man that Noggs had met in Smiley's bar, who had pimped for his wife, and shot Rice. He stood only yards away now, and Noggs could see the dark, sullen features and the rounded shoulders that no scarlet and brass would ever disguise. It was Whelan, sure enough, Noggs wished desperately it could be otherwise, or that he could have remained ignorant. It was a complication he could do without.

He turned, but he was too late. Whelan was staring directly at him.

* * *

'The auld Sergeant iss *sparklin'* with wit, look,' said Private John David Hughes. 'There iss nothin' like a funny *choke* after cold porridge and ye' buttons turned pluddy green wi' damp, see.' But Whelan was not listening.

Private Whelan's narrow little world had suddenly disintegrated. Twenty yards away, at the tail-board of an ammunition limber, stood a man he recognised, the sight of whom contorted his belly into cramping knots. Holy Mother of God. It was unbelievable, but there was no mistake. Whelan felt the bile rise to his throat.

It was savagely unjust. After everything — the flight to Dublin, then Brecon and the detestable Sergeant Gamble, the heat, lice and tick-flies of Natal, the brutalising discipline, the marching, sweat and mud — after all that, when at last he had decided that his crime must be forgotten and himself safe from pursuit, now there was this man, standing only yards away, looking at him. The first time we meet again, he'd said, will be the last. I'll see you hang.

* * *

All day, on the plain of Mahlabatini, on both banks of the Mbilane stream below the royal kraal, the Zulu impis had been gathering — not two, as the white men had been told, but twelve, totalling almost twenty-five thousand warriors. '*Abakw Ma-Nyismane belelesile*' they chanted, smeared with ochre and grease. 'The white men have come, and will be slaughtered. *Bulala*! The vast horde hummed, singing their praise songs and drumming their spears against their shields. Thousand after teeming thousand — umKhulutshane, uMbonambi, uMcityu — raised a pall of dust that hid them from Ulundi as they stamped and shuffled, their head-plumes a boiling sea that spread across the veldt for several miles. The time has come, 0 Great King! Let the word be spoken! *Bayete! Nkosi enkulu! Bayete!*'

CHAPTER THIRTEEN

It was oddly shaped, like a couchant lion — or, even more strikingly, resembling the Sphinx of the 24th's regimental badge. Although less loftly than the northerly Nqutu range, of which it was a detached spur, it reared conspicuously from the surrounding rubble-strewn veldt that sloped away, undulating, from its base.

For a number of reasons the declining skirt of Isandhlwana was a good site for a camp. There was wood and water within easy reach but, more important, the position was almost unapproachable from the westward because of the precipitous obstacle of the mountain, several hundred feet higher, behind it. The ground on both flanks was broken, stone-scattered, while the grassy plain to the eastward — from where any attack, however unlikely, could be expected — was visible for a distance of several miles, intersected by shallow gullies and spruits, but offering little cover.

The tent-lines were laid during the afternoon of the 20th, and by five o'clock most of the canvas had been raised, extending across the track which meandered on towards die Zulu hinterland. Behind the men's tents were the regimental wagons and the hospital and headquarters' tents, nearer to the hill, although straggling Boer wagons continued to arrive until well after dusk. It was a dry, dark night, and quiet, with the Kaffir vedettes reporting no movement on the surrounding veldt. The men ate well on fresh-killed beef, preserved potatoes, bread and tea, before seeking early blankets following a tiring day of marching and tent-raising.

Morning brought nothing more surprising than the arrival of 'F' Company of the 1st battalion, with Captain Mostyn and Lieutenants Anstey and Daly, having marched determinedly, almost without pause, from Rorke's Drift. The men were tired, dirty and sweat-streaked, but jubilant that they had joined the main body in time for the real fighting. There were back-slappings and hand-shakes, the ribald exchanges of men to whom abuse was an indication of comradeship. 'F' Company had come home, and the 1st Battalion was five companies strong. With five companies, bach, we'll knock spit out o' auld Bismarck's Prussian Guard, look you.'

It was probably true. Fit, and in good spirits, the 24th Regiment would have conceded nothing to any similar number of drilled troops anywhere in the world, given civilised conditions, and according to the rules. It was almost criminal to employ such men against ignorant savages with spears. As Private John David Hughes lectured, 'We're the flower of Her Matchesty's armed forces, see? Men of Harlech, boyo, that's what.' He raised a massive fist. 'Gif me one of them painted darkies on the end of this, look you, and he'll think he's been hit by a cartful o' pluddy Best Welsh Steam!'

It was a day of comparative inactivity; all were in need of a brief period of relief from hard marching. There were weapons to be cleaned, wagons located and stores checked, boots and clothing to be repaired. In addition, the orders for the 2nd Battalion of the 24th, with a battalion of Kaffirs, the mounted infantry and four guns, demanded an early dawn start, under Chelmsford's personal leadership, for the operation to the south-eastward. The veldt was wide and empty, and the vedettes, so far, had not 'flushed ebony'. The earlier report of two approaching Zulu impis was probably just a 'shave' — a rumour based more on hope than fact.

Noggs had avoided 'A' Company's lines. He needed time to think about Whelan. Even more, he needed advice, but he knew nobody here in whom he could confide safely. A few enquiries and little calculation would quickly lead to the identification of Whelan. There was only one person — William Mudford of the *Standard* — but he was thousands of miles distant. Even so, there was a way.

Noggs intended to accompany Chelmsford's sweep to the south-east tomorrow, but today he could write a report for Mudford — 'With the British Army in Zululand'. He could add a sentence in code, normally employed for conveying information of a delicate or exclusive nature, and Mudford, who knew the story of Whelan, could similarly reply.

And today almost for certain, Chelmsford would be sending a galloper back to Natal with despatches. Noggs' report could go with him, to Pieter Maritzburgh telegraph station thence via Cape Town to London. Even if weeks passed before a reply was received, there was little danger of

Whelan making off. He was as securely detained on the Zululand veldt as he might be in Pentonville Prison.

Of course, Noggs considered, his few coded words to Mud-ford might be the beginning of yet another news scoop for the *Standard*, while Forbes, Francis, Miers and the others were still impatiently stamping the decks of the ships bringing them to the Cape, but that was not Noggs' design. He only wanted, for the moment, to tell somebody, and Willie Mudford would do nothing rash.

First, Noggs decided, he would seek out Major Clery, senior of Chelmsford's staff officers, and ask permission to be allowed to send his report with the General's galloper. Undoubtedly there would be officers hoping to despatch private letters by the same means, and there was a limit to the amount a rider could carry.

He found Clery on the lower slope of the hill, in conversation with Lieutenant Melvill, Adjutant of the 1st Battalion, and Brevet Lieutenant-Colonel Degacher, commanding the 2nd. But, Noggs perceived, this was no time for asking favours.

'I know what you're thinking by your face, sir,' Melvill was saying. 'You don't like the position.'

Degacher was angry. 'It's a bloody pig of a position. It *looks* all right, until you remember we're fighting natives, not European troops. Dammit, Clery' — he turned to the staff officer — 'what in hell made you choose this ground? That broken approach is no greater obstacle than a ploughed field against Zulus. They'll charge home, I tell you. With the numbers we'll have here tomorrow we ought to be in laager — and there's not even a picquet in our rear!'

'Why do you want a picquet in the rear,' asked Cornelius Clery, 'when you've got the mountain?'

'It's *because* we've got the mountain, blast it, that we need a picquet,' Degacher insisted. 'Even if the Zulus can't attack directly from that side, Major, we want to know if they're there!'

Clery was equally annoyed with the censure in the other's voice. Degacher was one of those officers who pressed their own requirements without caring that compliance meant something else must be neglected. Clery shrugged. 'Well, sir, if you're nervous, we'll post a Kaffir picquet behind — at least until tomorrow. Then we'll need every native to make the track passable for the guns.'

Noggs walked back to the tent-lines with Clery. 'Degacher's damn right,' the staff officer admitted morosely. 'Last night an Inspector of the Mounted Police was making the same complaint to Colonel Crealock, the General's secretary. And do you know what m'Lord said? "Tell the police officer *my* troops will do all the attacking!" But it's bad business. The column's moving much too slowly. We're not carrying supplies for a prolonged campaign, and we can't spend more valuable time in making every halting place a bloody fortress. All the same' — he narrowed his eyes — 'my blood runs cold when I think of an open camp being attacked —'

* * *

But everything would be all right when the time came, Dyson had decided despite his superiors' misgivings. To the older men, he had discovered, things were never as good as they used to be, never as they ought to be. Either discipline was going to the dogs, or duties were too soft, or they just didn't breed real soldiers any more. 'Goddam, young Dyson,' he'd heard a dozen times, 'you ought to have served under Blenkinsop in 'sixty-four — a flogging every day except Sundays, b'God. Subalterns went white as sheets when they heard he was going to inspect —' In twenty years, Dyson mused, he'd be saying the same thing. 'Goddam, young Jones, you ought to have served under Harry Pulleine in 'seventy-nine. We fought bloody Zulus in those days —'

He had never thought about fighting Zulus before coming to the Cape. If he had thought about fighting at all, he had visualised massed regiments of grey-clad Russians, swirling snowflakes and a leaden sky, jingling squadrons of enemy cavalry, distant gun-flashes, and the ranks of his own company cheering as they fired. That was the popular picture of a battle drawn by artists who had never been nearer to a war than the annual manoeuvres at Aldershot.

But Zulus? He had heard that they moved across country as fast as cavalry and, the Boers said, the sight of a disciplined impi of two or three thousand warriors sweeping across the veldt, searching for its enemy, was something to curdle the blood. Young Zulus, on initiation, were required to capture a lion alive, or tread out a bush fire with their bare feet. When they killed, they slashed open the bellies of their victims, spilling the entrails. They ignored the possibility of death, which was pre-ordained, and nothing, the Boers warned, halted a charging Zulu except a heavy slug through his head. Hit him anywhere else, and he'll keep coming, with an assegai in his hand and slaughter in his heart.

Christ. When the time came, he hoped he behaved well. He wasn't sure.

'A' Company tents were to the southward of the Rorke's Drift-Ulundi track, the unprotected flank of the camp from which an even narrower hunting track twisted towards the Buffalo and Helpmakaar beyond. Behind the tents were the battalion wagons, with the outspanned oxen boredly chewing as the flies crawled around their bloodshot eyes. The sun of late afternoon was hot, and the British troops were in shirt-sleeves, busily applied to doing as little as possible. The bell tents, sleeping twelve to sixteen men, feet to pole, were oven-hot within, even with brailings raised, and a man would stream with sweat after only a few minutes' occupancy. Cavaye could have ordered drill, or inspections of kit, rifles or feet, but he did not. 'Don't chase 'em,' he growled. He paused, then frowned and said, 'Where's bloody Whelan?'

Whelan, b'God. The inadequate Irishman was conspicuous at any time, but never more than when he was absent. He was the Company's shabby joke, but the Welshmen tolerated him — only God knew why — and covered for him, black-balled his boots, buckled his complicated equipment, and nudged him into movement when, almost invariably, he failed to comply with a shouted command. 'Dyson, where's Whelan?'

'He's with the Sergeant's party, clearing rubble, sir,' Dyson offered. Dammit, there seemed an unusual interest in Whelan, with Norris-Newman last night, and now Cavaye. The scrubby Irishman was becoming a bloody celebrity.

'Parsons' party has been back an hour since,' Cavaye said. 'Dyson, I always get a prickly feeling in the back o' my damn scalp when I don't know where Whelan is. It's like leaving the bath running when you can't see it. Any moment, and it's too blasted late.' He sighed. 'I want to know where he is, Dyson.'

'Whelan, sir,' explained Sergeant Parsons, 'is picquet, like you said.'

'Picquet?' Cavaye frowned. 'What picquet?'

'The running spruit, sir, on the track.' Parsons lifted his helmet to scratch his cropped head. 'He said you'd ordered it, sir — an' orf he went in field order an' fifty rounds.'

'Picquet on the *spruit*?' Cavaye spat. Why the hell would I want a picquet on the spruit? Who's going to steal a bloody ditchful o' water?'

'I didn't arst questions, sir.' The Sergeant was hurt. 'Nobody gives 'imself picquet dooty fer nuthin, least of all Whelan. He jes' strapped up, sir, shouldered 'is bundoo, an' marched orf without a word.'

Cavaye stared, then, 'God Almighty. The bloody fool must have a touch of the sun; not that anybody'd know any difference, dammit. Mr Dyson' — he turned to his junior — 'for Chris' sake see what it's all about, will you?'

The spruit ran across the track, a half mile to the westward in the direction of Rorke's Drift, through a greeny-dun, stony veldt that undulated from horizon to horizon. Dyson reached the spruit in ten minutes, ill-humoured. A few Kaffir boys watered oxen at the churned edge of the stream, and there were several cooking fires trickling smoke skyward, but there was no red-coated picquet.

It was odd, even for Whelan, b'God. It would be dusk in an hour, and if the man really believed he was standing picquet he might be difficult to find. Confound the ignorant bastard. Exasperated, Dyson turned to retrace his steps, then halted. Confound the clod. There was a humped kopje climbing to his left, and he made for its crest.

From his new vantage point he could see, further westward, a scattering of native huts, deserted, and patches of mealie. Two hundred feet below him, on the track, a group of Kaffir scouts sat on their haunches, smoking, and he could just hear their distant chatter. The sun was in his eyes, and he shaded them with a hand, squinting as he surveyed the empty landscape. Then he swore, unbelieving.

A thousand yards across the veldt, barely discernible, was a scarlet fleck under a bobbing pin-point of white. It was Whelan, marching determinedly towards Rorke's Drift and Natal.

Dyson ran. The Kaffirs' chatter ceased as they stared at him from below, blank-faced. The sweat was soaking his shirt and his lungs ached. 'Whelan! Whelan!' Christ, this was ridiculous. It was bloody pantomime.

Whelan halted and turned. His equipment was awry and his solar helmet sat on his ears, from one of which he took a crumpled fragment of a cigarette and pushed it between his lips. 'Shure, an' I knew ut. Ef I marched fer a bloddy wayk there'd be no difference. Ut's the black luck ev a Whelan, sorr, an' thet's a fact. Everythin' I touches turrns ter shit.' Dyson heaved air into his lungs, incapable of talking.

'It wuz the land agent thet told ye,' Whelan resumed. 'But did he not tell ye the way ev ut? It wuz a bit ev sport, Rice sez — ter intimidate the bloddy Englishman. Mother ev God' — he shook his head — 'it wuzn't murrder I wuz thinking ev, sorr. Shure, an' there's plenty ev things I'd do, but niver murrder.'

Dyson stared at Whelan, uncomprehending. 'Murder?'

'Shure, an' the first toim we mate, he sez, will be the larst. I'll see ye hang. Who wud think he'd see me in *bloddy Africa*? Faith, an' I moight as well hev gone straight back ter Sergeant Cooley in Letterkenny, an' finish wid ut.' He hawked and spat. 'What's wrong wid killing a man thet's jes' murrdered ye' woif?'

Dyson drew a final, shuddering breath. Probably Cavaye was right. Whelan had a touch of the sun. There were orders on the daytime wearing of solar helmets, and typical of the man that he had ignored them. Still, Dyson grasped at a straw-

'The land agent,' he said. 'I don't remember his name.'

'Shure ye do, an' all, sorr,' Whelan frowned. 'Et's bloddy Norris-Newman.'

That was it. He had been trying to think of Norris-Newman who, in turn, had known about Dyson & Bradley, and had then enquired about Private Whelan, the least attractive soldier of the battalion. He, Dyson, recalled that the journalist, familiarly addressed as Noggs, had once been an officer on the North-West Frontier — but had he also been a land agent? In Donegal? And what was all this about killing a man, and a murdered wife?

'I remember,' Dyson nodded slowly, then, 'But there's always two sides of a story, Whelan. I'd like to hear yours.'

'Jasus, an' who'd belavve me against the agent an' Cooley, an' the Inspector from Strabane an' all? Didn't they suspect me fer Campbell's killing, sorr, whin I wuzn't nearer the house than thray bloddy miles? Et wuz Rice, shure enough, but he'll not be confessin' ter anythin', an' no jury ev Dublin shopkeepers wud belayve a bloddy bog-peasant from Donegal —'

'But I might,' Dyson insisted, 'if you tell me, Whelan.' He paused. 'Right from the beginning.'

Whelan eyed him doubtfully for several long moments, then shrugged. 'Faith, there kin be nuthin' lost, I'm thinkin',' — he unslung the rifle from his shoulder — 'an loikly nuthin' gained, but I'll tell ye, sorr — and' I'm spaykin' the truth, Holy Mary —'

They remained on their feet, facing each other and completely alone on the measureless, hushed veldt. The sun was sinking and, eastward, the sky was purpling over the rearing butte of Isandhlwana. Dyson felt the sweat of his body cooling, and his stomach reminded him that he had not eaten since midday, but he kept his eyes on the other's shadowed face, making no interruption. Whelan talked, sullenly at first, with the congenital, self-effacing bitterness of his kind. Progressively, however, his rancour subsided until it seemed that he was unaware of Dyson's presence, that he wished only to relieve himself of an intolerable burden. His story was confused in places, ungrammatical and laced with obscenities, but it told of cold winters, hunger and blighted crops, of red-haired Mary Whelan and Smiley's Bar, the Fenians and the talk of Captain Rice that he did not understand but which promised much. It told of hopeless rent arrears and the detested 'gombeen' money-lender, of Campbell and Norris-Newman, and then that final, rain-sodden day at the Glaziers' estate house, when he had seen Mary Whelan flung backward by Rice's shot.

'There was only one bastard I've iver wanted ter kill,' Whelan finished, 'an' that wuz bloddy Sergeant Gamble. Shure, I wid hev, ef it hadn't been fer the dummy cartridge an' all.'

The reference meant nothing to Dyson, but he did not question it. 'And now you're deserting on active service,' he said. 'How far do you suppose you'll get, Whelan?' He shook his head. You'll be lucky to get past the company at Rorke's Drift — and if you do, what then? Dammit man, you'll be dragged back in hours, chained to a log, and then court-martialled.'

'Court-martialled, es ut?' Whelan snorted. 'Es thet worse than the bloddy Assizes? B'Jasus, kin they hang a man twice? Ef I put a bullet through ye now, sorr, an' left ye dead, whit worse cud they do than bloddy string me up fer ut?'

Dyson was aware that he had left the tent-lines without his pistol. In enemy country, with or without Whelan, it had been a careless oversight. 'It'd make things a damn sight worse,' he retorted. 'They wouldn't bother to bring you back. You'd be ridden down and shot on sight before you even reached the river.' He paused. 'Good God, Whelan, be sensible. If what you've told me is true, I can't believe any court of law would hang you. It could be a manslaughter charge, and perhaps only a brief prison sentence. If you take my advice —'

'I don't want ter shoot ye, sorr,' Whelan replied. 'Ye'll understand thet. Mother ev God, I've nuthin' against ye, but ef ye go back ter the lines ye'll be heving the mounted poliss after me.' He lifted his rifle. 'I'm sorry, sorr. Ye've done nuthin' ter desarve ut, but et's you or me.'

Dyson watched the rifle muzzle rise to his chest. 'There's a Kaffir picquet just over that ridge, Whelan. They'll hear the shot. You're only delaying the inevitable, and this time there's no justification. It's just cold-blooded murder.' But his belly had turned to ice. 'And you're killing someone who's likely to plead for you. I think Norris-Newman's another, and even Captain Cavaye. You've got a clean record, even if you're not the regiment's prize soldier. A recommendation for leniency from your officers — perhaps even Lord Chelmsford — could achieve a lot, Whelan.' Any second, he tensed, he'd have a .45 calibre bullet tearing a hole in his lungs. 'Think about it, man.' And every further second he gained was precious.

The frowning Irishman was uncertain. His eyes flickered to the ridge, then back to Dyson. 'Shure, I'm not wantin' ter kill ye, sorr,' he repeated, 'an' thet's the truth. I'm not bloddy man enough fer killin'.' He calculated. 'Ef I came back wid ye, sorr, ye'll spayk fer me?'

Dyson nodded. 'I'll speak for you, Whelan. No — I'll do better than that. I'll not say a word unless Norris-Newman exposes you, and I'm not convinced he will. If you are arrested, I'll stand as "prisoner's friend", and I'll see that you get something better than a docker's brief defence.' By Christ, he seethed, I'm a bloody coward. I'm bargaining. If I were a stiff-lipped, hard-bitten Cavaye I'd demolish this illiterate little devil in a few contemptuous seconds, but I'm too damned terrified.

Whelan considered, his dark eyes suspecting. Then he jerked the cocking lever of his rifle and a brass cartridge spun to the ground. 'Orlright, sorr. I'll come back wid ye, son, Holy Mary, ye'll not sell me?'

Relief engulfed Dyson. 'I shan't sell you, Whelan. You can take my word for it. You misunderstood your orders, see? Perhaps you'll get a few fatigues, but that's all. Then we'll wait, and we'll cross our bridges when we come to 'em.' And I'm still alive, he breathed. Christ, I'm supposed to be an officer, a leader of men. God help me when I'm faced with charging Zulus. I should have stayed in Aston Manor, with an office stool, invoices in duplicate and Grand Hotel smoke-room gossip. It had been bloody easy miming heroics in the Birmingham warehouse.

CHAPTER FOURTEEN

Already, on 21 January, 150 Natal Mounted Volunteers and two battalions of the Natal Native Contingent had been ordered out, in two groups under Major Dartnell and Commandant Lonsdale respectively, to reconnoitre the area around Matyana's kraal — Ngnaba-Ka-Mazungeni — the intended target of Lord Chelmsford's first strike with half his force, south-eastward. Noggs had ridden with Dartnell's detachment, anxious to absent himself from the Isandhlwana camp and the proximity of Whelan for a few hours. He had not sent his despatch to Mudford in London, and he needed time to think.

It was a gruelling, frustrating march over switchback hills, with slopes thickly foliaged and thorn-cluttered, occasionally cleared for small native settlements and corn-patches. The white non-commissioned officers of the Natal Kaffirs were in bad humour, foot-sore, sweating, and cursing their charges. Tempers were not improved when the advance mounted element sent back a report that scouts had sighted a large force of Zulus, possibly fifteen hundred, strongly positioned on a steep krantz and taunting the white men below them who could do little without infantry.

The straggling, tired column stumbled on. Did these Zulus represent the impis reported to be advancing from Ulundi — so far southward? The reconnaissance force, largely Kaffir, was not competent to deal with large enemy concentrations, and within an hour it was plain that any such thought must be quickly abandoned. From a distance of almost three miles, on the slopes of the next range of hills, they could see the waiting enemy — all of two thousand armed Zulus in disciplined lines, and in the intervening valley the halted, uncertain Mounted Volunteers.

Encouraged by the arrival of the native contingent, and in a spirit of bravado, a small group of the volunteers cantered to within 800 yards of the Zulu position. Instantly, with beautiful precision and in complete silence, two companies of the enemy opened into skirmishing order with flanks running at incredible speed. Threatened with encirclement in seconds, the volunteers wheeled and galloped for the safety of their main body. In turn the Zulus halted, almost disdainfully, and withdrew slowly without a backward glance.

It was stalemate, with dusk approaching, and nothing promising except an uncomfortable night of open bivouac. Major John Dartnell, commanding, had no intention of retreating now that he had flushed ebony, but an attack on his part would be criminal folly. He despatched a note to Lord Chelmsford, requesting the reinforcement of two or three companies of Imperial troops by morning, and also asking for the rapid supply of blankets and provisions — the lack of which had already seriously undermined the precarious discipline of his mixed force. Before dark two disgruntled officers of the native contingent — Lieutenants Avery and Holcroft — mounted their horses to return to a more comfortable bed at Isandhlwana. They were never seen again.

It was a night of sleeplessness and discomfort. Dartnell's force bivouacked in hollow square, with the Kaffirs on three sides and the volunteers, with rifles loaded and bayonets fixed, on the other. In the dark distance the Zulus' hundred night fires hung suspended, and during the early hours the Kaffirs, startled by an unidentifiable noise, scrambled away from their positions to throw chaos among the tethered horses. Noggs, huddled and chilled, was trampled by a shying animal, and disgustedly sought a less exposed location where he might doze until dawn.

But before dawn a despatch from Isandhlwana, accompanying rations and blankets, told that Lord Chelmsford was already marching with six companies of the 24th's 2nd Battalion, Mounted Infantry, a further battalion of Kaffirs, and four guns, expecting to reach Dartnell's position by daybreak.

Tomorrow, then, Noggs brightened, he'd have something really worthwhile for Willie Mudford and the *Standard*.

* * *

At Isandhlwana, at 1.30 am, Lieutenant-Colonel Degacher had been roused by a staff officer with Chelsmford's instructions. He was to muster his battalion as quietly as possible and without lights, in light field order and with one day's rations, ready to march at 3.30 am for the Isilulwane hills to the south-eastward where Dartnell's force waited. The instructions added that the ambulances and their attendant bandsmen would not accompany the fast-marching column, but through an oversight this latter order was not passed on, and the ambulances and stretcher-men followed the infantry and guns as they rumbled over the rutted track towards the first yellow streaks of approaching dawn. Also, because of conflicting picquet duties, 'G' Company of the 2nd Battalion, under Lieutenant Charles Pope, remained at Isandhlwana with the five companies of the 1st. Better a warm blanket, the 'G' Company men gloated, than a stumbling, chilly march in the dew-soaked darkness.

They did not know, any more than Chelmsford, that the Zulu force facing Dartnell was totally unconnected with the army of Cetshwayo, but consisted of the warriors of Matyana, a recalcitrant chief who had decided that he would fight his own war rather than that of the Great King's. Retribution would certainly follow, but for the moment the King's supreme commander, Tshingwayo, was prepared to leave Matyana unmolested. Indeed, Tshingwayo mused, it would be most satisfying if Matyana's warriors were thrashed by the red soldiers. Tshingwayo did not like Matyana — but unwittingly Matyana was to prove an invaluable asset in splitting the forces of the invading Ma-Nyisimane. At this moment, however, even Tshingwayo could not predict that.

* * *

The Great King's regiments had halted in a wide, stony and scrub-scattered valley that rose from the Nqutu mountains, northward, and the uDibi boys, who carried for the men, unrolled the warriors' sleeping mats and passed around corn-cakes and slabs of boiled meat. Some drank from the great maguda water pipes to wash the sourness of yesterday's beer from their mouths, sucked on marijuana, or sniffed, hawking and spitting, at pinches of snuff — the crushed leaves of tobacco mixed with the ash of burnt aloe leaves. They were five miles from Isandhlwana, where the red soldiers were kraaled, but there was no intention of fighting today. The moon was dead. Today would be a day for resting, for story-telling and boasting. Tomorrow, at dawn, the regiments would attack.

A few had seen occasional white men — missionaries, traders, Boers — but almost none had seen the white men's red soldiers, and they were curious, speculating. There were stories, handed down through generations of tribal custodians, of the white men's first coming. They had come out of the sea, carried in the bellies of great sea-going animals with many legs. They wore the bright *tusi* sun metal on their bodies to stop the Bantus' angry spears of futile bone and brittle granite. Their hair was the colour of dull fire, and their skins were like dirty milk into which a little blood had been poured. They carried weapons of ravening iron which laughed to scorn the thick hide of the toothy lion. They wore bands of white around their heads as if to stop their flowing hair flying off their scalps. Their shields were round, with bosses of bronze reflecting the sun, and their battle-shouts were loud in the ears of the frightened Bantu. They killed with their iron swords. They speared with their lances and scattered the Bantus' brains to the seven winds with their axes of iron and bronze...

On 17 January the Great King had assembled his regiments on the plain at Nodwengu, near Ulundi. '*Uya kuhlasela-pi na*?' they had roared at him. 'Where wilt thou wage war, O King?' Twenty-five thousand assegais rose to the hot sky. '*A-yi-ze*! Let it come!' Twenty-five thousand right feet stamped, once, and the ground trembled.

Cetshwayo, in the leopard-skin that only a king might wear, spoke slowly to his gathered *indunas*. 'I am sending you against the Ma-Nyismane, who have invaded the land of the Zulu. You are to march your regiments against the red soldiers at kwaJimu, and drive them back into Natal. You will attack by daylight, for there are enough of you to swallow them up, as the serpent swallows the frog. And you will march slowly, so that you do not tire.'

They had marched slowly, six miles, to bivouac on the west bank of the White Umfolozi river. On the following day they marched a mere nine, to sleep at the military kraal of Isixepi, to eat, to drink beer, to boast. If the time had come to die, nothing -could prevent it. Conversely, if the time was not yet, then a man would not die, and he might take what risks he chose. But, of course, it was bad to talk of death.

On the 19th they had reached the grassy tableland near the Isihlungu Hills, and then, on the 20th, reached the Isepezi Mountain, to the southward, still undetected. It was strange that, while hourly Zulu scouts brought news of the white men's movements, the white men seemed blithely unaware of the approach of the vast Zulu horde. Next morning the regiments moved cautiously on, to the valley of the Nxcata stream, barely a twenty minutes trot from Isandhlwana.

It had been the Mounted Infantry, under Lieutenant Browne of the 1st 24th — a mixed collection of army cooks, storekeepers and bandsmen, and apparently the least proficient of the horsed units — who had yesterday reported increasing numbers of Zulus to the eastward and north-eastward. It was possibly the lack of confidence in enthusiastic foot-sloggers pretending to be cavalry that resulted in their report being allowed little credence, and sent most of them with Chelmsford's dawn march, where they would be under the constant eyes of officers who knew better.

'It's high damn time,' a young lieutenant grunted. 'Now, at least, we're going to find Cetshwayo.'

An old Boer voorlooper shook his head. 'No, *Roinek*. First, Cetshwayo will find you.'

On the lower slopes of Isandhlwana remained five companies of the 1st Battalion and one of the 2nd, two guns and seventy men of the Royal Artillery, thirty of the Mounted Infantry, eight mounted volunteers and police, four companies of Natal Kaffirs, and a few non-combatants including a bandmaster and four regimental boys. Lieutenant-Colonel Pulleine, commanding, had Lord Chelmsford's written orders: 'You will be in command of the camp during the absence of Colonel Glyn. Draw in your line of defence while the force is out, and draw in your infantry outposts accordingly, but keep your cavalry vedettes well advanced.' Although not specific, the orders strongly implied that the role of the Isandhlwana force was a defensive one. Chelmsford had already decided that, when his own force had dealt with the Zulus to the south-eastward, it would not return to Isandhlwana. Pulleine would be ordered to strike camp and follow the line of route of the advance column.

At Reveille the camp seemed oddly deserted and quiet, its expanse over-generous for the diminished complement that remained. The day promised to be fine, and Pulleine immediately applied himself to re-positioning his defensive perimeter. His regulars were going to be stretched dangerously thin; single companies were strung over a thousand yards with almost similar intervals separating them. Pope's 'G' Company of the 2nd was almost a mile in advance of the camp centre, the men grouped in fours and looking pathetically exposed, while the elbow of the L-shaped line was occupied by 300 Natal Kaffirs, only thirty of whom were armed with Westley-Rkhards carbines, and these issued with only five rounds each.

'It's as quiet as death, Willie bach,' said Private John David Hughes, scanning the empty veldt. 'Like when the auld steam engine stops pumping, look, an' all you can hear iss water dripping, an' seffen thousand pluddy feet between you an' the plew sky.'

'Aye, there's quiet for you,' agreed Private William Morgan. 'If those plack boyos are coming, Dai, they're not stampin' their pluddy feet, see.'

Whelan said nothing, but his silence was not unusual. He seldom volunteered comment, and for the moment he had more to think about than the prospect of a Zulu attack. Bedad, several problems would be solved if the blacks did oppose Chelmsford's sortie to the southeastward, and at least eliminate the threat posed by the agent, Norris-Newman. That would leave only Lieutenant Dyson. He, Whelan, was already regretting his confession of the previous evening. Was Dyson to be trusted? Or had he already gone blathering to Captain Cavaye or Colonel Pulleine? It was the cursed black luck of a Whelan that still dogged him — that had married him to a red-haired woman, blighted his Letterkenny holding, made him a murderer, and now taunted him with the reappearance of the land agent. Holy Mary, wuz there no bloddy escape fer a dacent man thet niver meant harrm ter nobody?

His comrades' conversation had died, dampened by the overwhelming silence. B'Jasus, it wuz bloddy quiet, an' they wuz right. It wuz bloddy quiet. Ye'd think everythin' hed stopped an' wuz listenin', waitin'. Even the auld Sergeant wuz standin' still, frownin' — and it tuk something outlandish to silence the vociferous Parsons.

It was almost 7.30 am.

'Christ,' said Cavaye, 'it's damn quiet — like flag day in Aberdeen.' He fingered a badly-shaven chin. 'If there's one thing that ruins my day, young Dyson, it's shaving in bloody cold water. A man's entitled to hot shaving water, blast it. If I'm ever promoted to that great Staff College in the sky' — he nodded upwards — 'I'll forgo my issue of a bloody golden trumpet, so long as I get *hot shaving water*' In the lines a bugle was sounding 'Cookhouse', and Cavaye tugged out his watch. 'You can let one man in three go to the field kitchens, Dyson — and try to find me some bloody coffee that's not full of mud.'

The men with their mess-tins had hardly reached the kitchens to queue for tea, stirabout, bacon and bread when a police orderly of the vedette, stationed two thousand yards to the north-east, flung himself from his saddle outside Pulleine's tent to report that three columns of Zulus were rapidly approaching. Within seconds the 2nd Battalion duty bugler was sounding Company Call, and men were running, flinging down their mess-tins to snatch up rifles and equipment. Lieutenant Pope's forward company came tumbling back to join the line of regulars spreading thinly in front of the tents, while Pulleine scribbled a brief note to Lord Chelmsford: '8.5 am. Report just come in that the Zulus are advancing in force from the left front of the camp.' The police orderly, scrambling back into his saddle, spurred his animal in pursuit of the column that had departed four hours earlier.

For a time nothing happened. The sergeants jostled the men into dressed spacing, and the men, grumbling good-humouredly, complied, slapping at flies on reddened necks. Officers searched the veldt with glasses, uneasy at the gaping distances between companies but silently assuring themselves that it was impossible for any force of spear-carrying natives to reach those gaps in the face of six hundred breech-loading rifles and two 7-pounder guns.

'Them pluddy vedettes, look,' complained Private John David Hughes, having been deprived of his breakfast, 'wouldn't know a Zulu from my auld Auntie Glynis at Abergwynfi, that made the cheese for Ellis Griffith's funeral, see.'

'I remember that cheese, Hughie bach,' reminisced Private William Morgan hungrily. 'With a piece of fresh loaf and a good onion, boyo, it was food for angels, look you.' He shook his head. 'Dai, a man could marry a woman with her knees glued together for cheese like that, see.'

'It's right you are, Willie bach. And beer, look. A woman that brews good beer iss worth two women that only brews pluddy tea, look,' Private John William Hughes ruled. 'Giff me a good terrier, a good ferret, an' a woman that makes good, strong cheese an' beer an' who doesn't mind a man passing a bit of wind occasionally —'

'In church and chapel,' Private Morgan nodded, 'let it rattle.'

'Jes' keep yer eyes ter the front, an' not so much clack,' admonished Sergeant Parsons, 'or I'll 'ave yer passin' bleedin' wind orlright, wi' two hours' soddin' pack drill. An' you, Whelan!' He wheeled on the

Irishman. 'Yer supposed ter be in *light field order*. That means "equipped an' armed ter fight one local action without demands on ordnance an' commissariat", see?' Parsons was remembering his Wellington. Whelan, I don't know what yer'll do to the Weedin' Zulus, but, b'Christ, yer scare the shits out o' me! Why don't yer stuff some soddin' paper in that 'at, so's yer can at least see where yer bleedin' going?'

'Goddammit!' Cavaye exploded, his glasses to his eyes. 'There they are, on the bloody plateau — like black bugs, Dyson!' He pointed.

On a flattened ridge of the distant Nqutu there were Zulus moving — an ominous, black froth stippled with colour, of tossing plumes, white-splashed shields and the glitter of steel. At almost three miles there was no sound, but it was a sight that most white men had never experienced. The soldiers were glancing at their officers, now also silent, but in seconds the indistinct, remote movement had gone, draining from sight beyond the hills northward. So fleeting had been the spectacle that it might have been an illusion, a flight of excited fancy, but they had all seen.

* * *

At 10 am the undercurrent of unease among the officers was dispelled by the arrival of a welcome reinforcement in the form of 250 Natal Native Horse, a rocket battery, and three more companies of Natal Kaffirs, under the command of Colonel Anthony Durnford, Royal Engineers. This was part of a secondary, reserve force earlier ordered by Chelmsford to enter Zululand by Middle Drift, forty miles away, primarily to meet the possibility of Zulus avoiding the main body and infiltrating into scantily garrisoned Natal. Durnford, however, was ill-suited for negative defensive duties, and Chelmsford had already reprimanded him for excessive enthusiasm, finally instructing him to bring his horsed detachment and rocket battery to support his own advance.

Durnford, tall and ruddy, lengthily moustached and pugnacious, shared with his General the frustration of military unfulfilment. More unfortunately, he was senior to Colonel Pulleine, commanding at Isandhlwana.

Durnford, however, was not immediately prepared to assert his seniority. He was not irresponsible, and he knew himself to be fresh to the situation while Pulleine was an experienced infantry officer with, for the moment, a superior grasp of events. Even so, the prospect was interesting. There were Zulu forces in the vicinity, apparently offensive, and he, Durnford, was technically the senior officer present. He confined himself to a tactful suggestion that Pulleine should withdraw his men from their tiring stand-to positions for a meal, emphasising that they should remain equipped and armed during the process. The far hills were now empty, and Pulleine had no hesitation in agreeing. Durnford sent fifty of his mounted men back on their tracks to escort and hasten in his following wagons, then joined Pulleine for a breakfast that both men were ready for.

CHAPTER FIFTEEN

'White people,' Sibindi told Nzobo, 'do not mate like the amaZulu, and white women do not bear children with blood and pain like black mamanas. They lay shining eggs that hatch little baanas the next day.' Around them, as far as the eye could see, were the massed impis, assembled in the immense half circle — *umkumbi* — in which they would go forward to battle, while the reserves sat with their backs to the fighting, forbidden to watch until they were called upon to participate. But Sibindi knew that these were not all. The horns of the great army lay out of sight, southward, and the uMcityu were in the shadow of the Nqutu range, northward. Stragglers from Ulundi were still joining, all with three days' provisions, and the boys of the iNtanga drove cattle in the rear.

The *iniangas*, the witch-doctors, whistling in order to communicate with die spirits, crouched among the tossing ocean of plumes, of flamingo feathers, lion skins, cowrie shells, white cow tails and owl feathers, sprinkling medicines and distributing emetics. Usibebu, the *induna*, pranced before his thousand inDlu-yengwe, promising that by sunset tomorrow all would have earned the head-ring, and the Great King would grant them fat wives, and cattle of their own. The uThulwana jeered. It required men to kill red soldiers with their big guns on wheels, not herd-boys in cow-hide collars pretending to be warriors.

Sibindi, vociferous champion of the inDlu-yengwe since he had fought with the black bull, rose to his full height, pointing scornfully. 'Who are these toothless old men who talk of fighting?' The uThulwana, with their ostrich feathers and green monkeyskin ear-flaps, were forty-five years of age. 'They should go back to their kraal and weed their mealie-fields! See, they tremble on their old legs, and their eyes are dim. How can these grey-heads keep pace with such as the inDlu-yengwe?' He snorted with contempt and his comrades hummed. There were other men climbing to their feet, shouting similar jibes, among them the uNokenki, the isaNgqu, the inGobamakhosi, the inDlondlo.

It was the eve of the battle, the time for shouting threats, for bragging of prowess and for generating within themselves an assurance of invincibility, so that when the massed, savage regiment stamped forward across the dusty veldt nothing would halt it except complete destruction. Once an impi was in motion, no warrior could hesitate or hold back, none might pause to throw his spear from a distance. A spear was for stabbing, hand to hand with an enemy, in an all-devouring, overwhelming charge that deluged like a black flood over everything that stood in its path.

The sun still required an hour to reach its highest, and when the men had eaten they would sleep under their shields, or lazily hone the blades of their assegais until they drew blood from a finger-touch. Some would dry-shave the heads of comrades with iron knives, smoke tobacco or wild hemp, or kneel about the witch-doctors as they threw their magic knuckle-bones of goat and baboon, to foretell tomorrow's battle. But none spoke of death. It was not good to speak of death.

They knew of Isandhlwana, shaped like a crouching lion, the great guardian rock beyond which was the Buffalo river and the beginning of the lands that had once been Bantu, but were now ruled by the Ma-Nyisi-mane, the white men. The warriors who had not yet washed their spears had been told by the *indunas*, the old scarred ones, that the red soldiers would have their wagons in laager, end to end, and would have dug pits or raised walls of stone. And the white men had big guns on wheels, hauled by horses. It was necessary to watch the big guns carefully, and when a red *induna* raised his arm, and the big guns flashed, the warriors should throw themselves to the ground, thus allowing the big bullets to pass harmlessly overhead. When the white men who served the big guns had been killed, the guns were useless.

Isandhlwana. The Little Hand Mountain. It was hardly a mountain, being only several hundred feet higher than the grass-covered hill below it, which in turn, sloped gently, eventually merging with the further, larger range of hills northward, the Nqutu. The resting Zulus could see the northerly hills clearly enough, but they could not see Isandhlwana to their south-westward, which was hidden by intervening, undulating veldt. But they would see it soon, first the encircling flanks, the horns, of the army, and then the frontal attacking chest, the solid centre — once loosed, beyond recall.

The sun was climbing, and soon it would be hot in the valley. Even the lone kite that floated high overhead would sink to earth, and the men would sleep, shining with sweat. Then night would follow, with the thousand children of the moon scattered like silver seeds across the sable sky, and then dawn again, the dawn when the spears of the amaZulu would be washed in blood, and the vultures and the hyenas would gather for the feasting.

But death was not to be kept waiting until tomorrow. South-westward, over the crest of the near, dune-like ridge that hid Isandhlwana from them, rode a man on a pony.

He was a Basuto, but not Zulu. He wore an ill-shaped hat wound with a scrap of scarlet rag, a dirty red tunic, canvas trousers that had once been white, with his bare feet thrust into the rawhide stirrups. There was a rifle at his back.

Surprise was mutual and paralysing. The rider wrenched his mount to a halt, staring incredulously at the valley below him, densely swarming with 20,000 armed Zulus. There were several seconds of stunned silence, and then the Basuto horseman turned, shouting. Below, thousands of warriors scrambled to their feet. '*Ayi hlome*! *Ayi hlome*!'

White-haired old Tshingwayo, veteran of a hundred vicious battles for Shako, Dingane, Mpande, and now supreme military commander under Cetshwayo, hissed angrily, and his *indunas* ran, hammering their spears against their cow-hide shields to draw attention to their bellowing for discipline and restraint, but to no avail. Thousands of men were tramping forward, slowly at first, and then breaking into a jostling trot, with the dust rising from their churning feet. Somewhere to the right, among the uDududu, there was a roar of 'Si-gi-di!' — the blood-chilling war cry of the Zulus — and it was too late. The black, boiling sea, plume-tossing and glittering rolled on, irresistible, towards the crest of the ridge, and towards Isandhlwana, which they could not see.

* * *

Lord Chelmsford's column had reached the Mangeni valley piecemeal, and soon after 6 am, in half light, a three-pronged advance was ordered against the hill on which the Zulus' fires could still be seen burning. This, then, was what they had come for, had marched hundreds of miles through dust, mud, teeming rain, flies, and blistering sun. It could be all finished with today, if Cetshwayo's army lay over that hill ahead, that the

Kaffirs called Isilulwane. Noggs climbed into his saddle, stiff and damply itching, and trying to shake off the ill humour with which he had survived an uncomfortable night. Dammit, he must be getting old. Time was when he'd spend a month of nights under conditions as bad, and never give a thought to it. After this, he mused, he'd best ask Willie Mudford for a less demanding assignment — society gossip or theatre reporting, say — when he'd be within easy reach of Williams's Boiled Beef Shop in the Old Bailey, Charlie Leybourne and Jenny Lind at the Lyceum, and could write his late-night copy over lobster kidney and a whisky noggin.

And Whelan. He had made up his mind over what he'd do about Whelan. It was nothing. Nothing at all. With luck, he'd not see Whelan again, and the man could go to damnation — but not through any action of Noggs'. The Irishman had killed Rice, but Rice was already a murderer, probably twice over. It was even possible that Whelan, unwittingly, had saved Noggs' life. Well, that was settled, then. Whelan could take himself to damnation and Noggs, for the first time in two days, decided that he was anticipating the coming day's action with new relish. Goddam, there was life in the old dog yet. Recklessly, he took a clean shirt and dry socks from his saddle-bag. Who could ask better than to see the sun rise over the wet African veldt with a breakfast of biscuits and stewed tea?

The Kaffirs went up the hill reluctantly, over-emphasising the difficulty of the ground, not anxious to be embroiled until the left and right encircling movements of mounted volunteers, police, and Imperial infantry had been completed. At the top, however, there were no Zulu hordes, only the glowing remains of fires and a few stragglers disappearing into the distance. The Kaffirs and their dispirited NCOs halted. Supplies of blankets, tea, sugar, biscuits and tinned meat had reached their camp hours earlier, but none had yet eaten, and morale could scarcely be lower.

It was odd, bloody odd, and Noggs, following the Kaffirs up the hill, was developing an uncomfortable feeling that something was not quite right. From the top of Isilulwane the view, still slightly hazed, was magnificent. Ahead, the green highlands of Zululand swelled and rolled to a distant, clouded horizon. Turning about, he could just distinguish the blurred shape of Isandhlwana, a three-hours' forced march away. It was unlikely that he would tread its slopes again if Chelmsford brought up Pulleine's command in support tomorrow.

Suddenly, there were shots from ahead, and Noggs kicked his horse forward. Bloody hell, was something happening? The ground fell away, and two miles across the slope he could see the volunteers and mounted police, in a long, ragged line spread across the grassland at full gallop in pursuit of fleeing, scattering Zulus. There were tiny puffballs of smoke mingling with the mist, and running, weaving men were falling. The Natal Kaffirs, encouraged, rose to their feet and broke into a shuffling trot, but Noggs was already flinging his horse ahead, groping at the damp leather of his holster-flap.

It was finished quickly, with eighty Zulus dead and the mounted men jubilant, some claiming that they had brought down their quarries at six hundred yards with their Martini-Henrys. Noggs, scribbling notes, thrust aside the sobering thought that eighty Zulus did not measure up to the two thousand that had stood on Isilulwane last night, and even two thousand did not nearly resemble the total of Cetshwayo's army. Well, the day was still young. There was time yet.

Lord Chelmsford and his staff had dismounted on the northern base of Isilulwane, where four companies of the 2nd Battalion 24th had halted. There were still groups of Zulus ahead, retiring mile by mile, seemingly towards the Ingutu Mountain, but there was time for tea to be brewed and a pipe of baccy. They had been hard-slogging for six hours and, sod it, there was Weedin' limits. The kettles, however, were hardly steaming when a dishevelled police orderly climbed from a sweating, lathered horse to present the General with a despatch from Isandhlwana. He had left the camp, he reported, shortly after eight that morning, at which time — he had seen it with his own eyes — strong Zulu forces were mounting an attack. There were startled faces among the officers surrounding Chelmsford, but he showed little concern as he read Pulleine's note aloud.

' "Report just come in that the Zulus are advancing from the left front of the camp." That's all.' He paused thoughtfully, then drew out his watch. 'The despatch is timed 8.5 am, it's now turned 9.30, and it will take at least three hours of hard marching to regain Isandhlwana. If Pulleine's had action, then it'll be resolved long before we can reach him.' He paused again. 'Pulleine's a competent officer, he has an adequate force, and by now he will surely have been reinforced by Colonel Durnford. No' — he glanced down at the despatch — 'there's no urgency suggested in his report. He's not asking for assistance. I think, gentlemen, that we can assume he is not in difficulty.'

Tensions relaxed. The General, of course, was absolutely right. With something like seventeen hundred men at Isandhlwana, of whom six hundred were regular infantry, no officer of Pulleine's experience would allow himself to be worsted by a few thousand Zulus like these just shot down on Isilulwane. Dammit, the boot was on the other foot. The lucky devils at Isandhlwana would be savouring the prospect of a horde of black primitives charging to suicide on their waiting guns.

Only Captain Redvers Buller, one of Chelmsford's aides, was still a little uneasy. With a colleague he rode back to the hill-crest, and from the additional height of a small tree they studied distant Isandhlwana through glasses. The lines of white tents were plainly visible, but they could see no unusual movement and all seemed peaceful. The General had been right, then. If Pulleine had indeed suffered an attack, he had successfully beaten it off.

It was almost 10 am.

* * *

At 10.20 am Pulleine and Durnford had finished a belated breakfast. There had been reports of the faint noise of firing heard from the south-east, which could only mean that Lord Chelmsford's column was in action, possibly against Cetsh-wayo's regiments. If so, what had been the Zulu force on the Nqutu hills, seen from Isandhlwana earlier that morning?

The frustration of Colonel Anthony Durnford was slowly increasing. Somewhere across that veldt a battle was being fought, and he wasn't involved. Blast it, was he to miss yet another opportunity? Already the Crimean War, the Indian Mutiny, die Abyssinian and Ashanti campaigns had passed him by. He had served in Ceylon, Malta and Gibraltar — garrison postings with never a shot fired in anger. Now, having at last achieved an active appointment, he was sitting in a hot, airless bell-tent drinking bad coffee while everything was happening only a few miles away.

'If the General is in action,' he calculated, 'the impi you saw this morning could be a wide out-flanking movement. If it circled and came up on the General's left or rear, there could be the devil to pay, Pulleine. These blacks move damn fast.' Even if Durnford was seeking an excuse for taking positive action, it was logical reasoning. 'You've a picquet to your rear?'

'No,' Pulleine admitted. 'It was withdrawn when the column left.' He swallowed at the last of his coffee. Blast it, his rear faced Natal and, with Chelmsford engaging the Zulus to his front, his rear should be safe enough. Besides, he'd had a bloody lot to think about during the past six hours, and his orders were vague. He didn't need Durnford to remind him of an elementary omission. Just *who* was supposed to be in command, anyway? It was a sensitive question, and neither wished to introduce it. Chelmsford, intending that the Isandhlwana force would follow him within twenty-four hours, had probably never given a thought to the fact that the transitional appearance of Colonel Durnford, four years senior to Pulleine, might present any problem. But it did, very quickly.

A frightened Boer of the vedette, still stationed on the plateau, came careering among the tent-ropes with a garbled story, in a mixture of Afrikaans and English, of Zulus approaching along the Nqutu hill-ridge. His information was second-hand and vague, and Pulleine, impatient, sent another rider spurring for the ridge for further information.

'I don't like sitting here, Pulleine, doing nothing,' Durnford decided. 'We might as well be in Aldershot for all the bloody help we're giving the General. These blacks know every inch of this ground, and if they're trying an outflanking movement, then we ought to hit them damn hard —'

Pulleine was doubtful. 'My orders don't provide for offensive action.' He took the paper from a camp table and read to Durnford. ' "Draw in your line of defence while the force is out, and draw in your infantry outposts accordingly, but keep your cavalry vedettes well advanced." In any language, dammit, that's defensive. Besides, we're only guessing at the Zulu's strength and their intentions. I've already sent a galloper to the General, so he'll know by now that we have the enemy in the vicinity. If he wants to change his orders —'

Durnford shrugged. 'Your man, or the General's answer, might not have got through. As I see it, Pulleine, we're here to fight Zulus, and if there's Zulus around we ought to fight them.' He paused. 'There's another thing. Your orders cover the force left here when the General marched this morning. They don't apply to the reinforcement I've brought in, so the situation's changed.' He stood, hands on hips, surveying the endless and empty greeny-dun veldt that was just beginning to shimmer under the sun's increasing heat. He held the final trump card, after all. Whether or not his seniority implied command of the Isandhlwana camp, Pulleine could not dictate the deployment of Durnford's own column, and there were ways of forcing an issue.

He had decided. 'I'm sending two of my troops of mounted Kaffirs to the plateau, then taking out two troops myself on an eastward sweep, with the rockets and a company of native infantry following — a reconnaissance in force. Between the two detachments, we might flush these black devils into the open. If we do, then we'll see. Perhaps we can draw them onto you — and you've got a thousand rifles and two damn seven-pounders. Mark you' — there was a fleeting moment of doubt — 'if I get into trouble, I'll expect you to give me support.'

Durnford beckoned at the Kaffir holding his horse, then turned back to Pulleine with a half grin. 'You wouldn't consider letting me have a couple of companies of your Imperials, I suppose, Pulleine?'

'The blazes, Durnford!' Pulleine snorted. 'Two companies? I've only got six, and they're spread blasted thin, with precious little behind them that counts for anything. Dammit, you're asking me to deliberately reverse my instructions, and your own intentions are open to question —'

Durnford's grin broadened. 'All right. I only asked.' He nodded towards the northward. 'It's that saddle, Pulleine — wide open. I'll give odds that the General's got Cetshwayo by the ears, but if there is a sizeable force up there on the Nqutu, and if it breaks past my detachments, you could have a nasty moment. It'd only need a company of your regulars on the ridge — and you can always pull back if things get hot.' He climbed into his saddle. 'There's nothing like being prepared, eh, Pulleine?' He kicked his horse into motion.

Colonel Pulleine watched, angry, as Durnford's mounted Kaffirs wound raggedly out of the camp-lines. Durnford turned to lift an arm in disdainful salute, and Pulleine seethed. The mule-drawn rocket-caissons swung to the flank of the shambling Natal irregulars following. Christ, the man was bloody impossible. Orders were orders, and Pulleine had his. They weren't stimulating, but they were part of a larger plan, and if every field officer twisted his orders to achieve personal ambitions then there was no point in having damn orders at all.

Pulleine stood by his tent, pensively, for a long time, and when Durnford's departing detachments were almost beyond sight, he stirred. 'Orderly! My compliments to Captain Cav-aye. He is to fall in "A" Company, ready to march and then report to me.'

It was wrong, and he knew it. The youngest subaltern in the battalion could have told him that, if threatened by attack, he should shorten his line, not extend it. Pulleine's every military instinct screamed at him to draw in his six regular companies, to form a hedgehog position with the sheet wall of Isandhlwana at its rear and the wagons and Kaffirs enclosed. A tight, compact formation, with concentrated volley-fire and ample ammunition reserves, could tear the heart out of the Zulus, whatever their number. But Durnford, damn him, thought he knew better, did he? And Durnford, not Pulleine, would have to answer to Chelmsford if something went wrong. It almost made a man wish — Pulleine pushed the thought aside.

* * *

Over the spur, almost a mile to the northward of the camp, and out of sight of it, Cavaye halted his company. It was a bloody odd assignment, and no mistake. He had seen, fleetingly, the Zulu impi earlier, and if that number of the enemy approached his position, then one isolated company of infantry could do nothing but fall back on the camp defence line, if it could — and it would be better there in the first place, blast it.

Already, on the spur, were the Kaffirs of the picquet, huddled together and sitting on their haunches. He could expect little from them; they would probably be a liability. He got his men extended, with a field of fire that commanded an easterly valley, but there was concealed ground on his left flank, and he didn't like it. Christ, he'd thought Pulleine had more sense. Everything was bloody wrong. What was one company expected to achieve in this undulating vastness?

'Dyson!' Bugger it, the lad wasn't ready for this sort of responsibility, but there was no choice — and he had Parsons, a damn good sergeant. 'Dyson, take a detachment of thirty' — it was a third of his strength — 'and take position five hundred yards further northward. You'll be out of sight, so you'll need a runner.' B'Christ, he needed more than a runner himself to communicate with Pulleine. 'And no bloody heroics, Dyson.

If you see Zulus, *fall back* You ought to have good warning. There's two troops o' mounted Kaffirs scouting to the eastward, sod 'em.'

Dyson detailed his men — Sergeant Parsons, Corporals Knight and Tarbuck, then Hughes, Morgan, Whelan, Pope, Sullivan — he knew the names now, and could put a face to each as Parsons shouted. They were simple, rough men, with simple ideals and with ambitions that seldom extended beyond today. Coarse-mannered, poorly educated and, with rare exceptions, interests confined to beer-swilling, petty gambling and prostitutes, yet they maintained an aggressive code of loyalty among themselves and an infinite faith in the ability of their officers to control their destinies. It was this latter quality that Dyson found disturbing. He already had the taste of ashes in his mouth. Sooner or later, he had always known, he must come to this moment of proving, and he was afraid.

Cavaye drew his subordinates aside. 'Now listen, young Dyson, because there's not much time for a lecture on applied tactics. The blacks haven't reached this far westward yet. If they had, those bloody Kaffirs wouldn't still be sitting on their arses. When they come — *if* they come — it'll be across that valley, see?' He pointed. 'Now, keep your detachment together, and make sure you've got an easy route for retirement. The men will fight more confidently if they know they can fall back without being overrun — and so will you.' His words were unhurried, assured, and Dyson nodded. 'All right then — off you go. And don't be afraid to take Parson's advice. He's done this before,' Cavaye lifted a hand to lightly touch Dyson's shoulder. 'Good luck, lad.'

When the leading bands of warriors reached the skyline, there spread before them a panorama of rolling veldt, stippled with grass and scrub, but almost treeless, bisected from roughly north to south by a wide spruit and, further, a dry donga. The lower slopes of Isandhlwana were still obscured, but there were mounted men on the plain immediately ahead, black men and white, in assorted garbs, in a long, ragged line that had just tugged to a surprised halt as the Zulus exploded like black spray over the lip of the ridge. But if the horsemen had been taken unawares, they recovered quickly. In a moment they were out of their saddles, flinging themselves to earth with legs splayed. There was a faint crackle of rifle fire, a sudden haze of smoke over the waiting horses, and among the Zulus a dozen men plunged, spinning. It had happened more quickly than a man could tell of it, and then the far enemy, unhurriedly, remounted, turned their horses' heads, and cantered away towards the south-west.

For minutes the proud discipline of the Zulu impis hung in precarious balance. Intoxicated by excitement the flanks of several regiments were intermingled with others, and Sibindi, Nzobo, and scores of the inDluyengwe found themselves irretrievably mixed with men of the rival inGobamakhosi. Northward, the uMcityu had streamed away, bloodlusting, and nothing now would check them. Elsewhere, however, die *indunas* were screaming for order, and stabbing at the headstrong. There would be a time and a place, they snarled, for blood-letting, and when it began it would be *impi ebomvu* — red war — to the finish. Slowly, reluctantly, the warriors jostled into untidy formation.

Today was not for fighting. Nothing of importance was done when the moon was dead, but what choice was there when the white men were only a gunshot away, and the uMcityu already advancing along the slopes of the Nqutu hills?

'*Dadewetu!*' Sibindi spat. 'Are we to cower here like frightened rock rabbits while the uMcityu do all the killing? Are there not enough of us to crush them like ants? They have killed. *Igazi li puma egazini*. Blood comes from blood, and our spears are still dry!' From the northward they could hear scattered rifle fire, which meant that the errant uMcityu were at grips with the enemy, but here, on the veldt, there was death promised for any warrior who sped ahead of the *indunas* in the van — not a clean death by spearing, but by having wooden pegs hammered up the nostrils into the brain.

Ahead the retreating horsemen had been joined by more — white men clothed in black, with white stripes down their breech-legs and white hats surmounted by little spikes. They fired again, but this time not dismounting, and their aim was unsteady. Even had every bullet found a victim, the fire of fifty or sixty horsemen could have little effect on a battle-horde that stretched almost two miles from flank to flank. They wheeled away again, splashing across the wide but shallow spruit to its *far* bank, still unhurried, but aware that a running Zulu could keep pace with a horse — and the Zulus were getting very near. The horsemen, indeed, as Sibindi had said, were a scattering of ants in the path of an elephant who could tread them into the earth, unaware even of their existence.

* * *

'We've got company,' Cavaye said. He could see the mounted Kaffirs spilling across the valley towards his position, and behind them, seconds later, the boiling deluge that swarmed in pursuit. Christ, the bastards were moving fast, and there must be all of two thousand — likely three. He lowered his glasses. 'Load. Range eight hundred yards — and wait for it. We'll let 'em get a bit closer.' The racing Zulus were veering to his left, so young Dyson should have them sighted by now. There'd be time for a half dozen volleys, and then they'd have to get to hell out of it, back to Isandhlwana, in two groups leapfrogging each other with covering fire. There was no need to send a runner to Pulleine; the mounted Kaffirs, already wheeling southward would reach the camp within minutes.

'Take your time,' he cautioned. 'Present. FIRE!'

But these, he did not know, were only the uMcityu, the runaway right horn of Cetshwayo's army. Out of Cavaye's sight, on the veldt below the Nqutu, more than twenty thousand rolled like black thunder towards Isandhlwana.

* * *

Five hundred yards northward, Edwin Dyson could see the uMcityu, and his belly knotted.

'They're getting pluddy close, look you,' said Private John David Hughes.

'Pluddy close, Dai,' agreed Private William Morgan. 'Pluddy close.'

'Holy Mary,' sniffed Private Whelan. He wiped the sweat from his eyes with a filthy hand, 'Did ye iver see anythin' loik us? Shure, there's ivery black haythen in bloddy Africa, howlin' an' scraychin'. Et's worse than St Partick's noight en Sackville Strayt!'

'Pluddy arse —'oles!' someone spat. 'Does the auld Colonel expect us ter stand in line against *this* lot, look you?'

It was unbelievable, and unbelievably terrifying. The entire middle of the valley ahead was a dense, chaotic, black ocean, heaving, tossing — and flooding forward with incredible speed. Nothing — and certainly not a single company of infantry — could hope to stand in the path of this all-devouring nightmare. But it couldn't be true. This was one of those crazed dreams from which a man awoke, sweating and trembling, but thereafter never spoke of his cringing terror, or the relief with which he heaved cold air into his lungs, and lay, wet and shivering. This must be one of those dreams.

'If yer can't stand the sight,' shouted Sergeant Parsons, 'then shut yer bleedin' eyes. I'll tell yer when ter open 'em. Pouches open, an' I'll strangle with 'is own guts the first sod ter fire without an order!'

'It's not rifles we want, Sergeant bach,' said Private John David Hughes, it's pluddy Gatlings, see?' The War Office still frowned on the multi-firing Gatling gun, for several reasons including its expensive consumption of ammunition. The same reason was behind opposition to the introduction of a magazine rifle. Give a soldier five rounds in a magazine, it was said, and he'd fritter away with his ammunition and devil take the cost. Oddly, the Navy, with far less justification, had the Gatling, and army commanders often faced the embarrassment of requesting naval gun-crews to support campaigns, hundreds of miles inland. It was a nuisance, because the blue-jackets were a different breed. Neither naval officer nor rating adapted kindly to the military brand of discipline, and an army sergeant could find himself flat on his back with a dislocated jaw for the minor oversight of entering the sailors' tent with his helmet on.

But this time there were no Gatlings with Chelmsford's column. He had sent them, and their crews, back to their ships as being unnecessary for his campaign.

From Dyson's right came the sudden chutter of Cavaye's rifle fire, and Parsons glanced at him expectantly. Dyson nodded. Toad!' he shouted. His voice, thank God, sounded a bloody sight better than he felt.

'About seven hundred, sir?' Parsons suggested.

'Range seven hundred yards,' Dyson ordered. 'Present' — he waited for them to steady their aim, then — 'FIRE!' He fumbled for his Webley, his fingers all thumbs.

His ears sang, and he was suddenly aware that he had never been in close proximity to thirty rifles being fired in unison. 'Load!' There was a chatter of cocking-levers. 'Present — FIRE!' Guiltily, he thrust his Webley back into its holster unable to cope with both pistol and binoculars, and grateful that Parsons' eyes were not on him. He focused with water-weak hands. Christ alive! There were Zulus down, tangling, like squashed black pumpkins among the scrub, and his own men were laughing. 'Did you see that, Willie bach? Flat as a board, boyo, and at seffen hundred pluddy yards, look you!' Christ, they were gems, these men of his. Bloody gems. He experienced a throat-choking surge of pride in these imperturbable, trusting scoundrels. 'Load! Present —'

B'God, he'd not scuttle back to Cavaye just yet. Not just yet. 'Fire in your own time!' he bawled. 'Pick a target, men, and aim low!' He had a few minutes — just a few minutes to gain control of the crawling revolt in his belly.

'Yew got bleedin' cloth ears, Whelan?' the Sergeant roared. 'Aim *low*, the officer said! Yer ain't shootin' soddin' pidgeons out o' trees!'

'If wit was shit, look you,' Private John David Hughes spoke from the corner of his mouth, 'the auld Sergeant would neffer need pluddy castor oil, see.'

The surging Zulus were close, damn close, and the thirty men on the spur could see the dyed head-plumes and jolting monkey-tails, the spear-points like black grass. Five hundred yards? The men were firing and reloading as fast as they could claw cartridges from pouch. Four hundred?

'Sir?' It was Sergeant Parsons' apprehensive voice, and he had good reason to be apprehensive. It was time to abandon this exposed hillside, time to rejoin Cavaye's detachment for the retirement on Isandhlwana —

'Mr Dyson, sir,' Parsons insisted. 'It's "F" Company — Captain Mostyn's lot — comin' up on our right.'

CHAPTER SIXTEEN

On Isandhlwana all had been quiet until several disconcerting things happened in rapid succession. Three horsemen from the mounted detachment that had left to sweep the Nqutu plateau that morning — one of them Captain Shepstone of the Natal Carabineers — came racing across the veldt, gesticulating wildly. The Zulus were coming, Shepstone shouted, pointing eastward, not just two or three thousand, but a colossal horde that overspread the entire plain. There was only one explanation. Whatever Lord Chelmsford was doing, he wasn't fighting Cetshwayo's main army, because it was here, every blasted man of it, avalanching towards Isandhlwana and only minutes away.

Before Pulleine had time to digest the information, two more gallopers arrived, rather less perturbed. They were from Lord Chelmsford, with a despatch ordering Pulleine to load his wagons, strike camp, and prepare to march his command to join the General's. The two men had left Chelmsford at about 10 am, with the General still following in pursuit of retreating scattered Zulus. They had had an easy ride, seeing nothing unusual. As they were leisurely making their report, Shepstone was impatiently trying to interrupt, to emphasise to Pulleine that every passing second was vital if he was to defend Isandhlwana against an attacking force outnumbering his regular troops by forty to one. 'Goddam, sir,' he broke in at last. 'I assure you matters are very serious!'

Pulleine, like most Queen's officers, had little regard for the military acumen of locally-recruited volunteers, and he was not to be hustled into action by a so-called Captain of the so-called Royal Natal Carabineers. The veldt to the eastward was empty, hot and shimmering under a vicious sun almost directly overhead, and he had been about to order his sweating men to a midday meal of boiled beef, dumplings and hard peas. Besides, somewhere on the veldt was Colonel Durnford — and Durnford knew it all, didn't he?

But from the northward saddle that linked Isandhlwana to the Nqutu there came an ominous and continuous rattle of rifle fire. It was Cavaye's company. Cavaye was in trouble, and he knew Cavaye. He didn't shoot at nothing. Cavaye was worth twenty of these festerin' colonial amateurs.

Pulleine glanced about him for a company commander, and found one. 'Captain Mostyn? You'll take your company out to support Cavaye, and smartly, please.'

'Not the saddle, sir!' Shepstone exploded. 'Cavaye's only got the rags of the Zulus' flanks up the hill! The main army's coming from there!' He flung an arm eastward. 'Christ, you've no idea!'

'Colonel Durnford is also out there, Captain,' Pulleine explained patiently, 'and I have no doubt he will have the situation well under control.' He turned to Mostyn. 'Captain —'

It was an ironic choice. Mostyn's "F" Company had reached Isandhlwana only after an exhausting march from Helpmakaar, and had scarcely regained breath. Still, they had raced here to be in at the kill, and there was apparently killing to be done on the saddle.

But Pulleine, largely through petulance, was compounding an earlier error of judgement. He was sending a second company to support a first, which should never have been detached in the first place.

* * *

Overflowing onto the plain, even the sure-footed Zulus could not maintain a headlong pace across a terrain laced with crevasses and treacherous with loose rubble, nor did the *indunas*, wise in war, want their warriors running at full stretch for four or five miles. The few, distant troops of horsemen were clearly engaged in reconnaissance, unlikely to stand and fight. They would fall back progressively to Isandhlwana, where the red soldiers and the big guns waited. There was little to be gained in attempting to overtake them.

But, surprisingly, the horsemen did stand and fight. Sibindi, his legs bloodied by thorns, with only fragmentary glimpses of the veldt ahead through a clashing tangle of shields and spears and leaping head-plumes, did not see the horsemen dismount again in the donga — the dry, twisting gully, with an escarpment of about four feet, that provided excellent cover for both men and animals. Sibindi was only aware that, this time, deliberate, accurate volleys were taking a noticeable toll of the warriors around him. He was treading over fallen men, retching in the dust, and the *indunas* were shouting for them to halt, to lie down. They could see only the white hats of the men in the donga; it was probable that they had been reinforced, but there was no need to expose warriors to their determined guns. In a few minutes the donga would be outflanked, and the white men must either abandon it or be cut to pieces.

And the warriors could see Isandhlwana, the grassy slopes of its base dotted with little white houses and wagons. But the wagons were not in laager, nor apparently, were there any pits or walls; swarming red ants were jostling into lines in the open as a bugle teetered urgently. It was true, the men in the donga were in danger of being outflanked. The uMcityu and umHlanga had already swarmed beyond their left and were wheeling in a massive pincer movement towards Isandhlwana, where the lines of red soldiers were wreathed in smoke and twinkling with gun-flashes.

From the halted inGobamakhosi, men who had guns were crawling forward to fire back at the donga, but they were poor marksmen, and it was unlikely that they would embarrass the well-hidden white men, who could pick them off at leisure. Behind, the crouching warriors hummed, and the *indunas* shouted. 'Be patient, children of Zulu, your hour will come! *Nirgama qawa*! You will destroy them all, but be patient!'

It was not easy to be patient, to remain crouched as bullets spat up the dust or stabbed through cowhide shield as if they were paper. Then the big guns vomited, and they could see the uMcityu scythed down in swathes. They hummed again. 'There will be many widows in the kraal of the uMcityu,' Sibindi said dispassionately, and Sigcewelegcwale, the *induna*, cursed the guns — not the guns of the white men, but those carried by Zulus. Guns ruined the discipline of a Zulu impi. Why, man questioned, should they charge with iron spears when they might lie in the grass and kill from a distance? But Zulus were not skilled with guns, not like white men. They did not fully understand the purpose of rear-sight and fore-sight, and often tended to hold the butt away from the shoulder to avoid its recoil, so that bullets were often yards wide at even short ranges.

'The white men's bullets are more than a harvest of mealie-coms,' Nzobo said. 'They have wagons full of bullets. Can this man fight bullets with his hands, as he fought the black bull?' He reached for the snuff-bag at his ear, and then contorted, his hand jerking to tear the thong bloodily from the lobe. He hissed. 'Ayeee!' There was a coin-sized hole in the centre of his chest, welling crimson. 'Sibindi, brother. *Na taka kufa*. I am dying.'

'It is a small hole,' Sibindi observed. 'When we have killed the white men, the *inianga* will mend it. It is a very small hole.'

Nzobo coughed. 'My shadow is weakening. *Na taka kufa*.'

'The *inianga* will mend it,' Sibindi nodded. The witchdoctors achieved a degree of success in treating flesh wounds by washing clean with warm water and applying bile from a freshly killed ox, or urine from ox or human, which had antiseptic qualities. A man with a serious wound, however, could hope for nothing but death, and rather than linger in agony for hours, perhaps days, he would ask for a swift, clean thrust of a companion's assegai, followed by a single slash of the same weapon to release his spirit.

'Is this man's spear sharp?' Nzobo enquired. There was a bubbling in his throat and his gaze was fixed. Sibindi shook his head. 'It is a very small hole,' he insisted. 'The *inianga* will mend it.' The duty asked him was repugnant, but it must not be shirked.

'My shadow fades,' Nzobo said.

'It is the sun,' Sibindi offered. 'The sun is a weakly thing — see? The sun is weary, for has not the moon plucked its feathers?' He shrugged. 'Tomorrow, when we have killed the red soldiers your shadow will be strong and black, like sable skin.' He did not recall a time when he had been without the companionship of Nzobo. They had crawled together as infants, fought with sticks as boys, herded the same cattle and, together, had submitted to the painful ceremonies of initiation to manhood. Sibindi could not visualise the progress of a single day without Nzobo.

When, together, they achieved their coveted head-ring and had taken their cattle from the King's herd, they would choose their wives, and get drunk, and jeer at the youths of the uDibi who had not yet washed their spears in the blood of the red soldiers. They would join in thatching their huts, in placing their hearth-stones. Their mealie fields, tended by their women, would lie together, and they would mate their cattle. Their firstborn sons would know two mothers, two fathers, and when he and Nzobo aged, they would join the elders in the *kgotla* when the evening sun was cool, smoking and spitting, remembering the great battles of which the younger generation knew nothing.

He climbed to his feet, reluctantly, standing astride the recumbent Nzobo, whose eyes, half closed, crinkled at the edges in a last grin. '*Safa sapela.* Release life, brother,' Nzobo gritted. A column of ants had climbed his out-splayed fingers to his forearm, and there was dust in the sweat of his face. Sibindi struck downwards, slashing, and blood vomited over his feet. Nzobo coughed once, jerked.

Sibindi stared at the blood, congealing and blackening in seconds. '*Indaba ipelile*,' he uttered. 'Thy will be done.' It was wrong, he fumed, that a fine warrior should be slain by an enemy that he had never seen. Man to man, spear to spear, strength to strength, that was how fighting should be. But a stinging bee of a bullet, from a half mile away, invisible and unchallengeable — this was not how a man should die.

A bullet struck a rock, inches from his foot, then whined away in a ricochet. Sibindi stooped to take up Nzobo's assegai. 'It shall drink, my Nzobo, in the hand of your brother.' He eyed distant Isandhlwana angrily. '*Basibukule itshe lineemamba*! They have unearthed a rock that hides a mamba!'

He was too angry to have observed that the white men in the donga were abandoning their escarpment and were remounting. The uMcityu of the uncontrolled right horn were streaming towards Isandhlwana, and the horsemen crouching in their saddles would be hard put to regain the safety of the red soldiers' lines ahead of the outflanking Zulus. '*Yize!*' shouted Sigcewelegcwale. 'Up! Children of Zulu! Up and destroy them! *Ni ngama qawu*! You are heroes! Now is the time for killing! *Yize! Yize!*'

The densely massed inGobamakhosi and uMbonambi, scattered with men of other regiments, rose to their feet, crashing their spears against their shields. '*Si-gi-di*!' — and then avalanched forward, towards the donga and Isandhlwana beyond. Underfoot the ground was iron hard, hot, thatched with yellowing grass and scattered with untidy clutters of grey boulders. The black hordes swarmed across the spruit, over the lip of the abandoned donga, and into the face of the first drilled volleys of redcoat fire. In their scores, warriors sprawled.

'Mostyn, b'Christ.' Cavaye raised himself from one knee. 'What in hell are you doing here?'

Captain Mostyn was breathing hard. 'Orders is orders. Dammit, I'm out of condition, Cavaye. I'll have to get out those dumb-bells that my sister sent me — when my blasted baggage comes up from Rorke's Drift.'

'Bugger the dumb-bells. I was just about to pull out of this confounded cactus. We're not going to live here, without a gnat's spit of cover, Mostyn. They're thicker than fleas in a Mongolian camel-blanket. And we shouldn't have been here in the first place. What's Pulleine thinking about?'

'I don't know, Charlie,' drawled Mostyn, drawing his pistol, 'and you're damn right, old son, We shouldn't be here.' The wax of his moustache was melting, but he sniffed it aside. 'My lads are between you and young Dyson's detachment, and he's blazing away like bloody fireworks. He's a good lad.' The green of the valley ahead of them was being rapidly blotted out by the black ink of the advancing, crawling tide of the enemy.

Mostyn's men had time for one volley before the scrambling withdrawal started, with Dyson's detachment on the left flank separated from Cavaye's, on the right, by "F" Company. The Kaffirs were already running. It was not a performance that would have earned approval in an Aldershot exercise; the line was erratic, the men firing, crouching as they scampered twenty yards, then turning to fire again, with the uMcityu creeping steadily nearer, cavorting, thrusting their spears at the air. Cavaye's right was vulnerable. A sprinting surge of the Zulus' left could outflank both companies and cut them off from the Isandhlwana, and Cavaye could not see the haven of the camp-lines yet.

And then he did. Suddenly, stumbling in the wake of his men, he saw both the Isandhlwana camp and the stretching veldt to its eastward, and in that first moment of vision he did not understand what he saw, nor wanted to. He grappled for cohesive thought, his eyes sweat-blurred, and interpretation came at last, like torture. The Zulus swarming on the heels of 'A' and 'F' Companies were piddling small beer. On the veldt below the saddle, it seemed, was every bloody warrior of the Zulu nation.

* * *

Pulleine had got away a final dispatch to Lord Chelmsford, by the hand of the General's own galloper, Captain Gardner of the 14th Hussars: 'Heavy firing to the left of our camp. Cannot move at present.' It was an odd message to send, miserably brief, reflecting little sense of urgency, and seeming to merely indicate that it was inconvenient, for the moment, to march. Minutes after Gardner had departed, the horses of the mounted volunteers and Kaffirs burst into view beyond the eastward donga, behind them the awesome flood of Cetshwayo's army.

* * *

Miraculously, 'F' Company and the segmented 'A' Company scuttled four hundred yards from the brow of the saddle before being compelled to turn and stand. They were still a thousand yards from the tent lines, their ammunition wagons, hospital tents, and the Union Jack that drooped over the battalion headquarters, but with the crowded uMcityu on their heels it would be ruin to run further. There was only one thing to do now — halt, take open order, stand firm, and wait for supports, if supports were available. If there were none, then they were, as Cavaye would have put it, in the bloody cactus.

Edwin Dyson, at least, was relieved to see, on his left and slightly to rear, the bayonets of Captain Young-husband's 'C' Company, and Lieutenant Georgie Hodson, fifty yards away, giving him a hurried, reassuring wave of a hand. Dyson returned an equally brief gesture, then got his detachment extended in time to receive the charging melee of the enemy. His left, then, was covered, and 'C' Company's in turn was against the wall of Isandhlwana itself.

The six regular companies were flung out over a defence perimeter shaped like a great inverted L. Towards the northward faced three — 'C' Company, then Dyson's detachment, Mostyn's 'F' Company, and finally the remainder of 'A' Company, under Cavaye, to the angle. Facing the eastward veldt were 'E' and 'H' Companies commanded by Lieutenant Porteous and Captain Wardell respectively, with the line terminated by the luckless 'G' Company of die 2nd Battalion under Lieutenant Pope which, righty, should have been with Chelmsford's column. The extra few hours of sleep the company had relished were going to be expensive. At the angle, or elbow of the line the Kaffir irregulars were clustered nervously about the two seven-pounders, a few erratically firing their rifles at the savage horror that bore down upon them. Free-born Zulus were a source of apprehension at any time for the Natal Kaffirs. The effect of twenty thousand of them was paralysing.

At full stretch and lathered, the mounted police and volunteers hurtled through the line and flung themselves to the ground, dragging their carbines from their saddle-buckets. The artillerymen were serving their guns like madmen, tearing blood-drenched furrows in the irresistible sea of ostrich plumes and otter tails. 'Faith,' Whelan spat, 'an didn't we have ivery black haythen in bloddy Africa the first toim? Now we've got twoice es many.' He aimed and fired. 'Pluddy hell.' observed Private John David Hughes. 'Did you see that, Willie bach? Whelan's hit a Zulu, look. There's a chance for us yet, see?'

B'Christ, there was no chance, Edwin Dyson decided. No chance at all. The end must come in minutes, perhaps seconds. B'Christ, what wouldn't he give, now, for just a dozen of those beautifully clumsy Gatling guns, lying uselessly in their crates in the Thomas Street warehouse, in Birmingham? Just twelve Gatlings, each firing a thousand rounds a minute, would dampen the vehemence of even these blood-hungry tribesmen.

What had his father intended for him? A commission in the Household Cavalry? He, Edwin, would need only one fitting of 24th scarlet, George Dyson had asserted. The second would be of Horse Guards' blue. At another time Edwin might have laughed. He still wore his first fitting of 24th regimentals, and young Austen Chamberlain could have a clear field in the smoke-room of the Grand Hotel. George Dyson's grief would be focused on the fact that his son had been killed by ignorant black men with spears instead of the Russian Imperial Guard in an assault in Kronstadt — and then he would speculate on how much Cetshwayo would be prepared to pay for twenty-three thousand Snider-Enfield rifles, slightly used.

'Ammo', sir!' Sergeant Parsons was shouting through cupped hands. 'I sent two men ter find our wagon, but they ain't back. We're near shot out. If we had ammo', sir, we could hold these bastards.'

Parsons' claim was optimistic in the extreme, but he could not know that, a thousand yards away, a dozen men from different companies were clawing the heavy ammunition boxes from the wagons, only to find them almost impossible to open. A sergeant hacked desperately with a hatchet, while other prised with bayonets that snapped, or kicked savagely with steel-shod boots. A few fortunates ran with hats or pockets filled.

'Fix bayonets,' Dyson ordered. He wasn't frightened any longer. A man was only frightened, he realised, while there remained the slightest hope of survival. When hope disappeared irrevocably, fear became replaced by a numb resignation. He thought he had two shots left in his Webley.

* * *

They had not expected the Ma-Nyisimane to be waiting, unprotected in the open. There were no wagons in laager. They could see wagons, but they were to the rear and flank, out-spanned and useless. There were no pits or walls, nor even barriers of thorny scrub to delay, if only for seconds, an attacking enemy. It was almost unbelievable.

The red soldiers faced them thinly in long lines, spread before their little white houses, presenting, to jolting eyes, chalk-slashes of scarlet and blue, capped by hundreds of white helmets that scarcely stirred. Were these all? And were the red soldiers so confident that so few could stand contemptuously in the open against a charging Zulu army?

There were ominous gaps in the Ma-Nyisimane's battle-line, wide enough for scores of warriors to pour. The red soldiers could not be such fools, could they? They stood, these white men, with every left foot advanced, their rifles rising in perfect unison, and the long knives, fixed to their barrels, glittering in the hot sunshine. What were such puny knives against die assegai of a Zulu warrior?

But there was nothing puny about the controlled shattering volleys of the red soldiers' rifles, slashing among the plumes and shields of the panting inGobamakhosi, hurling blood-coughing men to the ground. When the *indunas* shouted 'Um-*oya*!' the Zulus flung themselves to earth to avoid the big bullets of the big guns on wheels, but there was no avoiding the myriad, unseen, death-bringing hornets of the red-coated lines that fired, reloaded, and fired again as if controlled by a single finger.

The leather-tough soles of Sibindi's feet were shredded and bloody, and he did not know that a .45 calibre bullet had sheared through his shield, tearing the flesh from a forearm and baring it to the bone. Nzobo, he gritted, the sun will not sleep before red soldiers die under your spear, or Sibindi dies. *Ngitshlo*! I have said it. Today we shall stamp their bodies into the ground, and the hyena and the vultures shall be glutted —

'Up! Up! — Children of Zulu!' old Sigcewelegcwale shouted, his assegai aloft against the hot sky. 'Now is the moment you have waited for! Up! Up!' But hundreds of his finest warriors would never hear his entreaty. They lay where they had fallen — humped black mounds among broken feathers and bloody, splintered shields. A few crawled, pleading for *iKlwa* to release their spirits, as volley after volley of murderous rifle fire tore down their comrades still standing. It could not last. Courage was not enough when men could not reach within spear-thrust of an enemy, but must be scythed down helplessly, a hundred yards distant. What mattered a warrior's twenty — thirty — years of battle discipline if he could not even see the man he had to fight?

It could not last, but not for the reason that the *indunas* were beginning to dread. The blizzard of rifle fire was slackening noticeably. It was strange, hardly credible. The men of the inGobamakhosi hesitated, then edged forward, crouching and wary. A few stuttering shots still flung men to die dust, but the smoke that had obscured the skirt of Isandhlwana was dispersing. The red soldiers could be clearly seen now, and, with the constant chutter of gunfire almost silent, the Zulus could hear the white men's taunting shouts that invited the warriors to come forward and fight. Over all, the warriors could hear the sound of masculine singing, melodious and hymn-like — a song that they understood. Come said the battle hymn. Come, and we are ready. We are men of proud heritage, and give place to none. Come. You may kill us, but many of you will die in the killing. The lines of bayonets had not wavered.

> *And there'll we'll keep her banner flying,*
> *While the proud lips of the dying*
> *Echo to our shouts of defying —*
> *Harlech for the right!*

The massive Zulu encircling movement, more than two miles from one horn-tip to the other, closed around Isandhlwana.

Few of the warriors would ever know where or why the line first broke, but suddenly, in the face of the swarming uMcityu, there melted a gap of several hundred yards from which scores of terrified Kaffirs were flying, seeing the doubtful safety of the tents and wagons in the rear. It was a gap that the thinly-spread lines of red soldiers on either side could not hope to close nor, with ammunition spent, despite the flood of 2,000 uMcityu that poured into it. And pell mell on the heels of the uMcityu followed the unHlanga and the isaNgqu, screeching stabbing, blood-crazed.

Sibindi ran blindly. Before him the red-coated lines were stumbling backward, splintering into small groups of men who stood back to back, submerged in a consuming, black ocean that engulfed them from the front, flank and rear. In seconds the smaller groups were whirled away, helpless red flecks in an all-devouring maelstrom, but larger groups stood with bayonets thrusting — doomed but defiant, cursing and jeering at the crowded, maddened warriors who contorted and leapt about them. And the bayonets plunged, like the lash of a whip, to throat or belly, and warriors still fell as the white men jeered again.

But they could survive for only minutes. As every Zulu fell, a dozen trod ruthlessly over him. Beyond the confused melee, among the tents and wagons, warriors ran, scattering, slashing at reeling Kaffirs, at men still prising desperately at ammunition boxes, at bearded, shirt-sleeved Boers whose hunting knives and clubbed rifles flailed tigerishly before they, too, were submerged and overrun. Riderless horses and mules, gashed and terrified, flung themselves crazily among the fighting, until brought down, kicking, by shot or spear.

There would be no white men left, Sibindi decided, if he did not kill quickly. Nzobo's spear was still unwashed. Already the remaining, dispersed groups of red soldiers were dissolving, and still, impeded by the crush, he had not reached within spear's thrust of them. There was a flaring pain in his shield arm that he could not pause to investigate, his hand sticky with clotting blood. His feet and lower legs were crimson. Then, over the tangling sea of head-plumes, to the far right, he saw the red soldiers on the rising of the mountain.

They were the last formation of any strength or cohesion — forty, perhaps fifty, of the defence line's extreme flank. With fractionally more time when the Kaffirs had broken, these few had pulled back, wheeling to meet the crushing, outflanking horde that had swept the neighbouring companies to ruin. They had retreated stubbornly, yard by yard, firing coolly until their pouches were empty. They stood now, shoulder to shoulder, their bayonets raised as a solitary red *induna* shouted, ready to demand a final toll of their teeming enemies before they fell. Sibindi ran.

Every Zulu for a half century had practised to savage perfection the sequence of killing. It demanded that a warrior should meet an opponent's lunging spear with his shield and batter it to the left, outward. Momentarily unbalanced, the enemy would instinctively throw his own shield across his body; but in doing so would expose an armpit, into which, a second later, an up-slashing assegai would be buried. And

Sibindi had practised it to exhaustion, knowing well the shout of exultation that followed — '*Ngadla*!'

The red soldiers did not carry shields, and they held their knife-tipped guns with both hands like women hoeing mealies. Sibindi did not understand why this single line of white men had survived so long, nor why the ground before them was littered with Zulu dead, but there was no time for such thought. He was Sibindi, the Brave One, of the inDlu-yengwe, killer of the black bull, and in his hand was the spear of his brother, Nzobo.

He pushed himself through the gathered inGobamakhosi. 'Here is one of the inDlu-yengwe!' he shouted. 'Here is one who will show you how to kill! Watch, old men, and tell your grandchildren of it!' A warrior, jostled aside, snorted with disgust. '*Haul Indoda*! A man indeed!' The inGobamakhosi hummed, and Sibindi leapt at the red soldiers.

A man stepped forward to meet him — a short-statured man, dark-haired under a stained white helmet that shadowed his eyes. His blue trousers were crumpled, truncated, over heavy, dusty boots, and there were black sweat patches at the arm-pits of his tunic. 'Is ut a foight ye'll be wantin', ye black bastard?' he enquired, but Sibindi did not understand. He was such a puny man, and no match for a warrior of the inDlu-yengwe. Intent on parrying a thrust from the knife on the red soldier's gun, Sibindi threw his shield forward, unaware that his left elbow was shattered to splintered bone. Searing scalding agony clawed at his arm, shoulder and chest, and the fingers of his hand were nerveless. He shouted, puzzled, and the red soldier's knife thrust deep into his abdomen, tearing upwards. He fell on all fours, crouched and unbelieving. Nzobo, brother.

He lowered his face to the ground, his entrails spilling from a ripped belly, until the puny soldier's heavy boot flung him prone. 'Ye kin spit the bones out ev thet, ye haythen sod,' said Private Whelan, and turned away contemptuously. But only for a second. An inGobamakhosi warrior sprang, his assegai slashing viciously, Whelan sprawled, cursing his black luck.

Sibindi did not know. Nzobo, brother. The noise of battle was distant, muted, and all was dust.

* * *

Mostyn was gone, and Younghusband, and Charlie Cavaye, and Georgie Hodson. Furthest away, Lieutenant Pope's 'G' Company of the 2nd, with its flank in the air and nakedly exposed, fought for brutal seconds before being hacked down. The two seven-pounders were overrun, their blaspheming crews speared, while the dismounted police and volunteers, grouped together, threw down their empty carbines and died with knives in their hands. The Union Jack over the battalion tent was wrenched down by a screeching warrior, and a flailing, snarling boy soldier was raised by his heels and his throat cut. Infants, however vicious, did not qualify for a man's death by assegai.

Edwin Dyson's pistol clicked on an empty cylinder, and he hurled it with all his strength at the sweating black faces, feet away. It was here, he knew, and now. A man can die but once; we owe God a death. And let it come which way it will, he that dies this year is quit for the next. He grinned. Mason College, Birmingham.

'If you was to ask me, Willie bach,' said Private John David Hughes, 'you were a little bit *flat* with that last descant look.'

'You could be right, Dai,' Private Morgan nodded. 'The second time round, was it? Aye, it's haffing no practice, boyo. When this pluddy pantomime is finished, Hughie bach, we'll start practice *serious*, see —'

And that was only seconds before the last remnants of 'C' Company were swept away by the final, stabbing tide of inGobamakhosi.

CHAPTER SEVENTEEN

There is not much more to tell. At least, not much that does not follow a predictable pattern. Small nations that achieve an initial, shock success against a mighty one are seldom allowed a second bite at the cherry. And so it was with Cetshwayo.

Zulu witnesses, after the campaign, all told pretty much the same story: 'The English killed us, and we killed them, and the fight was kept up for a long time. The English troops became helpless because they had no ammunition, and were then killed... Before the soldiers knew where they were, they were surrounded from the west, attacked by the wings from the right, and the main body from the back. They tried to make an opening towards the front, but the Zulu army was too thick. With fixed bayonets, the men formed back to back. Some Zulus threw assegais, others shot, but they did not get close — they avoided the bayonet, for any men who went to stab a soldier was fixed through the throat or stomach. When a soldier was engaged with a Zulu in front, another Zulu killed him from behind. There was a tall man who came out of a wagon and made a stout defence when we thought all the white men were dead. He fired in every direction, and killed so many, but in the end he was shot.' Another claimed that the last survivor was a drummer of the 24th, who was seen to throw his short sword at a Zulu.

The official records, too, have an air of apology: 'Turn where we will, the same story of the disaster is traced in broad characters — extended formation against savages whose hand-to-hand fighting was alone to be feared, and failure of ammunition. When this failed, there was no hope. It is known that Quartermaster Bloomfield, 2nd Battalion 24th, met his death while trying with others to untie the ammunition boxes on the mules, and that mules with ammunition boxes on them were to be seen plunging and kicking over the field, maddened with fear. No arrangements had been made for the distribution of ammunition, and it may be mentioned that appliances for the purpose had been asked for...'

A handful of white men did escape the massacre, mostly Boers, but including six privates of the 24th — an officer's groom, two bandsmen, and three men with the rocket battery. So rapid was the action, however, that few dismounted Europeans had any chance. Lieutenants Melvill and Coghill, of the 24th, reached the Natal bank of the Buffalo, four miles away, with the Queen's Colour, before being overtaken and slain.

But what of Lord Chelmsford's column to the south-eastward? At the time that Isandhlwana was being overrun, the General was inspecting a new camp site near the Amangene stream. He was still here, later, when he received Pulleine's report regarding heavy firing. Again the distant shape of Isandhlwana was examined through glasses, but with the tents seen to be standing and all apparently peaceful, the second message inspired no more alarm than the first.

The shattering truth reached Chelmsford during mid-afternoon, from a number of sources almost simultaneously — again the underestimated Mounted Infantry, native scouts, and even an officer who had ridden unsuspectingly to within a few yards of the Isandhlwana tents before being fired on, but escaped by a miracle. Report after report, like horrifying shell-bursts, destroyed all remaining remnants of doubt. The Isandhlwana force was facing a devastating attack, and could even be overwhelmed.

Chelmsford's situation, only hours earlier following the familiar pattern of a leisurely colonial punitive expedition, was suddenly critical. There was still an unknown number of the enemy ahead of him, while in his rear was apparently a massive force attacking his base camp and supply train, and cutting him off from Rorke's Drift and Natal. Chelmsford's world was disintegrating, and a more sensitive man might also have gone to pieces. Chelmsford, however, was an orthodox soldier, and the moment was one for the rule-book orthodoxy. He did not know that the Zulu's casualties at Isandhlwana had been horrific, and that Cetshwayo, on learning the cost of his victory, had said. 'An assegai has been thrust into the belly of the nation. There are not enough tears to mourn for the dead.' The thousands who died before Isandhlwana were matched by the maimed who crawled and staggered for miles to die unseen, or survived as broken cripples. Never again would the proud Zulu impis tread the veldt like rolling thunder, all-powerful, irresistible. Private Whelan and Private John David Hughes had seen to that, boyo.

But we are ahead of our story. It happens when the pluddy fag ends are being swept up, look you.

Chelmsford, as Charlie Cavaye might have said, was in the soddin' cactus. He made his morale-boosting speech. While we've been skirmishing in front,' he confessed, 'the Zulus have taken our camp. There are ten thousand of them in our rear, and twenty thousand at our front. Men' — he drew himself up — 'we must win back our camp tonight, and cut our way back to Rorke's Drift tomorrow!'

'All right, sir, we'll do it!' they shouted. (Iss there a choice, bach?)

Screened by mounted detachments, the infantry moved off by fours from the left of companies, at company intervals, ready to form line and stand at any moment. There were thirteen miles of rough country ahead of them, with dusk falling, and as Isandhlwana loomed larger its outline became progressively less distinct. The men were tense, and there was little conversation, few sounds but the crunch of marching feet, the soft jingle of guns and caissons, the occasional nicker of a horse.

Noggs rode behind Chelmsford's staff officers. In an hour or two he might have a story to tell that would have the presses of the London *Standard* churning madly, the newsboys screeching, and the columns of the rival *Times* quivering with the rage of Crimean colonels, Basingstoke grocers and the Opposition front bench. On the other hand, of course, if Cetshwayo was anything less than a fool, there would be no story. Not a single man of Chelmsford's column would reach the Natal border alive.

By 7 pm the column was still two miles from Isandhlwana, and with darkness now almost complete the difficulties of the march were intensified. Horses and men stumbled into dongas or were sent sprawling by unseen rocks. Worse, the following Kaffirs, nervous of a Zulu attack, crowded on the heels of the regular infantry. It was clear that, in the event of an alarm, any defensive formation adopted by the redcoats would be thrown into confusion by the Kaffirs, who would be unrecognisable from the enemy.

But they were encountering familiar landmarks, and at 7.45 pm they stood only half a mile from the great black hump they knew to be their goal. Noggs, straining ears and eyes, could feel the sweat cold on his face. There was something weirdly wrong with the Sphinx-shaped mass ahead. There were no tent lights, no glimmer of guard lanterns, no red glow of field kitchens — nothing but blackness and an awful, blood-chilling silence. He heard the men around him sucking in their breath.

Lord Chelmsford's voice was low. 'Companies will form square and fix bayonets. Major Harness' guns will open fire with shrapnel on the neck of the saddle and the kopjie.' The bayonets of six companies rasped from their scabbards, clattering to rifle muzzles. There elapsed several seconds of further silence, and then the seven-pounders crashed in quick succession, like four giant hand-claps, followed almost instantly by a volley of echoes, flung back by the rock wall ahead and the distant Nqutu hills. The echoes jeered, faded, disappeared. There were no Zulu war-cries, no answering shots. The massive black Sphinx lay unmoving, shrouded in a tomb-like hush.

Only the dead remained on Isandhlwana.

CHAPTER EIGHTEEN

The Post Office at Green Point was thronged with officers seeking mail from home, and Noggs emerged into the street, tearing open with a dirty thumbnail the envelope with the London postmark. The breeze off Table Bay was warm and fresh in his face, and he breathed it gratefully. Beyond the southerly roofs of the Dutch-built houses, interwoven by trees, was the long, dominating shape of Table Mountain, its flat summit obscured by clouds.

London, 14 March 1879

My dear Noggs,

Absolutely splendid material from Cape Town, dear boy! There is not a rag in Fleet Street that's not puce with teeth-gnashing envy. We are being quoted in the House!

However, the final deliverance of the Zulus from primitive bondage is an assignment that does not need your unique qualifications, dear Noggs. I am sending MacKenzie on the African — a crude scribbler, but adequate for the purpose.

You, dear fellow, are for Egypt. Gordon is threatening to leave die Sudan and, if he does, blood will flow — and suddenly. Nothing is more certain. The Serapis, departing Cape Town on the 28th, will drop you at Gibraltar, and from thence the German takes you on to Port Said. Your passages are booked, and money for camels and equipment has been telegraphed to the British Agent. Be sure to boil all drinking water and keep your neck covered.

Dear boy, I remain,
Yours most affectionately,
William Mudford.

Noggs folded the letter, sucked his teeth thoughtfully, and then mounted the planked veranda of the Cape Royal Hotel. The Sudan, b'Christ. Willie Mudford's nose for a story sniffed out some bloody queer places. He needed whisky — a lot of whisky with ice, but there'd be no ice in this damn paint-peeling, fly-infested parody of an hotel. And he needed a bath more than anything. The armpits of his shirt were rotted, his boots broken, and the stink of his own body was in his nostrils. Several female coloureds rose from their haunches. 'Can I please yer, Captain? Short time? Very cheap.' They spoke in the guttural English of the Afrikaan, and he brushed past them, into the musty hotness of the clapboard building. His eyes, in the sudden gloom, were blind.

'Ah! Enter the special correspondent for the *Standard*, disguised as another native!' Francis Frances of *The Times* sat at the rickety bar, glass in one hand as he tentatively fingered a peeling nose with the other. 'Noggs, you're a sly devil, and no mistake. There's Gay and me with chilblains in Bulgaria, eating old goat and cabbage soup, while you've been drinking port with Lord Chelmsford and putting the Russians on page three with Mrs Beaton's Household Management.'

'Whisky,' Noggs said, 'and leave the bottle.' The bar, its smell and its shirt-sleeved, grimy bar-tender reminded him of something. Letterkenny, and Smiley's Bar. He filled his own glass and Frances'.

'I've been reading the casualty list,' Frances resumed more soberly. 'It was a damn bad business, Noggs. Why did it happen?'

Noggs winced as the raw spirit clawed at his throat. 'It was a bloody atrocity, and it didn't just happen — it was *imposed*.' He shook his head. 'They were good men, Frank — too good to be senselessly butchered because of a commander who hasn't the intelligence of a blasted wooden rocking-horse!'

'Chelmsford?' Frances shrugged. 'He's probably no worse than the other four hundred generals on the Army List, Noggs, Mark my words, he'll be promoted. The difference between success and failure is a hairline. He was unlucky —'

'*Unlucky*? By Christ!' His whisky spilled over his chin. 'You didn't see the Isandhlwana camp, Frank, next morning, when we moved in. Our men were crying like children — with sheer rage, Frank — and vomiting. It's not bloody pleasant, seeing men cry.' He paused as he tipped the bottle again. 'There were six thousand corpses, black and white, and a thousand animals — and every one gutted like a herring, spilling its entrails and bloating, with the flies like soot and a stench like you've never known. We buried them there, in pits, most of'em unrecognisable, but I saw Charlie Cavaye, Reggie Younghusband, Billie Mostyn, and young Dyson —'

'Dyson.' Francis Frances screwed up his eyes, then nodded. 'I saw his name on the list. Do you remember, Noggs — ?'

'The Travellers?' Noggs choked. 'George Dyson of "D & B"? Christ, I remember. Colonel Burnaby and the Horse Guards — and I recommended the 24th.'

'Ah, but I happened to read something about "D & B", old Noggs. Dyson Senior has made a big sale of Remington breech-loaders to some dealer in the Sudan, There's some nonsense being talked about a religious fanatic — a Mahdi — whipping up the tribes in the Kordofan area, south of Khartoum.' He eyed his empty glass meaningfully. 'It won't amount to anything, of course. The local Berbers — they're known as "Fuzzy-Wuzzies" — haven't the first idea about fighting. Gordon, with his swagger cane, and a couple of companies of British regulars, could drive the bloody lot into the Nile —'

POSTSCRIPT

It is difficult to terminate the account of Isandhlwana without mentioning Rorke's Drift, the mission station occupied by 'B' Company of the 2nd Battalion 24th. Sixty men under Lieutenant Gonville Bromhead, a few volunteers and departmental staff, the whole commanded by Lieutenant Chard of the Royal Engineers, successfully defended the post for twelve horns against the repeated attacks of three thousand Zulus, killing four hundred for the loss of only three soldiers. This resistance, the result of firm and able command, serves to illustrate what might have been achieved at Isandhlwana under different circumstances. It is of Rorke's Drift that our history books tell, but the quality and courage of its garrison were no higher than of the men of Isandhlwana. Courage, however, was not enough.

And Cetshwayo? Retribution was inevitable. No dark-skinned native king could be allowed to thumb his nose at the imperial might of Britain. A massive military force steamrollered into Zululand. Resistance was crushed and the royal kraal of Ulundi taken.

Cetshwayo, captured, was taken to London, his leopard-skin and assegai replaced by a smart English suit, hat, gloves and cane. He lunched with the Queen, and was eventually returned to an annexed Zululand, having cost the British £5,230,000 and the lives of nearly 2,400 troops.

Lord Chelmsford also returned to England to receive promotion and the GCB, but was never again granted an active command.

The Queen ordered that silver wreaths of immortelles should be borne on the staffs of the colours of both battalions of the 24th Regiment, subsequently retitled the South Wales Borderers, and now forming part of the Royal Regiment of Wales.

AUTHOR'S NOTE

What happened to the handsome hero of Victorian fiction — the man who overcame all obstacles, escaped death by inches, and always maintained a stiff upper lip? He disappeared, because, in a more critical age, he became too good to be true, and the harrowing situations in which he found himself (but always emerged unscathed) no longer exist. Besides, readers today demand better value than 'With one bound Jack was free!' Heroism has become unfashionable, yet in Victorian times those scarcely credible, cliff-hanging situations readily presented themselves in real life, and they produced their heroes, perhaps not always infallible or even handsome, but what other than unvarnished heroism can be attributed to men like Fred Burnaby with his ride to Khiva and his fight to the death at Abu Klea, to Lieutenant Lang and Major Reid in the Indian Mutiny, or to Lieutenant Chard at Rorke's Drift? Today, the vision of the gallant, blood-stained soldier with a broken sword in one hand and the regimental colours in the other, facing hopeless odds for Queen and country, may seem rather ludicrous, but it did happen.

It happened at Isandhlwana, in Zululand, in 1879 — an episode that our history books pass over quickly because it was an occasion when a British army, albeit small, was overrun and completely destroyed, not by regular soldiers but by half-naked unsophisticated African natives. Our Victorian grandparents, with their unrivalled experiences in colonial warfare, were at loss to find excuses for such a humiliation, and in the end decided not to talk about it. This was a pity, because it is very plain that the British troops involved were not defeated in the accepted sense of the word. They did not surrender or run away. They stood, as they had been taught to stand, and fought, *literally*, to the last round and the last man; they paid the price of political and finally tactical blunders over which they had no control; they were victims of the over-confidence of a General Staff with a fatally misplaced contempt for a courageous enemy. The British had not learned the lessons of the Battle of the Little Big

Horn, less than three years earlier, in which the American Custer and his Seventh Cavalry had been annihilated by Sioux and Cheyenne Indians.

Without exception, all the characters of this novel involved in the Zulu campaign were real people, but some licence has been used in presenting personal aspects of men of whom the only information available is a name and rank on a regimental muster list of 1879. Similarly, references to the causes of the Zulu War, which were prolonged and extremely complex, have been very much simplified. For more detailed accounts, reference should be made to a more erudite work, such as Donald R. Morris's eminently readable *Washing of the Spears*.

BIBLIOGRAPHY

Alexander, Michael: The True Blue: Rupert Hart-Davis, 1957.

Barnes, R. M.: A History of the Regiments of the British Army: Seeley, Service, 1950.

Becker, Peter: Path of Blood: Longmans, Green, 1962.

Binnis, C. T.: The Last Zulu King: Longmans, Green, 1963.

Blackham, Col. Robert: Scalpel, Sword and Stretcher: Sampson Low, Marston, 1926.

Briggs, Asa: Victorian Cities: Odhams Press, 1963.

Coates, Austin: Basutoland: H. M. Stationery Office, 1966.

Fauconnet, Max: Mythology of Black Africa: Paul Hamlyn, 1960.

Fortescue, J. W.: A History of the British Army: Macmillan, 1930.

King, C. Cooper: The Story of the British Army: Methuen, 1897.

Laver, James: The Age of Optimism: Weidenfeld & Nicol-son, 1966.

Morris, D. R.: The Washing of the Spears: Jonathan Cape, 1966.

Mutwa, Credo Vusa' Mazulu: My People: Blue Crane Books, 1964.

Norris-Newman, Charles L.: In Zululand with the British throughout the War of 1879: W. H. Allen, 1880.

Paton, Col. George: Records of the 24th Regiment.

Peterson, H. L.: Firearms: Connoisseur, 1964.

Petrie, Sir Charles: The Victorians: Eyre & Spottiswoode, 1960.

Ritter, E.A.: Shaku Zulu: Longmans, Green, 1955.

Rogers, H. C. B.: Weapons of the British Soldier: Seeley, Service, 1960.

Watteville, Col. H. de: The British Soldier: Dent, 1954.

Woodham-Smith, Cecil: The Great Hunger: Hamish Hamilton, 1962.

ACKNOWLEDGEMENTS

Acknowledgements also to Major G. J. B. Egerton, DL, and the regimental library of the Royal Regiment of Wales, Brecon; to the files of the *Southern Evening Echo*, Southampton; and to Mr A. Winship, of Sheldon, for his photography and research in the Isandhlwana area.

Printed in Poland
by Amazon Fulfillment
Poland Sp. z o.o., Wrocław